1 - Marriage

MARRIAGE
ACCORDING TO
THE NEW CODE OF CANON LAW

MARRIAGE

ACCORDING TO THE NEW CODE
OF
CANON LAW

by

Bernard A. Siegle, T.O.R., J.C.D., S.T.M.

ALBA · HOUSE   NEW · YORK

SOCIETY OF ST. PAUL, 2187 VICTORY BLVD., STATEN ISLAND, NEW YORK 10314

Library of Congress Cataloging-in-Publication Data

Siegle, Bernard Andrew.
  Marriage according to the new code of Canon Law.

  1. Marriage (Canon law) I. Catholic Church. Codex
Juris Canonici (1983). Selections. English. 1986.
II. Title.
LAW   262.9'4   86-10806
ISBN 0-8189-0497-6

Imprimi Potest:
Dennis L. Sullivan, T.O.R.
Minister Provincial

Nihil Obstat:
Robert J. Hospodar, J.C.D.
Daniel Sinisi, T.O.R.

Imprimatur:
† Michael J. Dudick, D.D.
Bishop of Passaic Diocese
January 31, 1986

Designed, printed and bound in the United States of
America by the Fathers and Brothers of the
Society of St. Paul, 2187 Victory Boulevard,
Staten Island, New York 10314, as part of their
communications apostolate.

2 3 4 5 6 7 8 9 (Current Printing: first digit)

FOREWORD

The teaching of the Church regarding the Sacrament-Mystery of Marriage and especially their canonical dimension, normally strikes the laity as being complex and difficult to understand. This is further complicated by the constant flow of new decrees concerning marriage. The publication of *Marriage According to the New Code of Canon Law*, which incorporates recent jurisprudence with the theologically maturing spirit of post Vatican II, should be a welcome aid to those involved in pastoral ministry, who must contend with the reality of today's world.

Emerging in the Church during the past several years is a growing awareness of its mission to the divorced and separated. Advancements in the behavioral sciences have given new insights into resolving the difficult state of life in which the divorced find themselves. Since there have been so many changes both in law and in the spirit of the Church, priests often find themselves in a quandary when confronted with a marriage problem. To rely upon their seminary training, especially if ordained more than ten years, is like trying to solve a computer problem with high school algebra.

While in every diocese there are experts in canon law, the visible presence of the Church for the People of God is the parish priest. He is the one whom they first approach. He enjoys the opportunity to offer his knowledge and pastoral concern for their spiritual welfare. Father Bernard Siegle's *Marriage According to the New Code of Canon Law* is a practical guide and informational source meant to assist priests in bringing the peace of Christ into the hearts of many troubled people.

As presiding judge of the Tribunal of the Byzantine Catholic Archdiocese of Pittsburgh, Father Siegle has experienced a daily encounter with marriage law. He has witnessed its developments and lived with the changes on a personal basis. *Marriage According to the New Code of Canon Law* shares those insights and adds a particularly useful dimension. It treats not only the matrimonial jurisprudence of the Roman or Latin rite but also includes commentary on the Motu Proprio *Crebrae Allatae*, the matrimonial law of the Eastern Catholic Churches. Promulgated in 1949, *Crebrae Allatae*, is of more recent vintage than the C.I.C. and included some updated interpretations of the universal law. Several decisions of the Commission for the Authentic Interpretation of the Code of Canon Law have been rendered since 1949, which are of prime importance for inter-ritual relations.

Diocesan officials and those engaged in pastoral ministry will find Father Siegle's book useful when dealing with marriage of different rites. Frequently, they encounter cases involving Catholics of the Eastern Churches and are in need of a reference source. *Marriage According to the New Code of Canon Law* is a readily available and updated source to meet their needs.

Michael J. Dudick, D.D.
Eparch of Passaic

PREFACE

Marriage According to the New Code of Canon Law has been written as a handbook for seminarians, priests and others who might be interested in the preliminaries and fundamental basic factors of Canon Law on Marriage. It is not intended to be an exhaustive work. Those interested should have their own basic library of canonical works, such as: *The Tribunal, Reporter, Marriage Jurisprudence, The Jurist, Studia Canonica, Annulments, Canon Law Digest,* and, most of all, *The New Canons of 1983* and its commentary.

This is a time of transition. Canon Law exists and is being reviewed constantly even though we do not have a completely new Code of Law as yet. Canon Law is not in a vacuum, as some might think. Immediately after Vatican Council II in the 1960s, many presumed that we would have a whole new set of laws, but nothing that radical appeared on marriage as such. We are still waiting. Codification is a long process.

This handbook, then, is being published to fill that void somewhat and to fulfill the requests of students who wish to update their knowledge on the latest positions in law.

This is a challenge, but, as everyone knows, as soon as a book is published, it is criticized. This is good. Constructive criticism is a factor every writer welcomes, but no writer can please everyone. Moreover, those who could write a handbook are hesitant to do so. "Better something doubtful or overbold, and therefore in need of forgiveness, than nothing at all," says Karl Barth. Therefore, I accept the challenge.

Marriage According to the New Code of Canon Law contains all the new laws of the Code of 1983. Commentaries are made on important issues which should provoke discussion with the hope of establishing a good theology of law.

It must be noted that the term "contract" is used sometimes in this work, but the existing jurisprudence and theology of law since Vatican Council II recognizes marriage as a "covenant." For clarification, I have used substantial material from noted authors such as Morrisey, Sanson, LaSage, Wrenn, Maida, Bevilacqua and others. This is being done for the benefit of all the readers of this book, especially for those in other countries who do not have access to this current material. Therefore, with the permission of the renowned authors, their commentaries are used.

As an official of the Metropolitan Archdiocese of Pittsburgh, Pennsylvania (Byzantine Rite) for the past 33 years (16 years as Officialis), many interritual problems have come to my attention, which I discuss in this work.

We must remember that Canon Law is a universal law binding both Catholics of the Latin rite and Catholics of the Oriental rite. It is necessary to state that law in general is divided into two categories, namely (1) Divine Law, and (2) Human Law. Divine Law is subdivided into (a) Divine Natural Law, which is the participation of the Eternal Law of God, placed in the very nature of things when created by God; and (b) Divine Positive Law, which is made known by God himself through divine revelation. Human Law is subdivided into Ecclesiastical Law and Civil Law.

The Church teaches that all authority comes from God because in God's plan we find an orderly government of the world. The Church upholds that God delegated his authority to two perfect sovereign societies independently and exclusively competent to regulate the affairs of mankind within its own sphere. These two societies we call the Church and the State.* The Church was established by God for the spiritual welfare of man in the world to help him attain his salvation. The State, on the other hand, was established by God for the temporal welfare of mankind.

Within the Church's exclusive realm of jurisdiction come the seven Sacraments instituted by Christ. Moreover, the Roman Catholic Church considers itself as divinely appointed guardian and interpreter of the Divine Positive and Natural Law. It considers the State the legitimate civil authority which God grants the authority to make laws, carry them out and pass judgment upon all things which pertain to the temporal welfare of mankind.

Since marriage is the foundation stone of human society, the Church considers this institution most sacred because it was instituted by God not man.

God made certain positive regulations concerning marriage, but all the other important detail requirements and restrictions follow from the very nature of marriage itself for the benefit of mankind. All marriages should be governed by the precepts of divine-positive and natural laws, regardless of the tenets or belief of the individuals contracting marriage.

Marriage is a (contract) covenant between a man and a woman who are juridically capable of contracting it, by which each gives and accepts the perpetual and exclusive rights to acts suitable for the generation of offspring. This definition pertains to all marriages, regardless of the subjective beliefs, or the lack of belief, of the parties who contract marriage. Therefore, all persons, regardless of their religious belief, who are not juridically capable, who do not give and accept the right to acts suitable for generation, or who do not give and accept the right perpetually and exclusively, do not make a valid contract. Therefore, unity and indissolubility are the essential qualities of every true marriage by the Natural Law and by the very definition and nature of marriage. Because of this, a valid marriage "contract" is much different from every other "contract," the marriage "contract" results in a bond and relationship sealed by God, who instituted it, between the two parties.

Therefore, the marriage covenant cannot be broken by mutual agreement of both parties; although the two made the mutual "contract," they cannot undo or break this bond since this covenant is governed by Divine Law. It is principally with this end in view that this work has been written, in order to bring up-to-date all the new legislation according to the recommendations of Vatican Council II, the Synod of Bishops, the Ecumenical Age, and the Laws of 1983. This work is intended for every priest and clergyman, as well as the teacher, lawyer, and other members of the laity to whom it may concern and who wish to be more knowledgeable about the marriage regulations in this modern age.

For those of Asia, Africa, Europe, India and elsewhere who have reported to me in Rome on the lack of progress in their tribunals, I can only recommend these words from the Allocution of Pope Paul VI to the Auditors of the Roman Rota: "The ministry of the ecclesiastical judge is pastoral because it comes to the aid of the members of the People of God who find themselves in difficulties. For them the judge is sympathetic to the one who has erred, recognizes the rights of one who has suffered harm, been calumniated, or unjustly humiliated. The judicial authority is in this way an authority of service, a service consisting in the exercise of a power entrusted by Christ to his Church for the benefit of souls.

"Prudence is not in fact to be identified with slowness which sometimes results in real injustice to the great harm of souls."

---

* This was debated in the *Lex Fundamentalis*.

TABLE OF CONTENTS

Appendices

MARRIAGE
ACCORDING TO
THE NEW CODE OF CANON LAW

NATURE OF MARRIAGE
General Principles

Canon 1055

§1. The matrimonial covenant, by which a man and a woman establish between themselves a partnership of the whole of life, is by its very nature ordered to the good of the spouses and the procreation and education of offspring; this covenant between baptized persons has been raised by Christ the Lord to the dignity of a sacrament.

§2. For this reason a matrimonial contract cannot validly exist between baptized persons unless it is also a sacrament by that fact.

1. Marriage As a Covenant

Since Vatican II the emerging concept of covenant has revolutionized the study of Canon Law, permeating the New Code of Canon Law of 1983 and specifically the entire system of marriage law. Although ancient in origin, the notion of covenant as the basis for Canon Law is new. To understand it let's look briefly at some of its scriptural foundation, keeping in mind that we do not as yet have an adequate theology of covenant.

The heart of the biblical concept of covenant involves an approach by God and a response from us: "This day you have accepted God's commitment, and God has accepted yours" (Dt 16:17). A covenant is a form of contract, but in it the details are not always fixed at once. The duties are not carefully spelled out from the beginning. Fundamentally there are no formal legal terms. The law becomes secondary and continuous, a contingent expression of commitment, legalistic prescriptions of rights and duties being wholly secondary, never overshadowing the basic commitment of persons in fidelity and spontaneity (cf. Jos 24:19-20).

Thus covenant is seen in scripture *primarily* as a personal relationship and mutual commitment, even though from a human point of view it must be specified by legal terms and prescriptions accompanied by warnings of what will happen if the covenant is violated. Scripture also presents covenant in the light of God's two great covenant virtues: his *faithful promise* which will never be broken (cf. Jr 31:31-34), and his *loving kindness* whereby he continually extends not only selfless, creative love, but also forgiving and redemptive love (Mal 2:14).

In the classic passage of the New Testament covenant theology (Ep 5:21-32) we have the first *explicit* application of the mystery of Christ's covenant love to the reality of human marriage. Contemporary sacramental theologians focus on this passage in order to give primary importance to St. Paul's description of the marriage of two believers as a reflection of Christ's covenant of redemptive love and fidelity with the Church, and as a sign or sacrament of that covenant. Thus marriage is a sign or symbol of Christ's covenant precisely because marriage is itself a covenant mystery if seen in relation to Christ's covenant with His Church.

In law, the three goods (*bona*) of marriage proposed by St. Augustine have expressed this reality clearly. However, in the context of the conciliar constitution *Gaudium et Spes* (no. 48), we can now say that:

1. the *bonum prolis* is the right to intimate sexual union having openness to fecundity — the capacity to be responsible parents, not only procreating, but properly rearing and educating a family.
2. the *bonum fidei* is the right to a marital love special to this exclusive and lifelong union — the possibility of loving and being beloved as the "only one."
3. the *bonum sacramenti* is that Christian love which signifies and partakes of the mystery of that unity and fruitful love which exists between Christ and the Church — the capacity for life and for all the essentials of marriage.

Given this perspective, marriage becomes the interpersonal human relationship most closely mirroring the covenant between God and his people, between Christ and his Church. It may be defined as a graced covenant of love and fidelity between two baptized persons which, when ratified and sealed in the flesh, has God as its author, witness, and guarantor of the indissoluble bond.

The idea of covenant which emerged from the Second Vatican Council, in opposition to those who wanted marriage defined as a contract, corresponds to an understanding of marital intercourse as mutual self-giving — not the single act, but the whole community of life and love viewed as mutual self-giving. And the stability of the covenant derives from its divine ordination, which is more than a merely factual arrangement. Marriage, therefore, can be described as the intimate partnership of conjugal life and love which is rooted in the conjugal covenant or irrevocable personal consent. The relationship of this sacred bond arises by that human act whereby spouses mutually bestow and accept each other. The marriage covenant of conjugal love is ordained for the procreation and education of children. In the total communion of life and love, the partners render mutual help and service to each other by an intricate union of their persons and of their actions.

The Importance of Conjugal Love

The role of conjugal love has not always been recognized as an essential element of Christian marriage. The 1917 Code of Canon Law presented marriage as a contract giving rights to the *ius ad corpus* without any direct reference to conjugal love. Pius XI, in his 1930 encyclical *Casti Connubii*, spoke of conjugal love with two definitions of marriage. In the contractual definition, conjugal love is a secondary end. In the definition of marriage as a "communion of life" between husband and wife, conjugal love appears within the higher dimension of mutual sanctification in the supernatural order and is referred to as the "primary cause and reason" for marriage (A.A.S., 22 (1930), p. 547-548). Herbert Doms, when writing in 1935 of the meaning and purpose of marriage described the meaning or essence of marriage as first and foremost a communion of life, and its purpose was placed in this context: the purpose of marriage is the community of two persons who make but one person, a community of life embracing the whole human being, from the spiritual sphere, through that of sense, and into the bodily. On April 1, 1944, however, the Holy Office stated that it could not be admitted that the secondary ends are not essentially subordinate to the primary end, but are equally principal and independent (A.A.S., 36 (1944), p. 103). Ford and Kelly taught that conjugal love was an essential end of marriage: "Conjugal love is the virtue by which man and wife wish to communicate to each other the benefits proper to marriage." Among these benefits are "the sharing of each other's lives in the work to which the very instinct of paternal love impel father and mother" (*Contemporary Moral Theology*, Vol. II, p. 110).

In *Gaudium et Spes*, the Second Vatican Council issued an outstanding compromise statement on the theology of marriage, indicating an important development in the Church's understanding of the nature of Christian marriage. A remarkably strong emphasis is placed upon conjugal love, noting that the intimate union which is a consequence of conjugal love demands permanence and exclusivity, a sharing of actions and the creation of a common conscience. The sacramentality of marriage is explained in terms of a transforming effect, first upon the husband and wife and then upon the family. The Council sedulously avoids the terminology of primary and secondary ends, especially in paragraphs 48 and 50 where the following is phrased with so much care: "*non posthabitis ceteris matrimonii finibus*" (which not making the other purpose of marriage of less account). Conjugal love, then, must be productive of intimacy, of mutual fulfillment and sanctification, and also be open to fruitful love. Conjugal love and the procreation and education of children are not two disparate and separate elements, but intertwined, interrelated and both essential.

The covenanting of love described in *Gaudium et Spes*, no. 49, will be a primary source of sacramental theology for years to come. This love will be evaluated in terms of compatibility (personality), comprehension (intelligence), agreement (will power), affection (sensitivity), and charity (grace).

The beautiful theology of marriage contained in Pope Paul VI's 1967 encyclical *Humanae Vitae* was effectively ignored because of the birth control debate. The term "ends" is not used at all. Instead we find a recital of the characteristics of human love — the first time, it seems, that an official document of the magisterium applies the new understanding of marriage initiated by the Council. The encyclical gives five characteristics of conjugal love (nos. 9-10):

— it must be *fully human*, an expression of the senses and of the spirit, arising from the unity of heart and soul, presented in the light of an integral vision of human perfection;

— it must be *total*, generously sharing everything in an oblative love that excludes selfishness and undue reservations;
— it must be *faithful* and *exclusive* until death;
— it must be *fruitful*, ordained toward the rearing of new life;
— it must be *moral*, in the sense that the responsible exercise of parenthood implies that husband and wife fully recognize their own duties toward God, toward themselves, toward the family and toward society in a correct hierarchy of values.

This renewed teaching, a consequence of a "covenant theology," understands conjugal love as more than a "secondary end" of marriage, more even than an integral part. It becomes *essential*, since conjugal love is necessary to the developing communion of life and love. Since the two elements of "covenant" and "conjugal love" are both outside the juridical sphere, a third new element arises to enable Canon Law to apply the teachings of the renewal theology: the gift of oneself in a communion of life and love.

The Gift of Oneself in a Communion of Life and Love

While no theologian can yet define the essence of marriage, the key is found again in *Gaudium et Spes* where it relates the Conciliar teaching to the ordinary jurisprudence of the Rota. Due to the fact that the collection of sentences is not published until ten years later, we are only able to discover from a study of decisions published in canonical periodicals some indication of the influence this new doctrinal approach has had in determining the outcome of certain marriage cases. For many years the aptitude to perform a connatural conjugal act was considered in Canon Law to be the sign and proof of a valid marriage. This approach was based on the premise that law must be grounded in facts or realities which can be perceived and demonstrated. In former days, love, which is something intimate and changing, did not seem to provide a reliable and stable criterion of life in common. However, with the development of the psychological sciences and the perfecting of testing techniques, specialists are now able to understand better the human personality with its characteristic traits, weaknesses and impulses. Hence, conjugal love enters the canonical sphere as an aptitude for the community of conjugal life.

The Conjugal Community of Life and Love (No. 48, *Gaudium et Spes*)

On February 25, 1969, a decision, given by the Rota *coram* Msgr. Lucien Anne, brought the Conciliar teaching to the level of law and marked an important breakthrough in juridical practice. According to him the statement of the Second Vatican Council has juridical significance. Indeed, it is concerned not so much with the *establishment* of the community of life as it is with the rights and obligations of this intimate community of life which has as its most specific element the intimate union of persons by which a man and a woman become one flesh, and to which, as a summit, this community of life tends. He defines matrimonial consent as an act of the will by which a man and a woman constitute between themselves a mutual covenant, or by an irrevocable consent, a perpetual and exclusive community of conjugal life, ordered by its very nature to the generation and education of children. Thereby, the formal substantial object of this consent is found not only in the perpetual and exclusive *ius ad corpus*, but it also includes the right to a communion of love, or a community of life which, properly speaking, is matrimonial, and gives rise to correlative obligations or the right to an 'intimate conjunction of persons and works' by which they complete each other and associate their actions to God in the procreation and education of new lives. While Anne broke ice in this matter, the sailing was still not clear. Indeed, for a short period of time it seems that other Rotal judges did not care to admit this new interpretation of law. We find a strong stand taken against it in a decision by Pinto, July 30, 1969, in *Monitor ecclesiasticus*, 96 (1971), p. 510-512, and in another by Palazzini as late as June 2, 1971 (still unpublished). Likewise, the recent lengthy decision of C. Raab contests the interpretation given to the Conciliar and Rotal decisions by a number of canonists. Nevertheless there now appears to be greater uniformity, with conjugal love accepted as a capacity to commit oneself to a life-long union and to share a significant degree of one's life with a marriage partner. (See, for instance, S.R.R., Dec., C. Fagiolo, October 30, 1970, still unpublished).

The interrelated fundamental finality of marriage can be seen not in the mere multiplication of human life, nor in the human development of the spouses, but rather in the fulfillment and propagation of a value, love, which transcends and incorporates those particular aspects in imitation of its supreme source, God, who is Love. The Church now incorporates this teaching and practice of the courts in its formal legislation. Church law defines marriage as an intimate partnership of the whole of life between a man and a woman which by its very nature is ordered to the procreation and education of children. By comparing this descriptive definition with Canon 1013 of the old Code, we can appreciate the great progress that has taken place since 1917: "The primary end of marriage is the procreation and education of children; its secondary end is mutual help and the allaying of concupiscence."

Other Developments

A further step in jurisprudence was the recognition of the *donatio*, the giving by husband and wife of the right to the community of life. At first the Rotal judges accepted this in the sense that if the couple *could* not give the right, the marriage was invalid (S.R.R., Dec., C. Fagiolo, October 30, 1970). The idea later evolved that if they *did* not give the right, whether they could or not, the marriage again was invalid. The most recent development seems to be the recognition of an important point made by Msgr. J. Serrano of the Rota: the necessity that there exist on the part of those entering an interpersonal pact of marriage the capability of doing so. Marriage requires that both parties be able to accept the full interpersonal relations of the marriage state, each partner sharing a *right* to interpersonal friendship through interpersonal conjugal understanding.

The Rights Entailed in the Community of Conjugal Life

In the Rotal decision given by Msgr. Lucien Anne on February 25, 1969, there is mention of the rights pertaining to the *consortium vitae conjugalis* as outlined in *Gaudium et Spes*, no. 48. But we find no detailed analysis of the rights which should be considered essential to any true Christian marriage as described in the encyclical letter *Humanae Vitae*. In a decision given by the Montreal Appeal Tribunal on April 20, 1972 (Prot. No. AQ 5/72, reprinted in *Studia Canonica*, 6 [1972], p. 99-104: G. Lesage, O.M.I., *The 'Consortium Vitae Conjugalis': Nature and Applications*), Father Lesage lists some fifteen elements, the absence of which to a vital degree would deprive a partner of an essential right of marriage. In his more recent study, "Evolution recente de la jurisprudence matrimoniale," Father Lesage has reworked these rights, grouping them into headings which would make them more easily distinguishable. While some canonists might not agree with each of his points, we must recognize that they constitute one of the earliest attempts to determine more precisely the rights involved in a Christian marriage. Following Father Lesage, these are the elements of the community of conjugal life, the absence of which to a serious degree would render the consent null and void:

Balance and Maturity Required for Truly Human Conduct

The person as an individual must be able to function as a rational being: a maturity of personal conduct in the relationships of daily life; a self-mastery, which is indispensable for any reasonable and human conduct; a stability of conduct and ability to adapt to circumstances.

Capable of Interpersonal and Heterosexual Friendship

The person must be capable of heterosexual and conjugal love: the respect for Christian morality and for the partner's conscience in sexual and conjugal relationships; respective responsibility of husband and wife in conjugal friendship; mastery of passions, impulses or irrational instincts which would place mutual understanding or life in peril.

The Aptitude to Cooperate Sufficiently to be of Conjugal Assistance to One Another

The person must be capable of acting as a social being: an oblative love which is not merely seeking egotistical gratification but the good and happiness of the partner; a respect for the personality or sensitivity of the other party within the affective and sexual orders; kindness and gentleness of character and manners in mutual relationships.

Mental Balance and a Sense of Responsibility for the Material Welfare of the Family

Needed are: respective responsibility of both husband and wife in providing for the material well-being of the home, stability in employment, budgetary foresight, etc.; mutual sharing and consultation on important points of conjugal and family life; objectivity and realism in the evaluation of happenings and events of family or conjugal life; lucidity in the choice and determination of the ends and means to attain them.

Psychic Capacity to Participate in Promoting the Welfare of the Children

Each of the partners must be capable of being a parent with a sense of moral and psychological responsibility for the generation, care, love and education of their children. If one of the spouses is radically unable, in spite of his or her good will, to meet these needs sufficiently, the other partner is deprived of an essential right of Christian marriage. A person incapable of fulfilling the object of the marriage promise enters into an invalid union. More will be said on this matter when we consider the defects of consent.

If other courts would devise similar criteria, their work would be simplified, especially in dealing with cases of lack of due discretion. It would also enable the jurisprudence of the Church to develop in accord with Conciliar teaching and recent advances found in Rotal decisions. To understand the position of the Church's marriage courts today, it is essential to grasp the principles underlying their practice.

2. Marriage As a Sacrament

Marriage is a visible sign instituted by Christ to give sacramental grace. This he did by making the contract the instrument by which sacramental grace is conveyed to the parties. The sign consists of *matter* and *form*: "The mutual and lawful surrender of the bodies indicated by *words* or *signs* expressing the interior is the *matter* of the sacrament while the mutual lawful acceptance of the bodies is its *form*" (Pope Benedict XIV). The matter, then, is the mutual offer made by the words or signs expressing genuine internal consent to the contract, while the form is the mutual acceptance expressed in a similar manner. For a valid contract, consent must be both interiorly genuine and mutually expressed externally.

The sacred quality of any marriage was emphasized by Pope Pius XI when he said: "The light of reason alone — above all, if we study the ancient records of history, if we question the unchanging conscience of peoples, if we examine the institutions and moral codes of nations — is enough to establish that there is in marriage itself a sacred and religious quality" (*Casti Connubii*). Even Pope Innocent III and Pope Honorius III "felt able to affirm without rashness and even with good reason that the sacrament of marriage exists among believers and unbelievers," says Pope

Leo XIII, meaning that these popes considered the act of marriage itself to be holy as a fact of nature willed by God.

Pope Pius XI continues: "The sacred character of marriage, intimately linked to the order of religion and of holy things, is the effective result of its divine origin and also of its purpose which is to bring children to birth and to form them for God, and at the same time to bind husband and wife to God in Christian love and mutual help; and finally, it is the result of the duty which is mutual to married union itself, instituted as it is by the all-wise providence of God the Creator, the duty to serve as a sort of medium for the transmission of life, by which parents become as it were the instruments of the almighty power of God." To emphasize still further that the sacred character of marriage is inherent in its nature, Pius XII reminds us that "even among those who are not baptized, legimately contracted marriage is, in the natural order a sacred thing" (*Allocution to the Sacred Roman Rota*, October 6, 1946).

When marriage is contracted between two baptized persons, that very fact makes it a sacrament because Christ elevated marriage to that supernatural dignity.[1] Thus marriage obtains its sacramental character from the moment of its celebration if the parties are already validly baptized, and acquires it later if baptism takes place after marriage. This raises the question of whether or not every contract of marriage is a sacrament for validly baptized Christians.[2] During the Code Commission's deliberations after Vatican II, Canon 1055 was challenged. Where there is a contract, there is also a sacrament, whether willed or not, whether the parties are suited for it or not, whether they are believing Christians or not at the time of the marriage. The Commission's suggested revision (Canon 242, §1.2°) reveals this conflict. Faith, they said, is important to all Christians. A literal definition of faith can be found in Hebrews: ". . . it is impossible to please God without faith, since anyone who comes to him must believe that he exists (6:6) and rewards those who try to find him." In other words, a *saving* faith is necessary; one should have a firm belief in the Incarnation and Redemption of Christ. Marriage, to be called sacramental, should be contracted in faith in order to receive grace, otherwise we are putting false labels, as it were, on products which are absent. For example, we could have two non-Catholics, baptized in infancy, who never had any connection with Christianity since, entering into a "sacramental" marriage. Can we put such a label on it? The same can be said for two non-practicing Catholics who have abandoned their faith or their Christian ideals. Perhaps the canon would better read: "When two *believing*, validly baptized persons contract marriage, this marriage becomes by that very fact a sacramental marriage." When this conflict was brought to the attention of those who formulated the final revision of the new Code, it was discussed briefly, then set aside. Maybe some future canonist will take up the dilemma again one day and subsequent revisions of the Code will be more precise.

Some non-Catholics also question the declaration of the Church that Christ instituted the sacrament of marriage, asking, "How did he do it and when?" "What words did he use?" Scripture gives no details whatsoever about this matter.

Canon 1056

The essential properties of marriage are unity and indissolubility, which in Christian marriage acquire a special firmness in virtue of the sacrament.

3. Purpose and Essential Properties of Marriage

Unity is one of the essential characteristics of every marriage whether Christian or non-Christian. By unity is meant oneness. A husband has only one wife; a wife has only one husband. Unity means that marriage can take place only between one man and one woman, in other words monogamy. The opposite is polygamy which can take the form either of polyandry which exists when one woman has several husbands, or polygeny which exists when one man has several wives. Polyandry seems opposed to one of the primary concepts of natural law. It is also opposed to the primary ends of marriage since it not only interferes with the love and companionship of the spouse, but is also the potential cause of sterility. If there are children, the paternity is rendered doubtful, in which case the education of the children becomes uncertain.

Indissolubility means that the contract of marriage cannot be dissolved at will or with the consent of the contracting parties but only through the death of one of the parties.

Canon 1057

§1. **Marriage is brought about through the consent of the parties, legitimately manifested between persons who are capable according to law of giving consent; no human power can replace this consent.**

§2. **Matrimonial consent is an act of the will by which a man and a woman, through an irrevocable covenant, mutually give and accept each other in order to establish marriage.**

4. Marital Consent

The covenant of marriage begins with the mutual exchange of consent between the two individuals entering into the marriage. Before the 12th century a conflict existed between the Church and secular authorities wherein parents or secular authorities attempted to secure economic, political, or familial gain by giving or withholding marital consent. This situation still exists in some countries, e.g., India, where dowries are still in vogue. A comprehensive treatise on consent will be found under Canon 1095.

Canon 1058

All persons who are not prohibited by law can contract marriage.

5. Freedom to Marry

This canon stems from the principle of the natural liberty of individuals. Marriage is a natural right because society is founded by God for the propagation of the human race. Hence, this right must be honored unless there is some just prohibition of law which would impede it. Since marriage between all validly baptized persons (Catholic or non-Catholic) is a sacrament, ecclesiastical authority must safeguard the sanctity of matrimony and does so by determining how, when and where the marriage will be celebrated. The prohibition mentioned in this canon occurs when there is some impediment which would render the marriage illicit or invalid.

Strictly speaking, an *impediment* is a circumstance which renders a marriage either illicit or invalid, e.g., impotency, the previous bond of marriage, affinity, etc. Error, force and fear (e.g., of coercion), are not impediments in the strict sense. Neither is a temporary prohibition which a bishop imposes because this prohibition is not imposed by law but by a precept of the ordinary.

Canon 1059

Even if only one party is baptized, the marriage of Catholics is regulated not only by divine law but also by Canon Law, with due regard for the competence of civil authority concerning the merely civil effects of such a marriage.

6. Authority of the Church Over Marriage of the Baptized

Divine Law: Whatever is required by the natural law for all marriage contracts is also necessary for a Christian marriage. All marriages are governed by the natural and divine positive law. Moreover, it must be remembered that marriage was restored to its pristine category (unity and indissolubility) by Christ not only for all Christians but for all people (A.A.S. 41-158).

Canon Law: Because marriage is a sacrament, the Church claims independent and exclusive right over marriages of all who are validly baptized, Protestants as well as Catholics. This power of authority has been given to the Church by Christ (Leo XIII, Encyclical *Arcanum*). The Church as such is the official custodian and interpreter of laws governing marriage. This jurisdiction — legislative, judicial and coercive — includes all marriages in which at least one of the parties is baptized. It has the power to establish both diriment and prohibitive impediments. It is competent to render decisions on matrimonial cases within the limits of the natural and divine laws.

Although the Church does not legislate directly for unbaptized persons (Canon 11), nevertheless whenever one of the parties is Catholic it claims direct jurisdiction over the entire contract of marriage and so indirectly over the unbaptized. The question is disputed, however, since a contract which is indivisible must be governed by one power or another, namely, the Church or the State. According to present jurisprudence, the right of the Church is upheld. Because Canon Law concerns itself with marriage as a sacrament and as a contract, the contract in a sacramental marriage is considered indivisible from the sacrament. The contract and the sacrament cannot be separated; they are one and the same. The priest present at the marriage does not contribute anything to the matter and form of the sacrament. The bodies of the spouses constitute the *matter* of the sacrament; the words they express represent the *form*. The same matter and form are found in the natural contract as well. Christ added nothing external to that contract. He merely raised the natural contract to the dignity of a sacrament.

Civil Law: According to this canon the civil power has jurisdiction over the civil effects of marriage, but not over the bond itself or what is essential to marriage. The civil effects are those which are separable from the substance of the marriage contract, e.g., a dowry, the tenure of property, the right of succession, the right of the wife to use the husband's name, etc. (Vidal, No. 10). If there is no infringement upon divine or Canon Law, the civil power may prescribe regulations which safeguard health and public order, just as it requires a license or the registration of marriage and these regulations must always be just and reasonable.

Form of Marriage for the Unbaptized: Since the Church does not claim any right over the unbaptized, these persons must be subject to some other authority in order to ensure that peace and public order as well as the good of the family and of society are maintained. Therefore, within the realm of the natural law, the State can determine the form and criteria of validity for the marriage of the unbaptized.

Oriental Dissidents: The Orthodox faithful are not subject to *Crebrae Allatae* (even though there are authors who think otherwise, e.g., Coussa, Pospishil, Herman and others). The Orthodox Churches are not bound by *Crebrae Allatae* because there are no conciliar or papal statements extant denying the Orthodox hierarchy the authority to make or change their disciplinary legislation. As a matter of fact, there are innumerable statements to the effect that the Latin Church is committed to uphold the laws, rites and customs of the Oriental Churches. Furthermore, Clement Pujol of the Oriental Institute, who studied the preparatory acts as well as the final document of the motu proprio, *Crebrae Allatae*, concluded that it was not the intention of Pope Pius XII to legislate for the Orthodox. Motivated by the pleas of Catholic bishops, the Pope promulgated the new legislation in 1949 *only for those Orientals in union with the Holy See*. To have tried to legislate for the Orthodox would only have exacerbated the present split between the Catholic and Orthodox communions. Pujol holds that the technical term "*christifideles*" — the same term used in previous documents in a similar context — refers only to Catholics. Moreover, it is a general principle of the Roman Church not to legislate for the Orthodox.

Canon 1060

Marriage enjoys the favor of law; consequently, when a doubt exists, the validity of a marriage is to be upheld until the contrary is proven.

7. Marriage Favored by the Law

Whenever a doubt arises concerning the validity of a marriage that was certainly celebrated, the marriage is considered valid until the contrary is proven with moral certainty. If there is a doubt of fact that the marriage was celebrated, but the parties are in possession of a decent public reputation as a married couple, the marriage is considered valid until proven otherwise. In all cases the presumption is in favor of the marriage, both in the internal and external forum. Since every presumption is a probable conjecture in an uncertain matter, the presumption holds whether the marriage is valid or invalid until proven definitely. This theory is based on the fact that one would take the risk of violating the natural law by making either decision. In the case of marriage, the Code Commission gave a decision that the presumption of validity with respect to a first marriage (in which a doubt arises) is sufficient to justify a declaration of nullity of a subsequent marriage, provided the case is being handled according to the ordinary course of law. This canon is applicable especially in the United States in bigamy cases.

The exception to this canon is provided for in Canon 1150. In case of doubt, the privilege of the faith enjoys the favor of the law. In other words, the presumption of Canon 1150 takes precedence over the presumption of Canon 1137 because the privilege of the faith enjoys the favor of the law when there is doubt as to the validity of a marriage contracted by the unbaptized. The doubt is to be resolved in favor of the faith, in other words, or in favor of the convert. A question logically arises: Why should cases of doubt of law not favor the individual in cases that are not in favor of the faith? The general rule is: Doubt of law favors the institution rather than the individual.

In his talk at the meeting of the Canon Law Society of America in

Denver, 1967, Msgr. Stephan Kelleher, J.C.D, brought to light some interesting facts about Canon 1137 which are worthy of consideration. He said: "The canon goes on to state that in case of doubt a marriage is to be considered valid unless the contrary is proven. This is the heart of our subject. When there are strong reasons favoring the invalidity of a marriage, must its validity be upheld because there is probability that it may be valid? It is with this question that we are primarily concerned ... Granted that marriage enjoys the favor of the law, what action may a person take to try to free himself from the bond of an unhappy marriage? What steps can be taken so that the force of presumption of Canon 1060 may be reduced? Can steps be taken so that, where the presumption stands, marriages may be dissolved?"

These solutions were offered: (a) establishing a revised judicial procedure whereby a judicial official grants annulments; (b) establishing a judicial or administrative procedure whereby an ecclesiastical official grants a divorce; (c) allowing a personal decision by a party or parties to a marriage that the marriage is null. "Can there be a judicial or administrative procedure whereby the Church will grant divorces, including divorces in sacramental, consummated marriages? The answer to this question lies with the teaching authority of the Catholic Church, guided in large part by scripture scholars and theologians. The ideal of the indissolubility of marriage is not at stake. Every divorce has elements of tragedy. There is a potential tragedy in any marriage if the parties do not initially intend a permanent marriage ... Granted the validity of the indissolubility of every marriage, is every marriage an ideal marriage? Given the fact that divorce is in fact almost as common among Catholics as among non-Catholics, does the present teaching of the Church contribute to the common good? My response to these questions inclines to the negative. In view of the number of persons who cannot go to the sacraments, does not present teaching derogate from the common good and adversely affect the spiritual lives of many individual persons? If the Church permitted divorce, would Catholics be in a more realistically effective position to influence civil legislation to sustain individual rights and to foster the common good? My response to these questions inclines to the affirmative.

"Canon 1060 states that, for the welfare of the community, the stability of the institution of marriage is to take precedence over the rights of individual persons. In our culture there is a fundamental error in a judicial system which is more concerned with protecting what it conceives to be the stability of a given institution than with the safeguarding of rights of the human persons involved in that institution. Canon 1060 is concerned primarily with marriages whose validity is in some way doubtful. There is an inconsistency between what this canon requires of Christian souls and what we have consistently been taught to require of souls in other moral situations. For example, when the Church recognizes the moral system of probabilism to be used in the sacrament of Penance, it is saying that we have no right to impose the stricter obligation upon a Christian soul when there is a reasonable doubt concerning the immorality of a certain action. In such matters the Church does not look primarily to the protection of the institution; she looks primarily to safeguarding the basic right of the Christian to be free from obligations other than those that are certain.

"Consistent logic, as well as the present conciliar teaching on the meaning of Christian freedom and responsibility, call for change in our outlook concerning doubtfully valid marriages. It would be well if we adopt the principle that where there is a preponderance of evidence that a marriage is invalid, or where there is solidly probable evidence that a marriage is not viable, the individual who so desires could be declared free of such a marriage."

We cannot deny that the privilege of the faith means in some cases that a person who is baptized enjoys more favors in the Church than an unbaptized person. Moreover, the privilege also means that a person who receives baptism acquires a more favorable position legally than he had formerly. In an Allocution of Pope Pius XII to the Sacred Roman Rota, he remarked that in approaching this type of case, we are not to be too lenient nor too strict. The *via media* should be chosen; first things should be put first; *salus animarum* is to be preferred to the letter of the law. In the words of St. Paul, "The letter kills; the spirit gives life." Pope Pius XI, who was a great defender of Christian marriage, has revealed in *Casti Connubii* that he too was greatly concerned with the sacrament of marriage but was never reluctant to use the privilege of the faith when cases were presented to him. Therefore, *salus animarum* should be the principle governing such cases.

Canon 1061

§1. A valid marriage between baptized persons is called ratified only if it has not been consummated; it is called ratified and consummated if the parties have performed between themselves in a human manner the conjugal act which is per se suitable for the generation of children, to which marriage is ordered by its very nature and by which the spouses become one flesh.

§2. After marriage has been celebrated, if the spouses have cohabited consummation is presumed until the contrary is proven.

§3. An invalid marriage is called putative if it has been celebrated in good faith by at least one of the parties, until both parties become certain of its nullity.

8. Types of Marriage

This canon spells out three legal terms: ratified, consummated and putative. The equivalent canon in the 1917 Code contains other terms with which we should be familiar because they are in common usage.

Ratum: a sacramental marriage which takes place between two validly baptized persons (Catholics and Protestants) but which has not been consummated by the conjugal act.

Ratum et Consummatum: a marriage which is both sacramental and consummated by the conjugal act. A marriage is not considered consummated by any act of sexual intercourse which may have occurred prior to a valid marriage. Neither is onanistic intercourse considered sufficient for consummation.

Consummatum et Ratum: two unbaptized persons enter into matrimony and later, after their marriage is consummated, receive baptism together.

Legitimum: a marriage between two unbaptized individuals.

Naturale: a marriage between a baptized and an unbaptized person. It is not a term found in the Code but it has been used by the Holy Office in one of its decisions (S.C.S. Office, Nov. 5, 1924). Such a marriage is not a sacramental marriage since the sacrament cannot exist in one party and not in the other in the view of those who use this term.

Putativum: an invalid marriage which was contracted in good faith by at least one of the parties, and it remains putative until the parties become aware of its invalidity. Children born of a putative marriage are considered legitimate on the principle that the ignorance of one or both parties regarding an impediment which invalidated the marriage and the absence of malice on the part of the parties is sufficient to legitimize the children and to differentiate the putative from the ordinary invalid marriage. The Code Commission was asked whether the word *celebratum* of Canon 1061, §3 is to encompass only marriages celebrated before the Church. The reply was in the affirmative (Jan. 26, 1949). Therefore marriages between Catholics and non-Catholics contracted outside the Church, though the Catholics are in good faith, cannot be called putative.

Attempted Marriage: an invalid marriage, strictly speaking, whereby at least one party to the marriage contract is cognizant of an invalidating impediment, e.g., a marriage which takes place without the proper form according to Canon 1108, §1.

Public Marriage: a marriage celebrated in the external forum or in some public way and recognized by the Church as valid.

Clandestine Marriage: a marriage contracted without the presence of the pastor and two witnesses.

Secret Marriage or *Marriage of Conscience*: a marriage contracted before the pastor and two witnesses but secretly for some very grave reason. These marriages are not recorded in the regular parish matrimonial register but entered in the secret archives in the chancery (Canon 489). One must have special permission to perform such a secret marriage (Canon 1130-1133).

Canon 1062

§1. A promise of marriage, be it unilateral or bilateral, called an engagement, is regulated by particular law which has been established by the conference of bishops after it has taken into consideration any existing customs and civil laws.

§2. A promise to marry does not give rise to an action to seek the celebration of marriage; an action for reparation of damages, however, does arise if it is warranted.

9. Engagement: Promise of Marriage

Engagement or promise to marry, a long-standing tradition, is still in vogue in some contemporary societies throughout the world. The Mosaic law gave juridic force to an engagement. Medieval Germanic law also gave legal status to engagement to the extent that infidelity while engaged was considered adultery. In Roman law, an engagement was considered as a wife purchase, but in the Church it came to be understood as a promise of marriage in the future. Nevertheless, there was (and in many areas of the world there still is) some form of monetary exchange (dowry) prior to marriage.

The new Code considers a betrothal or engagement merely as a promise to marry at some future time. This promise has moral force but does not bind legally; no person can be bound to marry against his or her will. Refinements of the law on engagements are left to the particular legislation of local episcopal conferences. There have been cases where one party to an engagement was sued by the other when the engagement was broken, demanding remuneration for expenses connected with wedding attire, orchestra, reception hall, and so on.

For individuals planning to make promises in an engagement, the following considerations are presented:

Nature of an Engagement: An engagement is a contract whereby two persons mutually promise to marry each other in the future. They must be capable of making this contract (for example, an engagement by minors would be valid but illicit). It is possible to have a conditional engagement.[3]

Form of an Engagement: The promise of marriage must be (a) in writing, (b) signed by the parties, (c) signed by the pastor or local ordinary or two witnesses in order to be valid. This will be determined by the local conference of bishops. If either or both parties are unable to write, an additional witness must sign the above-mentioned document for validity. All parties involved must sign in each other's presence. The contract may be made by proxy.

Binding Force of an Engagment: The parties involved have a grave obligation in justice to fulfill the terms of the contract (e.g., to marry at the time specified in the contract). An obligation of fidelity to one another arises to the exclusion of any third party, i.e., fornication with a third party would be unjust. Although the engagement contract is valid, it does not give rise to the right of legal action in compelling the celebration of the marriage. If one of the parties suffers harm, financial or any other, by the breaking of this contract, he or she may sue for damages.

Dissolution of the Contract: The contract can be dissolved by (a) mutual consent of the contracting parties, (b) papal dispensation, (c) a subsequent invalidating impediment which cannot be dispensed, (d) entrance into a religious institute, (e) reception of holy orders, (f) inability to change the object of the contract, i.e., one becomes a heretic, an alcoholic, mentally ill or mutilated.

Recommendations: With almost fifty percent of all marriages ending in divorce in the United States today, many priests have successfully initiated a program to reduce the number of divorces by using the protective Canon 1062 regarding the solemn engagement. Although this canon has been with us since 1917, it has so seldom been used that priests who have been approached by prospective couples have turned them away because the priest was not acquainted with the betrothal contract and ceremony. This laudable ceremony which is sanctioned by the Church should be introduced into our pastoral work and employed for all couples contemplating future marriage.

Historically, formal engagements were considered a promise of future marriage by Roman law and the Roman pontiffs. St. Thomas Aquinas referred to this engagement contract as a "quasi-sacramental." The Codes of 1917 and 1983 treat engagement as either bilateral or unilateral contracts. When the contract is made and accepted by both parties, it is *bilateral*; when made by only one and accepted by the other, it is *unilateral*.

The pastor is, of course, not bound to insist on a formal engagement contract, but use of the solemn engagement contract may serve to help stem the climbing divorce rate in our country today. The betrothal contract can act as a safety measure which provides an excellent opportunity for proper preparation and anticipation of many obligations, cares and responsibilities which every marriage presents to those entering this particular state of life.

It must be understood that the natural law requires no special formality, but that such a special formality or solemnity is required by the positive law found in Canon 1062. For this solemnity and for validity, the several conditions specified must be observed. It must be signed by both parties and by either the pastor or the local ordinary or at least two witnesses. Non-Catholics and even children with the use of reason can act as witnesses. The contract should be dated and the place indicated, but this is not required for validity.

Oriental Law: Unlike the Latin Church, the Oriental Church has retained the ordinary practice of formal engagement. The new Oriental

Code specifically treats of this solemn engagement in Canons §6 and §7.

Canon 6: §1. The promise of marriage, even though bilateral, or in the nature of a mutual espousal, is null in both forms unless made before the pastor of the local hierarch or before a priest to whom the faculty of assisting has been given by either of these.

§2. 1° The same pastor or local hierarch or priest designated by either, can validly assist at a promise of marriage who, by prescription of Canons 86 and 87 can validly assist at the marriage.

2° He who assists at a promises of marriage is by obligation bound to see to it that the celebration is entered into his book of espousals.

3° However, from the promise of marriage, no judicial action is made available for seeking the celebration of marriage; such action is granted for the repairing of damages if any be due.

Canon 7: The priest assisting at the promise of marriage must not neglect to impart to the Catholic parties the blessing prescribed by the liturgical books, if particular law provides for this.

This canon is practically the same as in the Latin Code, as you can see, except that it need *not* be made in writing. If a couple belongs to different rites, either pastor may witness the engagement. However, it may be more advantageous for the pastor who will eventually assist at the marriage to handle this matter.

Suggestions for the Latin Rite Ceremony

A brief talk may be given by a priest before witnesses telling the couple that the promises they will make to each other do not bind under sin. It is well that they come to make their engagement promises publicly and to ask the Church's blessing on such an important occasion in their preparation for the great sacrament of matrimony. An individual who enters a religious community prepares for his or her life by a novitiate; candidates for the priesthood spend many years in study and prayer; so also matrimony should be entered into with great care and consideration. Some instructions may be given regarding the couple's sincerity and devotion to one another as all listen attentively to the words of the priest.

Then standing, the couple reads the formula of engagement aloud together and signs it. The priest adds his own signature, stating that he witnesses to this proposal and declares the couple engaged in the name of the Father and of the Son and of the Holy Spirit. He may then sprinkle the couple with holy water.

An engagement ring (if given) may now be blessed using the formula: *Our help is in the name of the Lord.* Response: *Who made heaven and earth.* Priest: *The Lord be with you.* Response: *And also with you.* Priest: *Let us pray. Bless, O Lord, this ring which we bless in your name, that he who gives it and she who will wear it, keeping full faith with each other, may abide in your peace and in your will, through Christ our Lord.* All: *Amen.* In a double ring ceremony, the same formula is repeated for the woman.

If further solemnity is desired, the priest may read from John 15 and an appropriate hymn may be sung as a response by all those present. The engaged couple may then kneel before the priest who places his stole over their clasped hands and says: *May God bless your bodies and your souls. May he send his blessings upon you as he blessed Abraham, Isaac and Jacob. May our Blessed Mother keep you in her care. May guardian angels protect you from all harm and lead you on the path to holiness. Go in peace in the name of Christ the Lord.* All: *Amen.*

Sample Contract: We, the undersigned, being of sound mind and understanding fully the obligations to be assumed, do hereby freely and mutually promise to enter into matrimony on . . . . . *(day and date)* . . . .

Signature of Man . . . . Date . . . .

Signature of Woman . . . . Date . . . .

Signature of Pastor . . . . Date . . . .

(Church Seal)

---

1 Cf. Gasparri, *De Matrimonio*, I, p. 31.
2 A subject of much theological discussion and diverse opinions among Robert Bellarmine, Suarez, Sanchez, De Lugo, Gasparri, Cappello and others.
3 Mathis & Meyer, S.J., *The Pastoral Companion*, Chicago, 1961, p. 170.

Chapter One

PRELIMINARIES TO MARRIAGE

Canon 1063

Pastors of souls are obliged to see to it that their own ecclesial community furnishes the Christian faithful assistance so that the matrimonial state is maintained in a Christian spirit and makes progress toward perfection. This assistance is especially to be furnished through:

§1. preaching, catechesis adapted to minors, youth and adults, and even the use of the media of social communications so that through these means the Christian faithful may be instructed concerning the meaning of Christian marriage and the duty of Christian spouses and parents;

§2. personal preparation for entering marriage so that through such preparation the parties may be predisposed toward the holiness and duties of their new state;

§3. a fruitful liturgical celebration of marriage clarifying that the spouses signify and share in that mystery of unity and of fruitful love that exists between Christ and the Church;

§4. assistance furnished to those already married so that, while faithfully maintaining and protecting the conjugal covenant, they may day by day come to lead holier and fuller lives in their families.

1. Pastoral Care in Preparation for Marriage

Every pastor is a teacher. He must instruct. Therefore, he must have the right knowledge and understanding of the principles of Christian marriage and morality since the common good depends to a great extent on this. Today, when pornography and sex information of all kinds are being freely distributed to the young, the proper approach to instruction in sexual matters must differ markedly from what it was in generations past. In the 1917 Code, this canon cautioned pastors to avoid abruptness or embarrassing situations when counseling couples about to be married. There are various means and techniques for dealing with such delicate subjects. The priest should first acquaint himself with the person to be instructed and proceed according to individual circumstances. Different approaches are required in the cases of, for example, a nurse, an ordinary layman, or an illiterate person, even though the same essential doctrine must be imparted to each. This is stressed here because unfortunately mistakes have been made in the past in this regard. Every priest must use common sense and good judgment while at the same time facing facts. He must explain the principles of marriage and the responsibility married people have to society. He must stress the idea that marriage is not a private matter, that the common good plays an important role in this particular phase of any young couple's life.

The encyclical *Casti Connubii* deals with the nature and dignity of marriage, and a thorough course in this subject should be given in high schools and colleges. High school students are certainly not too young for this instruction, and many of them will not go on to college to be exposed to this at a more mature age. Many modern philosophies, incompatible as they are with Christian teaching, also undermine the common good of society. It is the pastor's duty to offset this by insisting on the proper instruction both of the young as well as of those about to be married.

Canon 1063 *obliges* the pastor to give proper instruction to parties wishing to enter marriage. He is to lay the foundation for their future happiness as well as provide solid instruction and preparation for the realities of married life. Many failures in marriage have been traced to priests who have been disinterested or gave no counsel at all.

Pre-Cana Programs

The *Prenuptial Investigation* involves an examination of each party privately and the publication of the banns in accordance with the directives set down by the local conference of bishops (Canon 1067). Such a thorough investigation prevents invalid marriages and at the same time protects the dignity of the sacrament of matrimony in the interest of the family and society.[1]

When danger of death is a factor, the law is not so strict. The couple merely declares under oath that they are baptized and not under any impediment of marriage. Should there be any impediments, Canon 1079 should be invoked.

Too many marriages have failed due to pastoral negligence in making proper investigations before the marriage. When searches are made in parochial files, some cases reveal that the pastor had no time to be bothered. Yet, if he had taken the time to check each couple according to this canon, he would have discovered that they were either not sufficiently instructed or that they entered marriage without the proper intention. All pastors and others charged with premarital investigation and instruction have the very grave responsibility to make these investigations properly and thoroughly.

If the party or parties involved are living at a distance from the parish, the pastor of their home parish will investigate the matter and send all his findings to the pastor who will assist at the marriage.

Each party should be interrogated separately. Many things are revealed when they are free to talk. (This is also advisable when a married couple initially comes for counseling because of problems in the marriage.) Prudence is mandatory in making the investigation, especially when dealing with non-Catholics. Priests should be open-minded, discreet and tactful.

Historically, the Holy See has tried to impress pastors with the seriousness of this great responsibility. In 1970 the Holy Office gave definite instructions regarding prenuptial investigations. Pastors were told to check carefully for impediments and to determine whether the parties were entering the marriage freely. This question was to be directed to the woman especially, as she was the one most likely to be forced into a marriage against her will. The Holy Office further demanded that priests and bishops comply with this regulation strictly.

In 1911 the Sacred Congregation of the Sacraments issued a decree dealing with premarital investigations, admonishing careless pastors in this regard. In 1921 pastors were again reminded of the evils connected with poor and improper investigations. The decree contained the following items of importance.

(1) Ordinaries were instructed to remind all pastors to refrain from assisting at marriages unless they had satisfactory *proof* of the freedom of the parties to marry according to Canons 1067 and 1068, and above all to

demand certificates of baptism of both if they were baptized in another parish.

(2) The pastor who assisted at the marriage was required to *promptly* inform the pastor of baptism of this marriage (cf. Canon 1103, §2).

(3) For security and expeditiousness, pastors were exhorted to send all necessary documents through their respective chanceries.

(4) Pastors were to consult the ordinary regarding transients (*vagi*), immigrants and migrant workers, except in cases of necessity or danger of death.

(5) If the pastor of baptism received a notice of marriage to be entered into the record and found that the party was married before, he was to consult the ordinary immediately.

(6) Ordinaries were instructed to impose necessary canonical sanctions on those pastors who were negligent in making proper prenuptial investigations.

The Sacred Congregation of the Sacraments, on June 29, 1941, issued an Instruction on the manner of making premarital investigations. It indicated that the pastor of the bride has the right and grave duty to investigate whether there are any obstacles to the marriage. He may conduct the inquiry regarding the groom or request the groom's pastor to do so. When the parties are from different dioceses, documents of investigation should be transmitted through the groom's diocesan chancery to the pastor of the bride; or if the marriage is to take place in the domicile of the groom, then the documents should be sent in the same manner to the groom's pastor. It is also suggested that the *nihil obstat* be obtained by the chancery of the place of marriage. Many chanceries have drawn up their matrimonial forms according to this Instruction.

Canon 1063 of the New Code is clear on the catechesis and preparation for marriage. Besides the pastor's own instructions, the Code specifies utilization of the media of social communications and the expertise of specialists such as physicians, psychologists, lawyers, counseling agencies, etc., before, during and after marriage. The new Code stresses the grave obligation pastors have, especially in view of the serious problems facing all marriages today. *Gaudium et Spes* describes marriage as being "everywhere overshadowed by polygamy, the plague of divorce, so-called free love and similar blemishes; furthermore, married love is too often dishonored by selfishness, hedonism and unlawful contraceptive practices.

Besides, the economic, social, psychological and civil climate of today has a severely disturbing effect on family life." And the Papal Commission on Marriage and the Family states: "The crisis which gravely affects the family in those countries [European and North American] arises directly from the development of a mentality which stresses material success, individualism, efficiency and a technology that is becoming more and more refined, and the development of a life style that stresses money, action and power."

For the well-being of Christian society and evangelization in general, Canon 1063 cannot be stressed enough. The pastor's obligation with respect to marriage in today's world is very grave. Every society has a right to expect maturity and a full Christian commitment from the individuals who marry. Canon 1063 names four explicit areas wherein pastors must assist in marriage preparation:

(1) General catechesis of all the Christian faithful on marriage;
(2) Proximate preparation of individuals planning to get married;
(3) Fruitful liturgical celebration of the sacrament of marriage;
(4) Ongoing marital assistance to couples who request it.

Pope John Paul II in a recent allocution on the family says: "More than ever necessary in our times is preparation of young people for marital and family life . . . But the changes that have taken place within almost all modern societies demand that not only the family but also society and the Church should be involved in the effort of properly preparing young people for their future responsibilities. Many negative phenomena which are today noted with regret in family life derive from the fact that, in the new situations, young people not only lose sight of the correct hierarchy of values but, since they no longer have certain criteria of behavior, they do not know how to face and deal with the new difficulties. Experience, however, teaches that young people who have been well prepared for family life generally succeed better than others."

Personal or proximate preparation for marriage means exactly what it says. In some dioceses, to save time, five, ten or twenty couples are gathered together and given a general marital instruction that never touches intimate problems or issues of personal relationship and growth. Such preparation courses are a waste of time and do nothing to obviate potential marital difficulties and possible divorce. Each couple's psychological and emotional maturity must be evaluated, and this cannot be done in a general setting. Furthermore, fundamental questions must be put to each couple, namely: What are their personal goals in marriage? What are their expectations? What do they see individually as their strengths and weaknesses? How do they intend to cope with their own weakness and those of their spouse in marriage? What is their financial situation and what are their economic goals? And finally, what is their understanding of family? What are their intentions with respect to children?

The exercise of the right to marry is relative to the capacity and willingness to live out the obligations of this great vocation. The parties must be fully aware that in time of conflict, arguments, and incompatible solutions, they should seek counsel from competent sources as needed.

Canon 1064

It is up to the local ordinary to make provisions that such assistance is duly organized, even after consulting men and women of proven experience and skill, if it seems appropriate.

2. Responsibility of the Local Ordinary

The local ordinary of every diocese has a primary obligation to provide forms of pre- and post-marital support. This includes providing assistance to people of various ethnic groups in his diocese. He is also responsible for evaluating family life as it actually exists, taking into consideration the customs of the people as well as their various economic and social conditions, in order to provide appropriate support for these people of God. On the basis of all this information, the local ordinary must organize diocesan marital programs utilizing the expertise of lay persons, professionally trained psychiatrists, psychologists, physicians, counselors, and so on. In so doing, the ordinary fulfills the prescriptions of Canons 212, §3 and 228, §3 which state that Christians have not only a right but a duty to offer advice and assistance to their pastors and dioceses. Ordinaries are obliged to exercise special leadership regarding the married faithful in their dioceses.

Canon 1065

§1. **If they can do so without serious inconvenience, Catholics who have not yet received the sacrament of confirmation are to receive it before being admitted to marriage.**

§2. **It is strongly recommended that those to be married approach the sacraments of penance and the Most Holy Eucharist so that they may fruitfully receive the sacrament of marriage.**

3. Sacraments Recommended in Conjunction with Marriage

The reception of baptism is necessary for the valid reception of the sacrament of matrimony. Confirmation, penance and the Eucharist are strongly recommended for Catholics who enter into marriage. Although reception of these sacraments is not necessary to insure the validity of the sacrament of marriage, the faith dimension of marriage as well as the ecclesial obligations that necessarily follow make full participation in these sacraments of the greatest importance.

Canon 1066

Before marriage is celebrated, it must be evident that nothing stands in the way of its valid and licit celebration.

4. Certitude of Valid and Licit Celebration

Baptismal Certificate: An Essential Document

If the parties were baptized in the same church where the marriage will take place, the proof of baptism can be found in the parish baptismal record. The pastor usually checks the records. If the parties were baptized elsewhere, then they must secure proof of the baptism from the church where it took place. The certificate will indicate whether the parties are free to marry. It will indicate whether the person was married before, received holy orders or made solemn religious vows.

Canon 535 obliges all pastors to record in the baptismal register of the parish all these important facts. For this reason Canon 1121 demands that pastors who assist at a marriage send a record of this marriage with the names, dates, witnesses, dispensations received, etc., to the church of baptism. Hence, a certificate of baptism will show whether there was a previous marriage, etc. Information of any marriage that has been declared null by the ecclesiastical court should also be included.

Where baptismal books have been destroyed, one trustworthy witness would suffice to prove reception of baptism, e.g., the godparent or the priest who baptized. In litigated cases, more proof is needed. Thus it is important that the pastor of a marriage insist on a baptismal certificate issued at least within the past six months. *Old certificates must never be accepted.* Pastors must also demand certificates of baptism from non-Catholics to determine just what type of dispensation is needed. If the parties are unbaptized, it is well to ask further questions. This information may prove valuable later on to some matrimonial tribunal.

Canon 1066 is self-explanatory, but it must be emphasized that besides the need to ascertain the legal status of the partners vis a vis a marriage and their lack of any impediments that would invalidate their marriage there are other factors to be considered before a marriage takes place: emotional and psychological health; acceptance of the Catholic concept of marriage; proper consent. Inadequate consent, for example, would be present in individuals indicating a desire for a wedding but a lack of desire for a real, true marriage. This kind of thing should be suspected when an engaged couple break up several times before marriage, when one party uses marriage to escape an alcoholic father or mother, when infatuation blinds one party to the objective facts of alcoholism, drug abuse or infidelity on the part of the other and causes that person to believe the other party will reform after marriage. In short, every pastor is bound by this canon to study the facts of each case, and the parties have a fundamental right in justice to a thorough, unbiased investigation of their intended marriage and a proper pastoral evaluation. If there is any indication that one or both parties show invalidating factors (e.g., not intending to have children; contemplating an open marriage with the possibility of other sexual partners; having in mind the remedy of divorce if things do not work out; symptoms of serious psychological disorder, etc.), this canon forbids the pastor to witness such a marriage. If he has thoroughly investigated the case and has serious doubts about a marriage, he must consult the local ordinary who can invoke Canon 1077 which deals with whether or not a marriage may be performed.

Canon 1067

The conference of bishops is to issue norms concerning the examination of the parties, and the marriage banns or other appropriate means for carrying out the necessary inquiries which are to precede marriage. The pastor can proceed to assist at a marriage after such norms have been diligently observed.

5. Conference of Bishops and Norms

The Code of 1917 was promulgated for the Universal Church. After several years it was realized that some laws could not be applied universally. Therefore, the new codification distinguishes between the universal law and the particular law of the Church. The 101 conferences of bishops throughout the world are permitted in particular law to establish norms for their own territories.

What is different in this new Canon 1067? It is substantially the same as that contained in the 1917 Code except that it is a universal law but one which the various conferences of bishops promulgate in ways appropriate for their territories. The obligation and purpose of Canon 1067 is to find impediments or other circumstances which would impede a valid and licit marriage. It is a fact-finding operation to determine whether one is eligible for marriage. To insure better scrutiny in determining eligibility for marriage since about one-third of the U.S. population changes residence frequently, tighter measures here were introduced.

Canon 1068

Unless contrary indications are present, in danger of death, if other means of proof cannot be obtained, it is sufficient that the parties affirm — even under oath, if the case warrants it — that they have been baptized and that they are not held back by any impediment.

6. Marriage in Danger of Death

Preparation for marriage requires a thorough investigation of the parties. Canon 1068 is an exception to this rule. Cases usually come up when priests or deacons are making sick calls or visiting hospitals. In such circumstances, individuals are discovered who have been married outside the Church, e.g., by a justice of the peace, magistrate, judge or non-Catholic minister, and their marriages are in general invalid due to lack of form, the parties having failed to be married in the presence of their proper pastors and two qualified witnesses for validity. In other cases a man and woman may have been living together but were never married, or were married but have some irregularity or impediment which must be dispensed. Canon 1068 applies to such people who are dying or are in danger of death who wish to be reconciled with the Church before they die. Since a full investigation cannot be made, only minimal information about their freedom to marry is required. The 1917 Code required an oath from the parties; this canon does not, unless there is a doubt. It must be affirmed that at least one party was baptized and that both are free of impediments or other invalidating factors. Canon 1079 explains in detail what is meant by "danger of death."

Canon 1069

All the faithful are obliged to reveal any impediments they are aware of to the pastor or to the local ordinary before the celebration of marriage.

7. Obligations to Reveal Impediments

For the preservation of the common good, the faithful are bound to reveal any known impediments which exist in the parties who are planning to marry. The announcement of banns (which is determined by local conferences of bishops) was a method used in the Code of 1917 for discovering one's freedom to marry. At this writing (1986), the bishops of the United States have not made a determination to require the publishing of banns.

Family members and close acquaintances have a particular obligation to reveal invalidating factors, such as mental illness, or invalidating intentions not known to the priest. Knowledge of such impediments obtained in sacramental confession, or through the medical or counseling professions, cannot be revealed. In the latter case, the information may be released with the written permission of the patients or clients involved. Mere suspicions are not acceptable.

Canon 1070

If someone other than the pastor who is to assist at the marriage has conducted the investigations, that person is to notify the pastor of the results as soon as possible through an authentic document.

8. Notification of Completed Inquiries

Whenever a premarital investigation takes place in one parish and the marriage is to take place in another, the investigation and preparatory information must be sent to the pastoral minister who will witness the marriage. An authentic document should be signed, sealed and sent to be filed in the archives of the church where the marriage takes place.

Canon 1071

§1. Except in case of necessity[2], no one is to assist at the following marriages without the permission of the local ordinary:

1° **the marriage of transients;**
2° **a marriage which cannot be recognized or celebrated in accord with the norm of civil law;**
3° **a marriage of a person who is bound by natural obligations toward another party or toward children, arising from a prior union;**
4° **a marriage of a person who has notoriously rejected the Catholic faith;**
5° **a marriage of a person who is bound by a censure;**
6° **a marriage of a minor child when the parents are unaware of it or are reasonably opposed to it;**
7° **a marriage to be entered by means of a proxy, mentioned in Canon 1105.**

9. Situations Requiring Local Ordinary's Permission

This list of marriages cannot be witnessed without the permission of the local ordinary except in cases of necessity. These situations may possibly endanger the parties to be married, their children or the community.

The Marriage of Transients

A transient (*vagus*) is a person who has no domicile, quasi-domicile, or an established residence (for example, people who are in a traveling circus, those who are perpetual wanderers, the homeless, migrant workers, immigrants, illegal aliens). Each case must be thoroughly investigated and referred to the local ordinary before considering the celebration of marriage.

Marriage Prohibited by Civil Law

Each individual State in the U.S. has its own civil requirements regarding marriage. Impediments to marriage in civil law include: existing marriage; lack of age by at least one of the parties; consanguinity within specified degrees; adoptive relationship; severe mental disorders; venereal disease; force, fear or fraud. In most States any of these factors would absolutely invalidate a marriage. Whenever civil impediments correspond to canonical impediments, they require a dispensation. Impediments cited in civil law that do not appear in Church law do not invalidate a marriage in the eyes of the Church. However, the civil laws should be respected and dispensations obtained where needed. In cases of conflict, the local ordinary should be consulted.

Marriage of a Person Bound by Natural Obligation Arising From a Previous Bond

The citation of natural obligations is something new in the Code. Even though a prior marriage is declared invalid in a formal case or is dissolved by the Church, there may exist obligations, e.g., to the children left behind or to the ex-spouse. Theoretically this canon would require the local ordinary's intervention in every marriage of a divorced person. Practically speaking, it applies only to cases where natural obligations had been neglected or would be seriously endangered by a second marriage. Cases must be examined carefully before granting decrees of nullity, since natural obligations were never stressed in the Code of 1917.

Marriage of Those Who Have Notoriously Rejected the Faith

This mandate pertains to one who rejects the faith outright, professes openly that he or she is not Catholic and refuses obedience to the Church and its laws. This differs legally from non-practicing Catholics who have passively abandoned the faith without signs of positively rejecting it. The law presumes that those who have openly rejected the faith and are hostile to it pose a danger to the believing party and/or to the Catholic offspring and are a scandal to the Church community. It should be understood as an ecclesiastical offense, a publicly known act committed under certain circumstances which can neither be concealed nor legally excused. This matter should be clarified in the beginning of the premarital investigation and referred to the local ordinary.

Marriage of Those Under Censure

Canons 1331, §1.2° and 1332 explain the solution to the problem by the nature of the censure and the offense upon which it is based. Reconciliation and remission of censure before the marriage could rectify the situation. The law here concerns those who are not reconciled. Two problems arise: (a) that the person will receive the sacrament of marriage while in a state of serious sin; or (b) that the offense will present a serious threat to the successful marriage covenant.

Marriage of Minors

A person who has not completed his or her eighteenth year is considered a minor (Canon 97, §1). If one or both parties is under eighteen and wants to be married, this case must be referred to the ordinary. The 1917 Code considered a minor one who had not completed his or her twenty-first year. Prior to 1917, the ages for a valid marriage were fourteen for males and twelve for females. The marriage of minors is strongly discouraged because they lack the emotional and mental stability and maturity to handle the responsibilities of married life. Furthermore, minors are subject to the judgment of their parents or guardians in the exercise of their rights. But even though minors are subject to their parents, the parents cannot force their children to marry or absolutely forbid them not to. Pastors should not proceed with the marriage of a minor if the parents are unaware of the intended marriage. Parents are to be informed and their advice considered. If the minor has a serious reason for not consulting his or her parents, the pastor should weigh the matter carefully before proceeding without the parents' knowledge. If there is some doubt, the matter should be referred to the local ordinary. Again, premarital counseling would clarify a minor's motives and eligibility for marriage by evaluating his or her strengths and weaknesses. If they exist, maturity and other factors necessary for successful marriage can be discovered and ratified by a competent counselor.

Marriage by Proxy

In general, all proxy marriages (Canon 1105) require the permission of the local ordinary. A proxy marriage is one that takes place without the parties being physically present to each other, one or both being represented by persons appointed to exchange consent on their behalf. As with other marriages, premarital preparations are necessary. Proxy marriages are a rarity, but situations do occur when one's physical presence is impossible, as for example, in military service, or when immigrants must be present elsewhere in order to secure a visa. (N.B. There must be a genuine intention to marry, not merely to enter the country.) Here again, the decision of the ordinary is necessary.

Marriage of Former Catholics

The norms for mixed marriages must be followed where one party has notoriously abandoned the faith, especially if he or she has embraced another sect. These precautions are necessary in order to protect the faith of the Catholic party and ensure the raising of the children in the Catholic faith. If the local ordinary is not satisfied that the legal requirements will be fulfilled, he has the right to refuse the requested permission.

Canon 1072

Pastors of souls are to take care to prevent youths from celebrating marriage before the age at which marriage is usually contracted in accord with the accepted practice of the region.

10. Marriages of Minors

This canon is based on the legislation of the Council of Trent and upholds the right of minors to marry, but it emphasizes their duty to parents and pastors. The implication is that minors can marry validly without their parents' consent. Although minors should consult their parents, such consultation in no way gives the parents any absolute right to command their children in the choice of a partner. If the parents have reasonable cause to oppose the marriage, and if they are insistent, the pastor should consult the ordinary of the diocese. Lack of parental consent in no way constitutes a prohibitive impediment. However, pastors and diocesan authorities are urged to give the matter close consideration because, even though minors have a right to marry, it is not always wise for them to use this right for economic, psychological and spiritual reasons. The best answer to this situation is often deferment.

Since most contemporary teenage marriages do not succeed, it is necessary to promulgate more stringent laws to curtail this problem. For those who are reluctant to resist teenage marriages, we recommend Anthony Bevilaqua's excellent survey, *Problem Areas in Chancery Practice: Refusal or Deferral of Baptism and Marriage* in the Appendix of this book. Tribunal experience reveals that contemporary teenage marriage is motivated by premarital pregnancy, rebellion against parents or authority in general, false expectations of marital happiness, false notions of success, escape from an unhappy home life, and the general encouragement of early marriage through peer pressure.

In dealing with marriage, the present Code portrays it as a comprehensive, interpersonal relationship demanding strength and maturity. While the Code recognizes the capacities and potentialities inherent in our contemporary youth, it stresses that everyone contemplating marriage should consider it seriously. Pastors and counselors need a consistent policy for dealing with minors who wish to get married. The Orlando, Florida, diocese has such a policy which can serve as an excellent guide to all.

Diocese of Orlando
POLICY RE: TEENAGE MARRIAGES

1. *Concern for Everyone's Welfare*

The Catholic Church is deeply concerned about the welfare of her members. She wants them to be happy and satisfied in this world and to be united with God, our Father in heaven after death. One of the greatest obstacles to achieving happiness and satisfaction is the break up of family life. This is especially true of families whose marriage began at an early age.

According to the National Center of Health Statistics, 56% of all divorces occur before the parties reach the age of 24. Thirty-three percent of all divorced couples are teenagers. Sixty-two percent of all divorced men and 75% of all divorced women were under twenty-five years of age at the time of their marriage. Norms for statistical evidence differ, but the inference is made: the lower the age of marriage, the greater the probability of divorce. The experience of Family Life Directors leads them to the same conclusion. Msgr. James T. McHugh, formerly of the Family Life Bureau of the National Catholic Conference of Bishops, indicates that seven out of ten marriages involving teenagers end in separation or divorce. In teenage marriages where pregnancy was a factor, 90% break up.

Church officials are very much aware of the fact that premarital pregnancy is on the increase. This factor puts extreme pressure on the teenagers to see marriage as a solution. In the "Lack of Form" cases handled by diocesan tribunals, it becomes clear that well over half of the broken marriages began with a pregnant girl.

These facts are understandable. They corroborate the legitimate presumption that many teenagers are not mature enough, emotionally, spiritually, intellectually, or financially to handle the rights, the obligations and the reponsibilities of marriage in contemporary society. This seems true even when one does not consider the factor of religion. Even a sturdy Catholic faith will not adequately compensate for the pressure put on youngsters trying to fulfill the responsibility of adults.

The right to marry is a natural right of high priority. It is not, however, an unrestricted right. Both Church and State can establish legitimate restrictions. Such restrictions must be founded on serious causes whereby the proposed marriage is shown to be in conflict with Christian revelation or posing a threat to the common good of society.

Church law has traditionally minimized essential personal requirements for marriage by saying: "All persons who are not prohibited by law can contract marriage" (Canon 1058). Canon 1083 establishes a minimum age for marriage, but this law is keyed to an understanding of marriage which concentrates on the biological capacity for reproduction. It was enacted at a time when life in society provided a setting in which one might hope for mutual stability. Today, in our present American culture, these guarantees are frequently absent.

Many counselors feel helpless in the face of teenagers who insist on contracting marriages that have little hope for success. Even though they may try to dissuade couples, they feel that the natural right to marry and the established canonical age make it impossible for them to refuse or even to postpone the marriage. However, the new Code of 1983 gives sufficient reasons to prove that postponement is the better decision.

Because of the romanticism to which couples are subject, many do not come to terms with the realities and responsibilities of married life. Sexual and emotional involvement blur their picture of the future and the demands that marriage will put on them. When the girl becomes pregnant, there is only a very low probability that she or the boy will seek counsel or search for possible alternatives to marriage. To protect their rights, to assure their future happiness and stability, every possible assistance should be given to help them understand if they are ready for marriage or not. Marriage is not a solution to problems. All too often it makes them worse.

Marriage entails serious responsibilities, moral, spiritual, sexual, familial, financial, societal. It takes a certain minimal level of maturity to fulfill those responsibilities. One who gives positive indications of possessing this minimal maturity should not be excluded from marriage. Anyone who does not give positive indications of possessing such minimal maturity is precluded by the natural law from marrying, since no one has a right to enter a contract which he or she is incapable of fulfilling. The fact that the individual believes himself to be capable or insists that he is so does not relieve the Church of the obligation to make its own judgment in individual cases.

Canon 1077 advises that "the local ordinary can prohibit the marriage of his own subjects wherever they are staying and of all persons actually present in his own territory, but only for a time, for a serious cause and as long as that cause exists." This canon supplies the legal basis on which a policy of selective postponement of an indissoluble sacramental marriage on the part of ill-prepared teenagers would be founded.

The Orlando policy attempts to guarantee: (1) The right to marry where both parties, though quite young, give evidence of required minimal maturity; (2) Wide enough consultation with experienced persons of good judgment to insure that the premarital evaluation is objective. This consultation should include both lay and clergy input; (3) The opportunity for the couple to avail themselves of prudent counselors who will help them face up to the serious aspects of the lifelong commitment that marriage demands; and   (4) The postponement of sacramental marriage until such time as an adequate level of maturity is reached by both parties.

2. *Diocesan Policy for Youthful Marriages*

When either party requesting marriage has not yet reached his or her nineteenth (19) birthday, the following norms will be observed in the Diocese of Orlando:

The date of the wedding may *not* be set until all the steps required herein have been taken.

There will be a three (3) month mandatory waiting period from the time of the first interview with the priest.

The priest and couple will have an in-depth interview.

Parents of both the boy and the girl will be interviewed by the priest.

The couple will be referred to Catholic Social Services for evaluation by a professional counselor.

The tribunal will authorize the marriage in writing to the referring priest.

3. *Guidelines for Priests*

When the couple first approaches the priest to make preparations for marriage, he should inform them of the diocesan policies regarding youthful marriages and assist them through its various stages.

The priest should conduct in-depth interviews with the couple (separately and together) in order to understand better their motives for marriage, level of maturity and readiness to receive the sacrament. These interviews will investigate factors which are influencing the decision to marry, such as pregnancy, family background, parents' attitudes, desire to escape an unpleasant home situation, degree of infatuation, etc.

The interviews will also consider the financial status of the couple including salary, savings, debts, ability to handle money and budget planning.

The spiritual status of the couple will be reviewed, emphasizing church attendance, reception of the sacraments, fidelity to religious instruction and attitudes toward divorce.

Other topics for discussion during these interviews include: courtship, sexuality, pregnancy, family relationships, personal goals and leisure-time activities.

The *Suggested Guide Questionnaire* which follows provides an outline for developing a fruitful dialogue with the couple. Not all questions are appropriate for all couples, but the material covered is generally applicable to most.

Following the interviews with the couple and their parents, the priest will complete a form which records his judgment of the couple and his recommendation regarding their suitability for marriage at this time. A copy is then sent to the Catholic Social Services office which will also be evaluating the couple.

Although this procedure is required only in cases of premarital pregnancies or when either party is under 19 years of age, the priest may fruitfully use it in situations where the parties are older but their level of maturity and understanding is seriously limited.

4. *Evaluation by Professional Counselors*

After the priest has interviewed the couple and their parents, he will refer them to Catholic Social Services for evaluation by a professional counselor.

The couple is to be referred to the Catholic Social Services office most convenient to them. Offices are located in Orlando, Daytona Beach, Cocoa and Lakeland. When the couple arrange the appointment, they may request that the interview be held in their city if they reside in an outlying area and are unable to travel to one of the above offices. This would apply to residents in such areas as Fort Pierce, Vero Beach, Ocala, Leesburg, Sebring, etc.

Catholic Social Services personnel may find it necessary from time to time to call on others in the diocese to assist in this evaluation process. This might occur when staffs are on vacation, during particularly busy periods, for the convenience of the couple, for purposes of confidentiality, etc. In such circumstances, a counselor would be selected from the following. [Names and addresses listed.]

The fee for the first counseling interview will be paid by the couple at the time of the interview. It is anticipated that most couples will require one or two interviews.

A summary of the counselor's assessment of the couple will be sent to the referring priest who will send the completed file to the tribunal.

The Catholic Social Services staff will be available for ongoing counseling, especially for those couples with negative evaluations.

The tribunal will request an additional report from a second counselor when there is one positive evaluation and one negative evaluation from the priest and the first counselor. Following review of these reports, the tribunal will notify the referring priest of the decision.

5. *Suggested Guide Questionnaire for Fruitful Dialogue*

PRESENT (Courtship)

1. When did you begin dating?
2. What attracted you to your fiancé(e)?
3. What kind of activities do you share together?
4. How often have you been seeing each other?
5. How did the subject of marriage arise?
6. When did you definitely decide to marry (formal engagement)?
7. Have you broken up during your courtship? Why?
   How do you deal with differences of opinion between you?
   Who usually gives in? Why?
8. Have you made any preparation for the wedding? Who? What?
9. What motives do you have for considering marriage now? Any hesitations about your decision?
10. Is a pregnancy involved?

(If Pregnant)

1. How long (have you/has she) been pregnant?
2. Who is the father?
3. Were you considering marriage before the pregnancy?
4. Are your parents aware of your plans?
5. Have you thought of other solutions?

(Religious Attitudes)

1. Describe your own religious beliefs and practices as well as those of your fiancé(e).

2. How does religion influence your present relationship?
3. Why have you come to the Church to be married?
4. What in your opinion are the most important elements of a (Christian) marriage?
5. Does the statement that marriage is a commitment for life have meaning for you?

PAST (Family Background)

1. Describe your own parents, brothers, sisters.
2. How do you get along with them?
3. Which of your parents is more dominant?
4. Which of your parents do you get along better with? Why?
5. Do you presently live at home? If not, why not?
6. What has been the degree of happiness or unhappiness of the relationship of your parents in their marriage? Are they separated or divorced?
7. How are the differences of opinions or quarrels solved by your parents?
8. What in your family experience do you resent most? What do you most treasure?
9. Describe your fiancé(e)'s family life. How does he or she get along with his or her parents?
   Which parent is dominant?
10. Do you think your fiancé(e) is marrying to escape unhappiness at home?
11. What do both sets of parents think of the marriage?
12. Has anyone tried to dissuade you from marriage?
13. What sort of relationship do you anticipate having with your parents and in-laws after the marriage?

(Education)

1. How far did you go in your formal education?
2. Did you enjoy school?
3. If further education is needed, how would you manage that?

(Life Experience)

1. Have either of you dated others?

Did either of you ever decide to marry someone else?
2. How much sexual experience have you had?
    Is this known to your fiancé(e)?
3. Do you both have close friends?
    How long have you known them?
4. Do you know many happily married couples?
5. Have either of you had any significant medical history (physical or psychological)?
6. Do either of you have any problems with alcohol, drugs, gambling?

FUTURE (In General)
1. Would you tell me why you and your fiancé(e) believe that you are mature enough to assume the lifelong responsibilities of marriage?
2. What are your strengths and weaknesses as you see them?
    How do you think they will affect your marriage?
3. What are your fiancé(e)'s strengths and weaknesses?
    How do you think they will affect your marriage?
4. Does your fiancé(e) have any characteristics that you would like to change after you get married?

(Finances)
1. Are you or your fiancé(e) working?
    Have you had many jobs?
    How much do you earn?
    How much have you saved?
    Any debts? How much?
2. How often do you speak about your future home? about furniture? future recreational activity?
3. Where do you plan to live?
    If with parents, what effect will this have on your relationship?
4. How will you help and assist one another in the beginning of your marriage?
5. What decision have you come to in regard to budgeting?
    What experience have you had in budgeting?
    Who will look after the budget?

6. How much do you think you will need in the beginning for living expenses per week?
7. Do you feel that you and your fiancé(e) have planned well enough for your economic future?

(Sexuality)

1. Have you and your fiancé(e) spoken about the number of children you will have? Do you both agree?
2. How many children do you plan on having? (This affords the priest or counselor a good opportunity for presenting the Church's teaching on family planning.)
3. What are your ideas concerning the place of sexuality in your forthcoming marriage?
4. How would you react to the possibility that your loved one would need affection and sexual expression more than you? What would be your responsibilities in this area?
5. What are some of the chief duties you will have as (Christian) parents? Do you look forward to these obligations?

6. *A Case to Ponder*

A girl, sixteen and pregnant, wanted to marry a boy of seventeen. The girl's parents would not hear of it. The parents of the boy were in favor of it because they knew many people who married at such an age with success. The couple presented a marriage license to the pastor and threatened to have a civil ceremony if he would not marry them. Although the couple were sixteen and seventeen, the license indicated that they were twenty one. The pastor called the chancery and got permission to marry them. The problem arose when the father of the girl threatened to sue the pastor because he was going to marry two youngsters who were legally under age. When brought before the civil authorities it was determined that the pastor had obtained permission merely to marry the couple, not to investigate them. Investigation would have shown that the civil marriage license was not valid. The case was dropped when the father was informed that a perjury charge could be brought against his daughter.

Pastors must point out to all parents and teenagers that venturing into the field of matrimony without enough formal training and education makes it difficult to say the very least to provide a home and raise a family.

One must compete with skilled professional people who are also looking for work. Jobs will be hard to get and promotions practically non-existent. After putting up with this situation for a time, the young couple usually becomes disgruntled and upset and eventually seeks a way out of their marriage. One third of all divorces stems from such economic pressures.

Due to the fact that 56% of all teenage marriages end in divorce, California introduced a State law in November of 1970 to make it more difficult for teenagers to marry: "To marry, any boy or girl under eighteen must get: Superior Court's permission (formerly only required for girls under 16); permission from parents or guardian; and premarital counseling can be required by the court."

7. Justice of the Peace and Marriage

Is a justice of the peace obligated to perform all marriage ceremonies that come to his attention? The answer is, "No." A justice of the peace is not required by law to perform a marriage ceremony. It is a privilege of his office to do so. Most judges of our Common Pleas Court refuse to perform marriage ceremonies, stating publicly that this is a matter peculiarly for a cleric. They too, though, have the right to officiate at a wedding. A justice of the peace is not obliged to offer his services to all callers nor can he be required to perform a marriage ceremony against his will. Before performing a marriage ceremony, a justice of the peace is not required to make any investigation other than to be satisfied that the parties are of age and that a marriage license has been issued.

Before a justice of the peace may perform a ceremony, the parties must present to him a marriage license which they have previously obtained from the marriage license clerk in the Orphan's Court Office. It is the duty of the license clerk to ascertain whether the parties are of age and otherwise free to marry, i.e., whether either party has a living spouse from whom no divorce has been granted. A justice of the peace may assist at the marriage of anyone in his office who brings to him the marriage license regardless of whether the parties reside outside of the country or State. He himself can perform the ceremony any place within the Commonwealth.

A priest who also holds the office of Justice of the Peace can refuse, as a justice of the peace, to perform the ceremony. Indeed, it would be his duty to do so. The same holds true for a Catholic layman who holds the office of Justice of the Peace.

---

1 Sacred Congregation of the Sacraments: Instruction on the Canonical Investigation, June 29, 1941. AAS 33-297.
2 "Except in cases of necessity" means that the necessity must clearly outweigh the possible dangers which may arise in particular circumstances. Premarital pregnancy is *not* considered sufficient reason.

Chapter Two

IMPEDIMENTS AND THEIR DISPENSATION

Canon 1073

A diriment impediment renders a person incapable of contracting marriage validly.

1. Diriment Impediments in General

The 1917 Code recognized two types of impediments: diriment impediments that invalidated a marriage unless dispensed by the rightful authority; and impeding or prohibitive impediments that rendered a marriage illicit but not invalid. Prohibitive impediments have been deleted from the new Code and the number of diriment impediments reduced. Down through the centuries, the Church has considered marriage to be the institution created by God for the propagation of the human race and the well-being of society. Abuses of the marriage bond were countered by appropriate legislation, new laws and precepts being enacted and others deleted as the circumstances warranted. Hence, when writing the new Code, a number of items were removed from the law of the Church because they were simply no longer of any use in contemporary society. As Father Ladislaus Orsy, S.J., put it: "Human laws are mortal, as people are. Once they have fulfilled their purpose, they should die. If they linger on, they are a burden and they drain the community of its life."

What is a *diriment impediment*? The term "diriment" from the Latin verb *dirimere*, means to destroy, annul or make something invalid. When applied to impediments, it indicates that these impediments to marriage are of such a nature that they destroy or annul the marriage if attempted without a dispensation. Canonists usually classify diriments into those of natural or divine law and those of ecclesiastical or Church law. Only the supreme authority of the Church has the right to declare authentically those cases in which the divine law forbids or annuls marriage (Canon 1075). This distinction between impediments of divine and of ecclesiastical law is of importance in questions of dispensation for the Church cannot dispense from an impediment of the divine law, but it can dispense from those created by her own law. In other words, the Church makes laws (ecclesiastical) for the common good and for the common good can dispense from them. The distinction is important in cases where unbaptized persons are involved, for unbaptized persons, though bound by divine law, are not bound by ecclesiastical laws (Canon 11). Canonists generally agree that impediments of the divine law are three: (1) an existing bond of marriage, (2) impotency, and (3) consanguinity in the direct line and to the second degree in the collateral line (cf. Canon 1094). Some canonists go even further considering disparity of cult, sacred orders and perpetual vows of chastity to be divine law impediments (cf. Canon 1088). Again, the Holy See alone is competent to interpret which impediments are of divine origin.

Canon 1074

An impediment which can be proven in the external forum is considered to be a public impediment; otherwise, it is an occult impediment.

2. Public and Occult Impediments

A public impediment is one which can be proven in the external forum; that is, the circumstances from which it arises are public. In most cases, facts can be proven in the external forum by: (a) authentic public documents (cf. Canon 1541), e.g., sacred orders, religious vows, disparity of cult, consanguinity, affinity, previous bond; (b) two trustworthy witnesses (cf. Canon 1574) who can testify based on their personal knowledge; or (c) with regard to official acts (cf. Canon 1573) one exceptional witness. A distinction is made between public and occult impediments because after a dispensation, public impediments become matters of public record. An impediment, occult by nature, would be a private vow, a crime arising from adultery or conjugicide, or occult consanguinity. An occult case occurs when an impediment is public by nature and occult in fact such as a case of consanguinity that is public by nature but not known in a new domicile.

Jurisdiction

A *forum* is a place for the transaction of official business, judicial or administrative. The *external forum* is the forum of the Church's external government. Here one is declared innocent or guilty in the eyes of the Church. The external forum is always exercised publicly, not secretly, and the findings become matters of public record.[1] Exercise of the external forum is non-sacramental but has juridical effects. The most obvious example of an external forum is a marriage tribunal. The *internal forum*, on the other hand, is the forum of one's conscience. Here one is innocent or guilty in the eyes of God. The internal forum is always exercised privately, not publicly. The internal forum may be sacramental or not. If sacramental, it takes place within the sacrament of penance, has no juridical effects, is never recorded and enjoys the seal of confession. If the internal forum is exercised non-sacramentally, it takes place outside the sacrament of penance, carries with it juridical effects and is always recorded,[2] but enjoys the status of professional confidentiality.

Canon 1075

§1. The supreme authority of the Church alone has the competency to declare authentically when divine law prohibits or voids a marriage.

§2. Only the supreme authority has the right to establish other impediments for the baptized.

3. Authority Empowered to Establish Impediments

No one except the Roman Pontiff can abrogate or derogate impediments of ecclesiastical law or dispense from the same unless this power has been granted either by the common law or by special indult from the Holy See. This canon deals exclusively with ecclesiastical law, for no human authority can abrogate or dispense from impediments of the divine law. The Holy Father can abrogate an impediment by removing it from the Code, or derogate it by eliminating only part of the law.

Canon 1076

A custom which introduces a new impediment or which is contrary to existing impediments is reprobated.

4. Customs That Are Reprobated

While custom is always the best interpreter of the law (Canon 27) and, in theory, may even have the force of law provided it follows the principles set down in Canons 23-28, this general rule does not include marriage impediments. Canon 1076 strictly prohibits the introduction of impediments based on local customs.

Canon 1077

§1. In a particular case the local ordinary can prohibit the marriage of his own subjects wherever they are staying and of all persons actually present in his own territory, but only for a time, for a serious cause and as long as that cause exists.

§2. Only the supreme authority of the Church can add an invalidating clause to a prohibition.

5. Prohibition of the Right to Marry by the Ordinary

The local ordinary may forbid a particular marriage only as long as due cause exists, for example, if there is danger of scandal, doubtful impediment, etc. The ordinary cannot prohibit a marriage under pain of nullity. Let's say an ordinary enacts a law that no marriage whatsoever can be celebrated in his diocese after 6:00 p.m. Would the marriage be invalid if this law were disobeyed? No, because since this canon forbids such a sanction, the marriage would be valid but illicit.

Marriage prohibitions under this canon may be imposed only in particular cases and not as a general rule, and the prohibitions may last only for as long as the serious cause for delaying the marriage exists. If a case in question involves emotional stability, it is advisable to take counsel with qualified psychiatrists, psychologists, or other experts before invoking this canon.

Canon 1078

§1. The local ordinary can dispense his own subjects wherever they are staying as well as all persons actually present in his own territory from all the impediments of ecclesiastical law with the exception of those impediments whose dispensation is reserved to the Apostolic See.

§2. A dispensation from the following impediments is reserved to the Apostolic See:

1° the impediment arising from sacred orders or from a public perpetual vow of chastity in a religious institute of pontifical right;

2° the impediment of crime mentioned in Canon 1090.

§3. A dispensation is never given from the impediment of consanguinity in the direct line or in the second degree of the collateral line.

6. Dispensations by the Local Ordinary and by the Holy See

The purpose of this law on impediments is to protect the parties, the community in which they live and the dignity of the sacrament of matrimony. There may be cases in which a dispensation would benefit the parties but be harmful to the community. Certain impediments reserved to the Supreme Pontiff cannot be dispensed by any other authority, e.g., impediments arising from sacred orders (bishops, priests, deacons), or from a perpetual vow of chastity in an institute of pontifical right, and the impediment of crime. We must keep in mind that this reservation also applies to permanent deacons who are unmarried at the time of ordination or to married permanent deacons who might want to marry for a second time.

If there is doubt about whether a situation or circumstance constitutes matter for an impediment, it can be dispensed in virtue of Canon 14, provided that it is not reserved, as in cases such as impotence, lack of age, public propriety and disparity of cult. Reserved impediments must be referred to the Holy See for dispensation. Bishops and priests apply to the Sacred Congregation for the Doctrine of the Faith; deacons to the Sacred Congregation for the Sacraments; and publicly vowed religious in pontifical institutes[3] apply to the Sacred Congregation for Religious and Secular Institutes. A distinction must be made regarding reserved impediments arising from sacred orders and perpetual vows of chastity and their obligation. Once a person is validly ordained a priest, the sacred orders never come into question — they always remain even though the ordained person is laicized. This loss of the clerical state and removal to the lay state does not in itself constitute a dispensation from the obligations of celibacy.

Canon 1079

§1. In danger of death, the local ordinary can dispense his own subjects wherever they are staying as well as all persons who are actually present in his territory both from the form prescribed for the celebration of matrimony and from each and every impediment of ecclesiastical law, whether it be public or occult, except the impediment arising from the sacred order of the presbyterate.

§2. In the same situation in §1 and only for cases in which the local ordinary cannot be reached, the pastor, the properly delegated sacred minister and the priest or deacon who assists at the matrimony in accord with the norm of Canon 1116, §2, also possess the faculty to dispense from the same impediments.

§3. In danger of death a confessor enjoys the faculty to dispense from occult impediments for the internal forum, whether within or outside the act of sacramental confession.

§4. In the case mentioned in §2, the local ordinary is not considered to be accessible if he can be contacted only by means of telegraph or telephone.

7. Marriage in Danger of Death

The local ordinary can dispense his own subjects in danger of death wherever they are staying (when on pilgrimage, visiting other countries, etc.) and all persons actually living in his territory from the form (pastor and two witnesses) and from *each* and *every* impediment of ecclesiastical law, whether public or occult, except the impediment arising from the sacred order of priesthood. Peace of conscience and/or legitimation of children as cause for dispensation have been eliminated from the new Code, but could still be cited. Affinity in the direct line of a consummated marriage has also been eliminated in the new Code, evidently because these cases are so few. Nor does Canon 1078 list direct-line affinity among the impediments reserved to the Holy See. When the ordinary cannot be reached, the pastor, a properly delegated sacred minister, or the priest or deacon who usually assists at marriages may also dispense. And if none of these individuals is available, a non-delegated priest or deacon may dispense (cf. Canon 1116, §2).

A priest with faculties to hear confession may dispense from occult impediments in the internal forum and may use this power even outside sacramental confession. There is no obligation on the part of the confessor to inform the ordinary of the dispensation. If there is a question of both public and occult impediments, the attending priest may act as confessor and dispense from the occult impediment and also from the public impediment, if recourse to the local ordinary is impossible.

Ordinaries of places are those mentioned in Canon 134, viz., bishops (residential, not merely titular or auxiliary, unless also a vicar general), an abbot nullius, a vicar general, an apostolic or papal apostolic, a prefect apostolic, or a temporary administrator during a vacancy.

This canon also states that the local ordinary is not considered available if he can be reached *only* by telephone or telegraph. It has been a long-standing custom that the telephone is not used to expedite dispensation cases where death is imminent. With respect to the telephone or telegraph, it is not at all impossible today to contact the Holy See by phone. However, the Committee for the Authentic Interpretation of the Code, way back on November 12, 1922, condemned the use of the telephone or the telegraph in such cases as being extraordinary means which are moreover unsafe. In this they were upholding a ruling of the Papal Secretary of State in 1891 who let it be known that "the Supreme Pontiff *orders* that all applications or favors made to the Roman Curia by telephone or telegraph shall be ignored, and that he wants the bishops to do the same."

Eliminated from this canon are the scandal and the giving of guarantee for dispensations from disparity of cult and mixed religion cases as requisites for the exercise of the powers granted in this canon. Though not, strictly speaking, mandatory, these two requisites should try to be fulfilled, where possible, as a precautionary measure.

The primary intention and reason for this canon is the salvation of souls. Hence, under certain circumstances such as distance from the Holy See, urgent necessity and the danger of death, this canon provides a means whereby the ordinary and others do not need to seek permission from Rome to grant certain important dispensations. Because the common law gives the ordinary these faculties, they are given also to the pastor and others mentioned in this canon.

Danger of Death

Danger of death in this canon does not refer to immediate or extreme danger (*articulo mortis*) but any ordinary danger which arises from internal or external causes. An internal or intrinsic cause could be an accident where a life-threatening injury is sustained, disease, illness, or a serious operation. An external or extrinsic cause might be a special or unusual circumstance that places persons in danger of death and which comes from two sources: natural and social. *Natural causes* include catastrophes and so-called "acts of God," e.g., earthquakes, epidemics, mine disasters, floods, etc. *Social causes* include disturbances of the peace and public order due to revolutions, insurrections, terrorism, invasion by enemies, military mobilization and cover civilians residing in war zones, those exposed to air attacks, people sent on dangerous missions, and prisoners awaiting capital punishment, etc.[4]

Certainty of death is not required but the law of probability is sufficient to use these faculties. If no actual danger of death is objectively present but is prudently determined to be probable, the faculties are valid and can be used. Other requisites for the valid use of these faculties include either peace of conscience or legitimation of children or both together. Peace of conscience is sufficient in itself. The ordinary or pastor who uses these faculties should keep in mind that it is unnecessary that both parties seek peace of mind, and the one who seeks it does not have to be the one who is in danger of death or the one who has the impediment to the marriage.[5] The reason for peace of mind need not be the need for sacramental absolution.[6] Indeed, it is not necessary that any confession be sacramentally valid, nor that absolution be given from an impediment in the internal forum, since the need may be to remove the proximate occasion of sin, or to ease some grave cause of contention, such as a legal controversy over property, reparation of injury, or loss of reputation.

Some Cases

Let's say a woman named Mrs. Smith, a Catholic, calls you about her unbaptized husband who is dying. They are not married validly. Mr. Smith wishes to be baptized and is willing to do anything to give peace of mind to Mrs. Smith. Mrs. Smith was a vowed religious before her marriage and was never dispensed from her vows. She is also Mr. Smith's second cousin. Mrs. Smith does not want to go to confession and the pastor cannot get in touch with the ordinary. The dispensation can be granted, however, and the marriage validated according to Canon 1079.

As another case study, let's assume that you are an assistant at St.

Mary's Church. The telephone rings at 2:00 a.m. Mrs. White tells you that her husband is at the point of death and would like to have a priest come to him as soon as possible. Mr. White is a Catholic. You hear his confession and through it you learn that he and his wife were married in the Baptist church and that the marriage was never validated. There are three children (6, 8 and 10 years of age) and another child is on the way. The three children attend Catholic school. Mrs. White, who is unbaptized, is Mr. White's second cousin. Mr. White mentions that he is a former seminarian who received the subdeaconate, but due to an argument with his bishop, he left the seminary without dispensation and later married. Mrs. White knows nothing of this because Mr. White has successfully concealed it from her. Mr. White is now very sorry for what he did and wishes to die in peace. He begs you to straighten out this marriage, telling you that Mrs. White will cooperate but is ashamed of witnesses being present. Describe point by point how you would handle this situation.

Canon 1080

§1. Whenever an impediment is discovered after all the wedding preparations are made and the marriage cannot be deferred without probable danger of serious harm until a dispensation can be obtained from competent authority, the following persons enjoy the faculty to dispense from all the impediments with the exception of the ones mentioned in Canon 1078, §2.1°: the local ordinary and, as long as the case is an occult one, all persons mentioned in Canon 1079, §2 and §3, observing the conditions prescribed in that canon.

§2. This power is also operative for the convalidation of a marriage if the same danger exists in delay and there is insufficient time to have recourse to the Apostolic See, or to the local ordinary concerning impediments from which he is able to dispense.

8. Marriages in Urgent Necessity

Whenever all things are prepared for the wedding and one discovers an impediment which is diriment, the ordinary may dispense for all ecclesiastical impediments except those mentioned in Canon 1078, §2 if there is not enough time to approach the Holy See. Scandal must be avoided and whenever it is a mixed marriage, requiring a dispensation of mixed religion or disparity of cult, the necessary promises should be made. According to the probable opinion, the ordinary can dispense even from the juridical form of marriage (priest and two witnesses). Pastors and confessors have the same faculty, in the same circumstances whenever the ordinary cannot be reached or whenever he can be reached but the occasion of doing so would involve a danger of disclosing the secret.

Impediments need not be discovered only on the day of the wedding when the couple has already arrived at the doors of the church, or a few days before. This canon applies any time an impediment is discovered and grave injury would be caused by postponement. Also, if the wedding must be celebrated within a shorter time for some reason, this canon may be used. If the ring is not engraved or the invitations have not been sent out as yet, the privilege may still be used if other preparations are made. Even if the parties withheld the fact of the diriment impediment until the day of the wedding, a dispensation could be given according to this canon.

If there is little time available for seeking dispensations, then this canon can also be used. Of course it must be kept in mind that no extraordinary means to save time, such as telephone or telegraph, are to be used. Causes for dispensation under this canon could be loss of reputation of the parties, serious family rifts, financial loss, possible loss of employment, deportation and so on.

Absolute certainty is not required in order to make use of the faculties of this canon; probable danger of great harm is sufficient. The probability depends on a reasonable estimation of possible serious consequences, e.g., scandal, family feuds, loss of finances, danger of breaking the sixth commandment, loss of reputation. If there is a doubt whether the reasons are grave enough, this doubt is sufficient to grant the dispensation. Precautionary measures must be taken that no scandal will result, and guarantees must be given if a mixed marriage or disparity of cult case is involved. It must be noticed that the pastor's faculties are limited by occult cases whenever the ordinary cannot be reached, or where trying to reach him would violate a secret, natural, professional or sacramental (Jone, Oesterle).

According to some canonists, if the pastor approaches the ordinary for a dispensation and the ordinary fails to respond, the pastor may go ahead according to Canon 1080 whenever a grave and urgent cause is present. In such a case, he should at once notify the ordinary of the dispensation and the circumstances of the case. This also holds true for impediments public in nature and occult in fact, which we call an occult case, as when a pastor forgets to obtain the dispensation and realizes this only on the day of the wedding.

The dispensing powers of this canon (*omnia parata sunt*) extend also to the revalidation of a marriage. If the impediment is discovered shortly before the ceremony and there would be delay or great harm to the parties themselves or to the children, this canon may likewise be invoked.

Canon 1081

The pastor or the priest or deacon mentioned in Canon 1079, §2, is immediately to inform the local ordinary of a dispensation granted for the external forum; it is also to be recorded in the marriage register.

9. Record of Dispensations for the External Forum

The pastor or sacred minister who performs the marriage and grants the dispensation for it in the external forum must inform the ordinary and must see to it that a notation of it is recorded in the marriage register of the parish in which the marriage took place. Dispensations granted in the internal forum are neither sent to the local ordinary nor recorded in the marriage register.

Canon 1082

Unless a rescript from the Penitentiary states otherwise, a dispensation from an occult impediment granted in the internal non-sacramental forum is to be recorded in a book which is to be kept in the secret archives of the curia; if the occult impediment becomes public later on, no other dispensation is necessary for the external forum.

10. Record of Dispensations for the Internal Forum

The secret archives (Canon 487) are kept locked in the chancery. Only the bishop and the chancellor have a key, and no one may licitly enter without the permission of the bishop, or of both the moderator of the curia and the chancellor, or of the vicar general and the chancellor.

1 Always recorded in the parochial records and the diocesan chancery.
2 Recorded in the secret archives of the diocese or the Sacred Penitentiary in Rome.
3 The local ordinary may dispense from a vow of chastity of one who is in an institute of diocesan right.
4 Dowdell, *Celebration of Marriage in Danger of Death*, Vatican Press, Rome, 1944, p. 529.
5 Clays Bowaaert-Simenon, *Manuale Juris Canonicis*, Gandae et Leodin, No. 250.
6 Bouscaren-Ellis, *Commentary on the Code of Canon Law*, Bruce, 1956, p. 487.

Chapter Three

DIRIMENT IMPEDIMENTS

Canon 1083

§1. A man before he has completed his sixteenth year of age, and likewise a woman before she has completed her fourteenth year of age, cannot enter into a valid marriage.

§2. It is within the power of the conference of bishops to establish an older age for the licit celebration of marriage.

1. Want of Age

A man before the completion of his sixteenth year and a woman before the completion of her fourteenth year cannot contract a valid marriage. Although the marriage is a valid contract after the aforesaid ages, nevertheless pastors should deter young people from making such a contract before an earlier age than is the custom in their respective countries.

The natural law indicates that children who have sufficient discretion, a general knowledge of what marriage means, and are willing to enter into marriage may marry validly. You will notice that the actual power to generate is not spoken of here since it is the consent of the parties, not carnal relations, that validates the marriage contract. Mental capacity, therefore, is absolutely required.

The restriction in this canon in one of ecclesiastical law. The canonical impediment of age binds only the baptized, whereby it recognizes a marriage to be valid only when the parties have completed the canonical age: 16 for males and 14 for females. A boy born on September 2, 1975, will canonically complete his sixteenth year only after midnight on his sixteenth birthday, i.e., on September 2, 1991. He could not get married on the day of his sixteenth birthday as it would be invalid. Similarly, for the girl. She cannot contract a valid marriage until the day after her fourteenth birthday. If parties marry while under the established age, the impediment ceases when they come of age; however, the marriage remains invalid and validation becomes necessary according to the form of marriage.

Canon 1084

§1. Antecedent and perpetual impotence to have intercourse, whether on the part of the man or of the woman, which is either absolute or relative, of its very nature invalidates marriage.

§2. If the impediment of impotence is doubtful, either by means of a doubt of law or a doubt of fact, a marriage is neither to be impeded nor is it to be declared null as long as the doubt exists.

§3. Sterility neither prohibits nor invalidates marriage, with due regard for the prescription of Canon 1098.

2. Impotence

The codifiers have not defined impotency, and canonists do not agree as to its real definition. All agree, however, that when there is an incapacity or inability to have natural sexual intercourse, this case would constitute impotency and would invalidate the marriage. The inability to perform a natural sexual act, namely, penetration of the vagina by the male organ and the emission of true semen in it, is called impotency. Impotency is present when a man is deprived of both testicles; when he cannot have an erection; when his sex organs are not of proportion; when a woman has no vagina; or when she has a vagina that cannot be penetrated.

All agree that sterility occurs when natural sexual intercourse can take place, when all the organs necessary for generation are present and intact but the man or woman are not capable of generating offspring. This happens when the parties are too old; when women have reached the age when ovulation ceases; when a woman has no ovaries or uterus or when a man has testicles that produce little or no viable sperm.

The human act of copulation (*copula*) and the physiological process that takes place in a man or woman for the generation of children are the two primary aspects of reproduction. The physiological process includes the development of the ova in the ovaries of the female and sperm in the testicles of the male. When copulation takes place during a fertile period, the sperm goes from the vagina to the uterus and on to the fallopian tubes of the female. At the same time the ovum or female germ cell released from an ovary of the female meets the sperm somewhere en route. When the sperm penetrates it, they are united. This union is called fecundation. From the point of fecundation, a human being in its embryonic stages begins to grow. This embryo descends from the tube and enters the uterus where it attaches itself to the uterine wall and develops to maturity. After approximately nine months, a child is born. Now whatever hinders the human act of generation, that is, normal copulation, is considered impotency. Whatever hinders the physiological process is considered sterility. (N.B., The medical profession does not accept this distinction, the canonical definition of sterility being considered impotency by the medical profession.)

When is copulation in itself suitable for generation? This is not clear. If a woman lacks ovaries or has had a hysterectomy, obviously her acts of copulation are not suitable for generation because, though intercourse is possible, the organs are lacking which are essential to begetting offspring. Decisions of the Holy See have consistently ruled that as long as a married couple are capable of having normal conjugal relations, they are not impotent. Of primary importance is the fact that the conjugal act depends on the human will, not on the physiological process which follows the act. If the parties are able to perform the conjugal act, that is sufficient. The fact that they are incapable of having children is a defect of nature.

There are six kinds of impotency recognized in Canon Law:

Antecedent:	impotency that existed before marriage.
Subsequent:	impotency that arises after marriage.
Perpetual:	impotency that cannot be cured by licit means and is not dangerous.
Temporary:	impotency that disappears naturally or can be cured by licit means.
Absolute:	impotency that renders the marital act impossible with any person.
Relative:	impotency that renders the marital act impossible only with certain persons.

If impotency is doubtful by either doubt of law or doubt of fact, marriage can take place even though this impediment is of natural law. Since it is difficult to solve such doubts, even though probable and prudent, the Church maintains that the natural law giving a right to marry must prevail.

If there is a doubt regarding the impediment of impotency before the marriage, a medical examination should be made. After this investigation, if the doubt persists, the marriage may take place.

If a couple after marriage has tried having marital relations and a doubt regarding the impediment of impotency arises, an investigation as to whether the impotency was antecedent and perpetual must be made. If it is certain that antecedent and perpetual impotency is present, the process of a declaration of nullity should be initiated.[1]

Code Commission Findings

The Code Commission for the revision of Canon Law considered various aspects of impotency and the following are some of the interpretations that the Commission feels must enter into findings of impotency.[2]

1. The husband's penis must be capable of penetrating the wife's vagina.
2. The ejaculate need not contain true semen.
3. Ordinary insemination is required, without consideration of the nature of the seminal fluid.
4. The copulation need not be accompanied by complete orgasm or sexual satisfaction on the part of both husband and wife.
5. True copulation does not exist if it occurred violently.
6. True copulation does not exist if aphrodisiac means are required.
7. True copulation exists even if the wife experiences great pain, provided she consented to the act.
8. True copulation and consummation do not exist when anticonceptual devices affect the physical act itself.
9. True copulation and consummation do exist when the anticonceptual devices do not affect the physical act itself.
10. Double vasectomy does not constitute masculine impotency.
11. A woman who has an artificial vagina inserted before marriage is to be considered potent.

12. A woman who simply has a closed vagina or one that is equivalent to closed is not to be considered impotent.
13. A woman who has a tubal ligation is to be considered potent.
14. It is not yet decided whether functional impotence constitutes a diriment impediment of impotence.
15. It is not certain whether impotence is an impediment of the natural law or one arising from the very nature of marriage (Canon 1084, §1).
16. If the impediment of impotence is doubtful either by doubt of law or doubt of fact, marriage is not to be prohibited, nor, as long as the doubt remains, is it to be declared null (Canon 1084, §2).
17. Sterility does not prohibit marriage or render it invalid, unless the sterility was fraudulently concealed (Canon 1084, §3).[3]

Congregation for the Doctrine of the Faith

"The Sacred Congregation always holds that those who have undergone a vasectomy cannot be impeded from marriage just as others in similar circumstances cannot be impeded when their impotency is not shown to certainly exist.

"Now, however, having reviewed this position and after study by this Sacred Congregation and by the Commission for the Revision of the Code of Canon Law, in a plenary meeting on Wednesday, May 11, 1977, the most eminent and reverend Fathers of this Sacred Congregation, postulating for themselves the following questions, decreed the answers:

1. Whether the impotency which invalidates marriage, consists in an antecedent and perpetual incapacity, either absolute or relative, for accomplishing conjugal copulation? Answered: Yes.
2. Given an affirmative answer, whether there is necessarily required for conjugal copulation, the ejection of semen produced by the testicles? Answered: No.

"And in the Audience of Friday, May 13, 1977, given to the undersigned Prefect of this Sacred Congregation, the Supreme Pontiff, Pope Paul VI by divine Providence, approved this decree and ordered its publication.

"Given at Rome, from the Palace of the Congregation for the Doctrine of the Faith, May 13, 1977."

Canon 1085

§1. **A person who is held to the bond of a prior marriage, even if it had not been consummated, invalidly attempts marriage.**

§2. **Even if the prior marriage is invalid or dissolved for any reason whatsoever, it is not on that account permitted to contract another before the nullity or the dissolution of the prior marriage has been legitimately and certainly established.**

3. Prior Bond of Marriage

This impediment is of the divine law and binds all men both Christian and pagan without exception. One who was married before is forbidden to marry again, unless the first marriage is declared null or has been dissolved. The Privilege of the Faith is the only exception to this rule insofar as the first marriage is dissolved, not before, but at the very moment the second is contracted.

A prior marriage is dissolved by the death of one of the parties whereupon the surviving party is free to marry. This freedom must be verified by:

1. Authentic documents: death certificate, ecclesiastical or civil. Where the ordinary does not require a *nihil obstat*, the pastor may allow the new marriage to take place.
2. Proof from witnesses when authentic documents are not available. These, of course, are submitted to the ordinary for the *nihil obstat*.
3. Presumption of death process[4]: Strict proof of death is impossible in some cases and in such circumstances the proper authorities can decide with moral certainty on the basis of the presumption that the party is dead.[5]
4. Cases decided by the Sacred Congregation of the Sacraments: AAS III-26 (1911); AAS VII-40, 235:476 (1915); AAS VIII-151 (1916); AAS IX-120 (1917); AAS XIV-96 (1922); Instruction AAS III-102 (1911); Instruction AAS XIII-348 (1921).

It must be noted that in presumption of death cases, the validity of the second marriage depends upon whether the former spouse is actually dead. Permission is by no means a dispensation. If the spouse should still be living, the second marriage is invalid. "What God has joined together let no man put asunder."

Instruction of the Holy See

1. Prolonged absence, civil declaration or other presumptions of death considered by civil law are insufficient.
2. Interested parties should obtain, if possible, official documents proving the death of the party concerned. The departments of vital statistics sometimes provide important information of this kind.
3. When official documents are not available, testimony of two trustworthy witnesses should be obtained, provided these witnesses: knew the deceased; know the fact of his death; agree on the circumstances, e.g., time and cause; and state whether they were related to each other, or even friends or associates of the deceased.
4. One first-class witness of the deceased may suffice if this witness can provide adequate circumstantial evidence.
5. Sometimes hearsay evidence may suffice (*tempore non suspecto*) should it coincide with information already available.
6. Presumptions based on age; moral character; physical or mental status; affection for his or her family; correspondence (letters); or any circumstances which would give reason to presume that the spouse would be heard from if he or she were alive are conjectures.
7. Rumors should be investigated if there is any foundation for assuming they may lead to useful information.
8. The results of investigations made through newspapers, radio, TV, government agencies or the FBI could be used if sufficient grounds are present for the presumption.
9. Whenever any other serious doubts are present, the matter must be referred to the Holy See (AAS XXXI, 252: July 2, 1898).
10. References to other cases may be invoked as for example:

    (1) *Earthquake in Messina — 1908*:   The Sacred Congregation of the Sacraments demanded that each case be investigated separately according to the decree of 1898.
    (2) *Russian-Japanese War*:   A decree of 1910 gave the same instruction as in §(1). Incidentally, lapse of time in this case was only three years. The decision gives a good review of circum-

stances which might be applicable in time of war, flood, earthquake, etc.

Cases Involving Servicemen or Veterans

Whenever a tribunal is handling a case of this kind, it may be necessary to conduct a special investigation in order to obtain information or additional information about a case already started concerning the party in question. The following address may be helpful: Military Ordinariate, 832 Varnum St.. N.E., Washington, D.C. 20017.

Declaration of Nullity

1. Lack of Form

A prior attempted marriage is proclaimed invalid by the declaration of nullity because of the defect of form (Canon 1108). No formal process is used here. The ordinary, after close examination of the following documents, is the competent authority to declare the nullity: (1) certificate of baptism; (2) certificates of confirmation and first Holy Communion; (3) record of any civil marriage; (4) record of divorce (photostat from the clerk of the Circuit Court); (5) sworn statement that the marriage was never validated in the Church, i.e., celebrated in the form prescribed by the Church.

2. Diriment Impediment

The ordinary may grant a declaration of nullity regarding a prior marriage by simple summary judicial process (Canon 1686) based on the following diriment impediments: (1) disparity of cult; (2) holy orders; (3) solemn vows; (4) ligamen; (5) consanguinity; (6) affinity.

3. Other Causes

Declarations of nullity regarding a previous marriage can be based on defective consent, impotence, force and fear. In these cases a formal judicial trial must take place and two concordant sentences rendered (cf. *Instruction of the Sacred Congregation of the Sacraments*, August 15, 1936, Art. 220).

The question of a presumed death is considered only indirectly under the impediment of ligamen (a previous and existing marriage) because many of these cases are introduced for processing without any direct reference to the ligamen impediment.

A common law marriage is one that omits the canonical as well as the civil form of marriage and the parties live together as husband and wife. This is a marriage without any ceremony whatsoever, that is, without either minister or witnesses assisting. The man and woman live together as husband and wife and act as such before society. Whenever common law marriages are permitted, civil law requires (assuming no impediments) that the parties exchange their consent mutually. The matter and form are not determined by civil law and hence are considered immaterial. Civil law requires that the parties have the intention to contract a marriage here and now (*de presenti*) and that they cohabit with each other. This third condition required by civil law seems to be a contradiction. It is difficult to see how this condition can be a constituent of a common law marriage. Objectively speaking and also from the canonical point of view, the mutual consent and the proper intention are sufficient. Cohabitation is merely a proof of such a marriage. To retain it as a condition to constitute the marriage seems to be unnecessary.[6]

The contemporary trend of living together without benefit of marriage has been so prevalent throughout the western world that it is possible to overlook the fact that some of these marriages could be common law. Each case must be studied separately.

Principles

1. The fact that a man and woman live together for many years is not automatically construable as constituting a valid common law marriage. The first two conditions mentioned above, mutual consent and intention must be fulfilled, otherwise the relationship amounts to mere concubinage, even though people may publicly consider them married.

2. It is often erroneously believed by clergy and laymen alike that relationships of this kind are not valid common law marriages, when they actually are. These cases should be carefully checked. After a divorce, individuals may find it inconvenient to have their relationship classified as a common law marriage and may prefer another sort of nomenclature. In such cases their stories about their relationship often vary.

3. Catholics cannot contract a valid common law marriage.

4. Unbaptized parties must observe the prescribed form of the civil law. If common law marriages are recognized by the Sate, then the unbaptized contract valid common law marriages in that State. If it is

forbidden by the State, then the common law marriage would be invalid. The State regulates the form of marriage for them.

A common law marriage is recognized as valid by the Church when it occurs between two baptized non-Catholics as well as between an unbaptized person and a baptized non-Catholic, irrespective of the civil law of a particular State, because these people are subject to the laws of the Church. Therefore, these cases must be carefully scrutinized by pastors and especially by the chancery to ascertain whether such common law marriages constitute an impediment of a prior bond, in which case it would invalidate a subsequent marriage. We should keep in mind that the solution of such cases is *not* determined by the fact that the civil law recognizes such marriages as valid, but rather by the very fact that mutual consent and proper intention in virtue of the natural law was or was not given. It must also be kept in mind that for such people no legislation exists requiring a specific formality for the celebration of their marriage.

5. When the parties to a common law marriage wish to become Catholics, in those States that prohibit a common law marriage, they must obtain a license and renew their consent in order to fulfill the requirements of civil law. It is also advisable that the same procedure be followed even in those States that recognize common law marriages despite the fact that they do not require it.

6. Regarding convalidation of a marriage in civil law, this is done by reason of the theory of consent persevering and this applies only to the marriage of the unbaptized.

7. Unbaptized persons who contract a common law marriage are bound by the diriment impediments of civil law.

8. If one or both parties to a common law marriage is a baptized non-Catholic, these parties are not bound by the impediments of the civil law, but are bound by the diriment impediments of the ecclesiastical law.[7]

Proving a Common Law Marriage

1. According to Canons 1059 and 1060, a common law marriage of a baptized non-Catholic enjoys the presumption that it is valid. When such a marriage lacks proof, i.e., registration of witnesses to same, the testimony given with an oath of the parties themselves can be accepted as proof of their marriage, provided no other marriage is prejudicial to this testimony.

2. Cohabitation and public knowledge of marital status establishes a presumption of a common law marriage. The presumption is corroborated by various concomitant circumstances:

(1) when both parties register as husband and wife at hotels when traveling;

(2) when the man introduces the woman in social circles as his wife;

(3) when the couple acts as husband and wife in legal matters such as

(a) having a joint bank account,

(b) filing joint income tax forms,

(c) registering together when voting,

(d) making out their last will and testament in such a way that he legally considers her his wife and vice versa,

(e) taking out insurance policies declaring the other party as beneficiary,

(f) when the income tax report of the man has any reference to the woman as his wife,

(g) when the couple refers to themselves as Mr. and Mrs. in public,

(h) when the couple registers at the post office or in the telephone directory as husband and wife,

(i) when the couple intends to live this way until death.[8]

Questionnaire to Determine Common Law Unions

1. Do you believe in the sanctity of an oath?

2. Do you realize the gravity of perjury and its serious consequences?

3. Do you solemnly swear to tell the whole truth and nothing but the truth in answering all the following questions? [This oath should be made touching the Holy Gospels]

4. Fill in the following:

Name ....

Address ....

Place of Birth .... Age ....

Occupation ....

5. Father's name ....

Mother's maiden name ....

6. Were you ever baptized, sprinkled or christened in any religion? If so, when? Where? What denomination?

7. Have you ever lived with anyone in a common law union? With whom? Was this party married before he (she) lived with you? If so, when? Where? With whom? Was the former spouse living at the time you lived together?

8. What is the present name and address of the person with whom you lived in common law?

9. Was this party ever baptized, christened or sprinkled in any religion? If so, when? Where? What denomination?

10. How long did you live together?

11. When did you begin living together?

12. Where did you spend this time together?

13. Why was there no marriage ceremony?

14. Did you look upon yourselves as husband and wife? What was the opinion among your relatives, friends, neighbors, trades folk, etc? Give names and addresses.

15. Did you call yourselves Mr. and Mrs.? Did you ever register at work or for income tax purposes, charge accounts, insurance, mail box and telephone directory as "Married"?

16. Did others consider you as married to each other? Who? What is their present name and address? Why did they consider you married?

17. Did you consider that you had a right to him (her)? Why?

18. Did you ever tell him (her) that this was no marriage? Did you ever tell anyone else? Why? Address? Why did you do this?

19. Did you ever mention that you really should get married? To whom? What is their present name and address? Why did you mention this? What was the answer to this?

20. Did you intend to live this way until death? Did either of you make a will? How did you provide for the other party?

21. Did you own property together? In what name was it listed?

22. Did you have any children? Were they registered as children of Mr. and Mrs.?

23. Did you think it was a sin to live this way?

24. Did the other party consider it a sin to live this way?

25. Did you ever go through any kind of a marriage form together, i.e., in which marriage consent was expressed, even privately?

26. [Additional questions may be appended at this point.]
27. Do you swear to the truth of the above statements?

Canon 1086

§1. **Marriage between two persons, one of whom is baptized in the Catholic Church or has been received into it and has not left it by means of a formal act, and the other of whom is non-baptized, is invalid.**

§2. **This impediment is not to be dispensed unless the conditions mentioned in Canons 1125 and 1126 are fulfilled.**

§3. **If at the time the marriage was contracted one party was commonly considered to be baptized or the person's baptism was doubted, the validity of the marriage is to be presumed in accord with the norm of Canon 1060 until it is proven with certainty that one party was baptized and the other was not.**

4. Disparity of Cult

This canon deals with: (1) persons born in the Catholic Church; (2) persons received into the Catholic Church from heresy and schism; (3) persons doubtfully baptized.

A marriage is considered null when contracted between a non-baptized person and a person who was baptized in the Catholic Church or who has been received into the Church from heresy or schism.

If the party at the time of the marriage was commonly held to have been baptized, or if his or her baptism was doubtful, the marriage must be considered doubtful (Canon 1060) until it is proven with certainty that one party was baptized and the other was not.

Background

The natural and divine laws govern the impediments of mixed religion and disparity of cult because of the possible consequent danger to the faith and morals of the Catholic party.

In the Old Testament we have a positive law which forbids marriage between a Jew and a Gentile (Ex 34:16 and Dt 7:3). Marriages between Jews and Christians in the early Church were considered legitimate by Christian emperors who had a great deal of influence on Church councils in this regard. From the 12th century to 1917, all marriages were considered invalid which were contracted between a baptized person and a non-baptized person, unless a dispensation was obtained. Because this legislation included baptized Protestants, many marriages were null in the eyes of the Church. The impediments of mixed religion and disparity of cult are considered to be from divine law if there is a danger of perversion either to the Catholic party or their offspring, and a dispensation cannot be given until the danger is removed. However, this is considered to be only a prohibitive impediment of the divine law, since we have no positive proof that such a marriage is, indeed, invalid by divine law.

Ecclesiastical Law

According to the 1917 Code, mixed marriage was a diriment impediment regardless of whether there was a danger or not to the faith of the baptized Catholic. If for example, the facts of a case showed that children were being raised Catholics and the wife practiced her Catholic faith without interference from her unbaptized husband, these circumstances were not considered sufficient in themselves to warrant a guarantee. Before 1917, the diriment impediment existed for all marriages of one probably baptized or for heretics, schismatics and the unbaptized. Since 1917, the impediment exists only for marriages where one party is not baptized and the other is baptized in the Catholic Church, or converted to it from heresy or schism.

The Oriental Code

There are distinct differences between the Latin Code and the Oriental Code of Law on this point. Canons 60 and 61 of the Oriental Code state: "A marriage contracted by a non-baptized person with a baptized person is null." This implies that baptized non-Catholics (including Oriental schismatics) cannot validly marry a non-baptized person. Hence, the Oriental Code, dealing with the impediment of disparity of cult, is more restrictive than the Latin Code, it being similar to the Latin legislation before 1917. This impediment is retained according to the particular discipline. It also includes Oriental schismatics and retains the impediment of disparity of cult.

In ecclesiastical circles there are discussions about returning to this pre-1917 legislation, the idea being that it might help stem the high divorce rate which results among the great number of non-Catholics who enter into such a marriage or wish to enter into such a marriage with Catholics and who must resort to the complicated and involved process of the Privilege of the Faith. If the pre-1917 legislation were in place, our chanceries, so the thinking goes, would not be bogged down in all the necessary paper work and routine in which they are now involved. It would all be solved simply by a declaration of nullity, as in the Oriental Church.

Conversion to the Catholic Church

The second item considered in this canon is conversion to the Catholic faith from heresy, schism or any other religion. The manner in which conversion to the Catholic Church takes place (after which the member is called a convert) is governed by the so-called ABC formula: (A) Adjuration of heresy and profession of faith; (B) Baptism which is given conditionally; (C) Confession sacramentally with conditional absolution. If the individual was baptized validly in a heretical sect, A and C alone are used. If never baptized, the person is baptized absolutely.

There is a basic disparity or inequality regarding religion between a Catholic and non-baptized person. After questioning the party concerned, relatives, friends and acquaintances should be questioned and records of churches where the non-baptized party lived for more than six months should be investigated. One should try to find out if other members of the family were baptized, if the parents were baptized and whether they were religiously inclined. If doubt exists then there is a strong presumption that the party may have been baptized. If the parents were religious, we can presume that the children were baptized. Baptism is not usually presumed if the parents of the non-Catholic party frowned on baptism, did not have any children baptized, felt that baptism should be postponed until the child was old enough to decide for itself or had no records in the church.

Cases of Orientals and Unbaptized Persons

Mary, though baptized a Byzantine (Ruthenian) Catholic, was brought up from childhood in the Latin Church where she attended

Mass and received Holy Communion. Later when she planned her marriage with a non-baptized person, the pastor of the Latin Church obtained a dispensation from the disparity of cult and performed the ceremony. Some time later the marriage ended in separation and divorce. Mary then married another non-baptized person outside the Church, but later this person wished to take instructions and become a Catholic. Mary now wants to have her second marriage validated. And it can be because the Latin rite ordinary had invalidly granted the dispensation from the disparity of cult. The Latin ordinary had no subject and therefore no jurisdiction in this case, even though Mary had attended the Latin Church for the whole of her lifetime.

Susan, a Byzantine Catholic in the U.S. Army, plans to marry a non-baptized person in the city where they are sojourning. The chaplain went to the local ordinary of the place, obtained the dispensation from disparity of cult, and performed the marriage in the parish church. Some years later Susan separated and got a divorce. Her marriage was declared invalid because the Latin ordinary did not have jurisdiction for either of these two parties. If the chaplain had obtained the dispensation from the Military Ordinariate, however, the marriage would have been valid. It should be noted that the ordinary of the Military Ordinariate in the USA enjoys faculties for Catholics of both the Eastern and Latin Rite Churches in the service.

Who are considered Catholics?

1. All adults who are validly baptized in the Catholic Church.
2. All children of Catholic parents. Also those of a mixed marriage who have been baptized with the intention of belonging to the Catholic Church.
3. All persons in danger of death who have been baptized by a Catholic. This may be baptism conferred by a layman or a priest, even though the party was unconscious at the time.
4. Children born of non-Catholics or of an invalid marriage are validly baptized in the Catholic Church when their parents' consent is given and a promise made that the child will be brought up as a Catholic.

Manner of Baptism

The baptism takes place with the remote matter, water, and the proximate matter, the washing or ablution by infusion, immersion or aspersion. When any of these is used, the one baptizing must use the form simultaneously: "I baptize you in the name of the Father and of the Son and of the Holy Spirit." A moral unity must exist between the ablution and the form. Protestant ministers must have the proper intention and they have this proper intention when wanting to do what Christ did in instituting the sacrament or when following the scripture as all Christians do in conferring baptism. When the proper ritual of baptism is used we can presume the proper intention. This brings up the question: Then are non-Catholics baptized validly? If the minister used the proper matter and form and does what Christ intended, the baptism is valid. Hence we cannot say, as some erroneously believe, that all non-Catholic baptisms are invalid. Ordinarily, doubtful baptisms are considered valid. The Holy Office has written the following to certain ordinaries in the U.S. about this matter:

"Whether baptism conferred by the Disciples of Christ, Presbyterians, Congregationalists, Baptists, Methodists, is to be presumed invalid, when the necessary matter and form were used, because the minister did not have the intention to do what the Church does, or what Christ instituted, or whether such baptism is to be considered valid unless the contrary is proven in a particular case. *Reply*: In the negative to the first part; and in the affirmative to the second part."[9]

In other words, baptism in these particular sects is considered valid until the contrary is proven.

Doubtful Cases

Case #1: Father A, after conducting a baptismal investigation, was sufficiently satisfied with a beautifully embossed baptismal certificate from a certain non-Catholic church stating that the person concerned was baptized. Father B, however, had doubts about the baptisms performed in that church. A further investigation took place. The rector of the church of baptism directed the investigators to his curate who took care of such matters. When asked what form he used, the curate was confused. "Do you have a baptismal font?" he was asked. He replied that he did not use one. "Do you issue certificates?" His answer was: "All the members of our church are baptized in this church when they sign our Golden Book of Baptism. We then issue the certificate. This was the case regarding your party."

Case #2: One non-Catholic minister stated that he baptized more solemnly than Catholics do. While he poured rose water on the person to be baptized, his wife sang with the accompaniment of the organ from the choir loft, after which he issued a certificate of baptism.

Case #3: Mary, a divorced non-Catholic, was now taking instructions and wished to marry a Catholic, if her Privilege of the Faith appeal was granted in Rome. In the process it was discovered that her minister had issued a baptismal certificate, thus making her first marriage a *ratum* marriage, since her former husband was also baptized. Mary protested that she had never been baptized. Investigation was made and the records showed that the former minister had entered Mary's baptism several times and then only partially, not like the others. These records showed that Mary was baptized one day after the wedding, when she was on her honeymoon. Moreover, the date of marriage, October 12, was tampered with and changed to October 13, meaning to show that the baptism had occurred on the earlier date. The present pastor stated that the former minister was 80 and very forgetful, the reason for his retirement. Evidently the old man had begun entering the marriage record into the baptismal book when he realized that it was the wrong book. He let it go and did not finish the entry. The fact that the entry was incomplete, the minister forgetful, the date changed, the time of baptism listed when the party was away, plus additional evidence given by relatives led to the conclusion that Mary was never baptized. All this substantiated her statement, and the Privilege of the Faith appeal was granted.

The Synod of Trullo (691) and the Impediment of Mixed Religion[10]

The controversy over the impediment of disparity of cult (mixed religion[11]) enacted by the Council of Trullo (A.D. 691) went on for several years. As a result, in the Latin Church the impediment of mixed religion has not been an invalidating prohibition of marriage since the thirteenth century. In the Eastern Churches, the severity of the prohibition was once sharpened by conflicts regarding christological issues, but here, too, the impediment has not been considered diriment for hundreds of years. Since Vatican II both the Latin and Eastern Churches accept the sacramentality of marriages of baptized persons and the intimate relationship existing between Christian marriage and the eucharistic community of the Church.

Since there is a common bond of belief today in the sacramental hierarchical dimensions of marriage, it is difficult to understand the contradiction between the publicized jurisprudence of the Roman Rota and the pastoral practice of the Orthodox Church regarding the impediment of mixed religion. The conflict exists between the interpretation of the binding force of Eastern law derived from Canon 72 of the Council of Trullo and various canonists. Canon 72 stated that marriage between Orthodox and heretics is forbidden under penalty of excommunication and must be dissolved. On the basis of a canonical theory of jurisdiction followed in recent years, the Orthodox faithful are still considered bound to the impediment enacted by this Council.

The earliest use of the impediment of the Council of Trullo as a possible ground of nullity is found in a private reply given to the Bishop of Worcester by the Sacred Congregation of the Oriental Church on December 1959.[12] Since then we have public record of the fact that this impediment has been upheld by the Oriental Congregation and used to invalidate many marriages by the Congregation of the Doctrine of the Faith, and more recently by the Roman Rota. Two cases (*"documentum libertatis"*) were granted by the Holy Office, February 10, 1960. Five more such cases were reported in the Roman Replies for 1965. The *Canon Law Digest Supplement* through 1965 records three cases. In each of these one party was a validly baptized member of the Orthodox Church and the other, a validly baptized Protestant. All of the marriages occurred before the motu proprio *Crebrae Allatae*, May 2, 1949. It was Cardinal Cousa's contention that after this motu proprio, Canon 72 of Trullo was abrogated for the Orthodox. He was wrong.

Crebrae Allatae was not intended for the Orthodox and therefore Canon 72 of Trullo still holds. Moreover, a rescript dated May 22, 1969 declared invalid the marriage of an Orthodox with a validly baptized Protestant contracted in 1956: *Constare de invaliditate matrimonii in casu ex*

72 *Concilii Trullani quod adhuc suam vim tenet.*[13] This now clearly contradicts the former theory and sustains the opinion that the motu proprio did not affect the matrimonial law of the Orthodox Churches.[14] To understand the controversy better, one should read "The Impediment of Mixed Religion."[15]

At first, decisions regarding Canon 72 of Trullo were handled administratively and reserved explicitly to the competency of the Holy Office. Subsequently, in particular cases, local ordinaries (Latin and Oriental) were instructed to decide the cases. By virtue of the apostolic constitution *Regimini Ecclesiae Universae* of August 15, 1967 and the decree *Integrae servandae* of December 7, 1965, these cases should now be handled judicially, with appeal to normal tribunals of second instance and then, if necessary, to the Roman Rota.

Canon 1087

Persons who are in holy orders invalidly attempt marriage.

5. Sacred Orders

Sacred Orders are the subdiaconate, diaconate, priesthood and bishopric. Subdiaconate, though still a sacred order for the Oriental Church, was discontinued in the Latin Church on September 14, 1972. This canon establishes an ecclesiastical impediment which has been in effect for the Latin Church since the Council of Trent though it had its origin in the Lateran Council of 1139. Prior to that time, celibacy had been encouraged in the Church since the fifth century. Being an ecclesiastical impediment, it could be dispensed by the Holy See, but this is seldom done for members of the priesthood.

In Oriental Law this legislation is similar to the Latin Code, with the subdiaconate still retained. It is a major or minor impediment depending upon whether the particular rite demands of its priests the observance of celibacy. In danger of death, Canons 1079 and 1080 provide for dispensation from the subdiaconate and diaconate.

Clerics who are constituted in major orders when they attempt marriage, even in a civil ceremony, incur an *ipso facto* suspension (Canon 1394). By common law such clerics lose their ecclesiastical office and become irregular. On May 4, 1937, the Sacred Penitentiary added a more severe penalty for a priest who attempts marriage, namely a *specialissimo modo* censure reserved to the Holy See. However, the new Code makes no mention of this censure.

Canon 1088

Persons who are bound by a public perpetual vow of chastity in a religious institute invalidly attempt marriage.

6. Perpetual Vows

Anyone who attempts marriage while in perpetual vows has this marriage rendered invalid by this canon. Vows taken in a religious institute are public and are either simple or solemn. The distinction between these is the fact that a vow is solemn if it is acknowledged as such by the Church; otherwise it is simple. The new Code makes no distinction between solemn and simple vows in this canon. They must be public (accepted in the name of the Church by a legitimate superior) and perpetual.

A religious in perpetual vows who is not a cleric and who attempts even a civil marriage incurs an automatic (*latae sententiae*) interdict. If a cleric, he also incurs an automatic (*latae sententiae*) suspension (Canon 1394 §1 & §2).

A person in perpetual vows can obtain a dispensation from his or her vows from the Holy See. Until that dispensation has been received this canon retains its full effect.

Canon 1089

No marriage can exist between a man and a woman abducted or at least detained for the purpose of contracting marriage with her, unless the woman of her own accord chooses marriage after she has been separated from her abductor and established in a place where she is safe and free.

7. Abduction

The Council of Trent combined the factor of abduction with that of force and fear in this ecclesiastical impediment. The Code now includes not only abduction but also any violent detention of a woman. It also indicates that even if she consents while still in the place of detention, the marriage would still be null because she must be brought to a safe place to make the consent freely. A distinction, however, should be made here. Suppose a man abducts a woman in order to have sexual relations, and not to marry her, but the woman afterwards consents to marry him. In this case, there is no impediment. But if she is abducted for sexual relations and afterward is detained for the purpose of marrying, the impediment would exist. Note that since this is an ecclesiastical impediment, it does not affect the unbaptized.

Canon 1090

§1. **A person who, for the purpose of entering marriage with a certain person, has brought about the death of that person's spouse or one's spouse, invalidly attempts such a marriage.**

§2. **They also invalidly attempt marriage between themselves who have brought about the death of the spouse of one of them through mutual physical or moral cooperation.**

8. Crime

This impediment arises between a man and a woman when either one murders his or her own or the other's spouse for the purpose of marriage to one another. The conflict or incompatibility arises between the taking of a life (murder) and the attempt to marry as a result of that crime.

The 1917 Code included adultery as one of the crimes which rendered a marriage invalid if it took place between two persons who promised marriage to each other (Canon 1075 of the Old Code). If such a case should come up, wherein adultery and promise to marry took place before November 27, 1983, it would have to be judged by the Code of 1917. This new canon is not retroactive.

The first degree of this impediment considers the actual murder of one's own spouse or the spouse of the other party. The intention to marry need not be mutual; it could be on the part of only one party. Neither is a mutual promise required to incur this impediment as such. If one party is ignorant of the intention of the murderer to have his or her spouse murdered, the impediment arises.

The second degree involves a mutual agreement (conspiracy) on the part of both parties to murder the other spouse. In both the first and second degree, the moral or physical cooperation on the part of both would give rise to the impediment of crime.

A dispensation for crime cannot be granted by the ordinary but by the Holy See (Canon 1078, §2.2°).

The impediment may be dispensed by the local ordinary or those mentioned in Canon 1079, §2-§3 when one of the guilty parties is in danger of death. It may also be dispensed in cases in which (*omnia parata sunt*) all is prepared for the wedding (Canon 1080). If the case is public, only the local ordinary may dispense; if it is an occult case, it may be dispensed by the ministers mentioned in Canon 1079.

Canon 1091

§1. **In the direct line of consanguinity, marriage is invalid between all ancestors and descendants, whether they be related legitimately or naturally.**

§2. **In the collateral line of consanguinity, marriage is invalid up to and including the fourth degree.**

§3. **The impediment of consanguinity is not multiplied.**

§4. **If there exists any doubt whether the parties are related through consanguinity in any degree of the direct line or in the second degree of the collateral line, marriage is never permitted.**

9. Consanguinity

Consanguinity is the relationship between persons based on carnal relationship or carnal generation. Consanguinity does not arise from blood transfusions. Consanguinity exists in the direct line if one of the persons is the *direct* ancestor of the other, that is, persons who descend from each other, such as father, daughter, granddaughter, great-granddaughter, etc.

The indirect line is usually called the collateral line. It exists when neither person is the direct ancestor of the other but both are descended from a common ancestor, as for example, brother and sister, first cousins, etc.

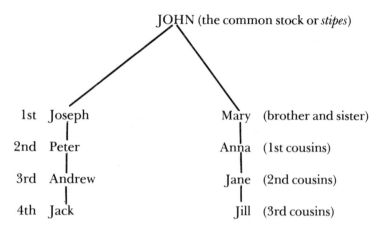

JOHN (the common stock or *stipes*)

1st	Joseph	Mary	(brother and sister)
2nd	Peter	Anna	(1st cousins)
3rd	Andrew	Jane	(2nd cousins)
4th	Jack	Jill	(3rd cousins)

5th   [No dispensation needed — 4th cousins]

In the preceding diagram Joseph and Mary are brother and sister removed one degree from the common stock, John; Peter and Anna are first cousins and two degrees from the common stock; Joseph and Anna are related in the second degree touching the first (*in secundo gradu tangente primum*), or uncle and niece; Andrew and Anna are related in the third degree of the collateral line mixed with the second degree, i.e., second cousins first mixed; Andrew and Jane are related in the second degree (second cousins).

Marriage between brother and sister is probably null in the natural law itself. The Church never grants a dispensation in such a case or even when it is probable that the parties are related in this manner. If non-baptized people are related in this way and already married, the Holy Office does not forbid a priest to baptize them.

A special instruction of the Sacred Congregation of the Sacraments, August 1, 1931, deals with uncle/niece marriages. No dispensation will be granted without very special reasons. The ordinary himself must write the petition to Rome for such a dispensation or at least sign the petition and give his views on the reasons the couple have for asking such a dispensation (AAS XXIII, 1931, p. 413). Marriages between cousins, aunts with their nephews, or uncles with their nieces should be discouraged.

It must be kept in mind that there is no impediment of consanguinity unless one of the parents of one party wishing to get married was at least a first cousin of one of the parents of the other party.

When determining the degrees of relationship, use the following:

(1) To make two persons brother and sister, give them common parents.

(2) To make two persons first cousins, give them a common grandparent.

(3) To make two persons second cousins, give them a common great-grandparent.

(4) To make brothers,

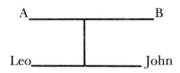

(5) To make brothers half-brothers,

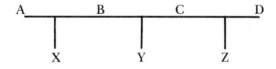

The degrees are computed in this way:

Direct Line: Compute it according to the number of generations, or according to the number of persons in the line without counting the ancestor (*stipes*).

Collateral Line: Compute it according to the number of generations in one branch if the branches are equal. If the two branches are unequal, count the longer branch (Canon 1091, §2).

A Case in Point

Jack and Mary come to your rectory to arrange for their marriage. Jack tells you that he is Mary's mother's first cousin and that he is also Mary's father's nephew. How are Mary and Jack related? Do you need a dispensation? (Ans. They are blood relatives in the second and third degrees in the collateral line from their common ancestors. Therefore, a dispensation is needed.)

Canon 1092

Affinity in the direct line in any degree whatsoever invalidates matrimony.

10. Affinity

Affinity exists only between the man and the blood relatives of the woman and likewise between the woman and the blood relatives of the man. It is computed in such a way that the same persons who are blood relatives of the man are related by affinity in the same line and degree to the woman and vice versa.

Affinity stems from a valid marriage. It extends to all degrees in the direct line. A man could not, for instance, marry his wife's mother, grandmother, daughter or granddaughter. The brothers of the husband, however, are not related by affinity to the sisters of the wife.

The Church rarely dispenses from affinity in the direct line. Henry VIII of England got a dispensation to marry Catherine, his brother's wife. Arthur, Henry's older brother, is said never to have consummated the marriage. When Henry VIII decided to marry again, he claimed that the affinity dispensation was invalid, even when given by the Pope because it was an impediment of the divine law.

The 1917 Code granted the faculty to dispense from all ecclesiastical impediments except that of affinity in the direct line of a consummated marriage. This rule holds for cases prior to November 1983 because this canon is not retroactive. In 1957 the disputed question was whether affinity contracted in infidelity became an impediment for marriage which was entered into after baptism even of only one of the parties. The answer was affirmative (AAS 49-77).

Twenty-six States in the United States do not cite affinity as a marital impediment. The following States, however, do have degrees of affinity laws that annul marriages: Alabama, Georgia, Iowa, Kentucky, Maine, Maryland, Massachusetts, Connecticut, Delaware, Michigan, Mississippi, New Hampshire, Oklahoma, Pennsylvania, Rhode Island, South Carolina, Tennessee, Texas, Vermont, Virginia, Washington, West Virginia and the District of Columbia. Every State varies regarding this impediment. Alabama forbids a son to marry his stepmother or the widow of his uncle. A father may not marry the widow of his son, nor the daughter of his wife, nor the daughter of his son. It is best to check the laws and statutes of each State.

Case #1: Joseph marries Mary who dies within a year. Joseph then wants to marry Mary's sister, Ann. Can he do so?

Case #2: Susie and Lea are sisters. Helen and Rose are sisters. Susie and Lea are first cousins to Helen and Rose. John marries Lea. How is he related to the other three in virtue of the impediment of affinity?

Oriental Law

The diriment impediment of consanguinity and affinity differ as to the manner of computation and applicability. Canon 66 of the Oriental Code provides that marriage between blood relatives in all degrees of the direct line are null and void. Furthermore, blood relations in the collateral line nullifies marriage up to the sixth degree inclusive. In case of a doubt concerning relationship in any degree of the direct line or up to the second degree of the collateral line inclusive, marriages are never permitted. Canon 66 has a fourth provision not to be found in its Latin counterpart, Canon 1092. This provision gives the Oriental version of Canon 96 of the 1917 Code, namely, the manner in which the degrees of consanguinity are to be computed.

The Oriental Code computes the degree of consanguinity by taking into consideration all generations on both sides of the collateral line, whereas the Latin Code takes into consideration only the one, the longer line. At first sight the casual observer might be inclined to think that this computation is the same as the third degree in the Latin Code, but this would be true if there were an unequal number of generations on both sides of the line. However, if one side of the line should have four or five generations and the other one or two, the Latin Code would permit marriage in the fourth and fifth generations whereas the Eastern Code would prohibit the same. Interritual marriages frequently occur and hence a situation might take place where a Latin would plan to marry an Oriental to whom he might be related in the fourth or fifth degree of consanguinity, often in the collateral line. According to his own law, the

Latin may contract marriage validly, whereas the Oriental could be disqualified from contracting a valid marriage without a dispensation. Which law prevails? Cappello[16] proposes the principle of communication of freedom from the Latin subject to the Oriental party. Moreover, if there still remains doubt regarding this (doubt of law) Canon 4 could be applied which states: "When there is a doubt of law, laws do not bind even if they be nullifying and disqualifying ones. . ." E. Herman disagrees with this interpretation,[17] and we might add that several other authors agree, suggesting that the safest route would be to obtain a dispensation from the proper Eastern hierarch (ordinary) who can dispense the Oriental party.

The Oriental Code recognizes as a diriment impediment affinity between blood relatives of the spouses and the so-called affinity *ex trigeneia* which arises from two valid marriages (even if not consummated) when the spouses contract marriage successively with the same third party or with two different persons related to each other by blood. For example: John marries a widow, Margaret, who had a son Joseph by her first marriage. Some time later Margaret dies and John marries another person, Susan. John subsequently dies and Susan wishes to marry Joseph. In this case, we find that there exists the impediment of affinity arising from "trigeneia," the degree of affinity of Susan's late husband, John to Joseph. The degree of John's affinity to Joseph then depends upon the degree of consanguinity of John's first wife to Joseph. Since Margaret was Joseph's mother (1st degree), we have simple affinity in the first degree between John and Joseph and we find then that Susan is related in the same degree of affinity to Joseph arising from "trigeneia," or a successive marriage with the same third party, namely, two different persons related to each other by blood.

In the direct line affinity nullifies marriage in all ascending and descending degrees as in the Latin Code but, unlike the Latin Code, marriage contracted in the fourth degree inclusive in the collateral line is also considered null. Affinity (*ex trigeneia*) which exists between the blood relatives of the two parties nullifies marriage up to the fourth degree inclusive.

Canon 1093

The impediment of public propriety arises from an invalid marriage after common life has been established or from notorious and public

concubinage; it invalidates marriage in the first degree of the direct line between the man and the blood relatives of the woman, and vice-versa.

11. Public Propriety

It must be noted that this impediment arises from an invalid marriage, consummated or not consummated and it must be from concubinage which is either public or notorious. Hence, any attempt at marriage in the first degree of the direct line between the man and the blood relations of the woman would render this attempted marriage invalid. What kind of invalid marriage are we considering here? The Code does not distinguish; neither shall we.

In 1929 the Code Commission did give a definition regarding public propriety insofar as it decided that this impediment does not arise from the mere fact of a civil marriage when there is no cohabitation (AAS 21-170). An invalid marriage is one that has the appearance of marriage but is invalid because of some diriment impediment, force or fear, or lack of consent, etc.

Concubinage is present when two people live as husband and wife with the intention of having sexual relations even when this union does not have the appearance of a marriage. If it is publicly known, the impediment arises; if it is not publicly known, there is no impediment. For example, John and Mary live in concubinage in a hotel where they are thought to be man and wife. There is no impediment, however, since the crime is not public.

The unbaptized are not bound by this ecclesiastical impediment. It binds directly a baptized and only indirectly an unbaptized party. However, the unbaptized are not bound by the impediment if they give up their concubinage at the time of conversion. If they continue after the baptism, they incur this impediment.

Unlike affinity, this impediment extends to the direct line only not to the collateral line.

An invalid marriage is different technically from concubinage. Both are similar insofar as both are immoral, these people having no right to the conjugal act. They are different insofar as an invalid marriage has some juridical act involved (the ceremony which accompanied it), whereas in concubinage no such act took place. A marriage is considered invalid only when the prescribed form is used and a diriment impediment is present. It must be remembered that we can obtain a sanation for an invalid marriage, but we cannot sanate a case of concubinage. When a sanation to an invalid marriage is given, the consent to the marriage must be persevering at the time the sanation is granted. In applying for a *sanatio in radice*, every priest should keep in mind this difference between concubinage and an invalid marriage. A dispensation for a *sanatio* for a concubinage case would not be valid.[18]

Canon 1094

They cannot validly contract marriage between themselves who are related in the direct line or in the second degree of the collateral line through a legal relationship arising from adoption.

12. Legal Relationship

This impediment depends on a real or true legal relationship of child to parent, which relationship is not so by nature. People who marry a second time have an option to adopt the children of the other spouse. This is not considered legal relationship for the purposes of this canon; instead, this would be an adoption giving rise to the impediment of affinity.

When a legal adoptive relationship ceases by some action in civil court, the basis for the impediment is removed. As noted in the canon, this impediment invalidates a marriage regardless of whether any civil law prohibits or invalidates a legal relationship arising from adoption. And since this is an ecclesiastical law, it does not bind non-Catholics.

---

1   Bouscaren, I. Lincoln, S.J., *Canon Law Digest*, Vols. II, III, IV.
2   Cf. *Communications* 6 [1974], pp. 177-198.
3   Cf. Carr, Aidan. "Sexual Impotency & Sterilization," *Homiletic and Pastoral Review*, Jan. 1978, pp. 65-68, Questions & Answers.
4   Instruction of the Holy See: AAS 2-199 May, 13, 1868.
5   "Presumption of Death Case," *The Jurist*, July 1959, Vol. XIX; cf. also *Canon Law Digest*, Vol. I, p. 508.
6   Long, Joseph, *A Treatise on the Law of Domestic Relations*, 3rd ed., Indianapolis, 1948, p. 91.
7   Cloran, Owen M., *Previous and Practical Cases on Marriage*, Vol. I, Bruce, 1960, pp. 231-235.
8   Doheny, *Canonical Procedure in Matrimonial Cases*, Vol. I, Bruce, 1937.
9   Sacred Congregation of the Holy Office, Dec. 28, 1949, AAS 41-650.

10 *Letter of the National Conference of Catholic Bishops* (USA), January 14, 1974.

Your Excellency: In the past few years there have been several questions presented to the Committee on Canonical Affairs regarding the processing of marriage cases involving Eastern Orthodox with non-Catholic Christians. The Committee asked the Canon Law Society of America for assistance, and we have now received an extensive report from a committee headed by Father Edward J. Luca of the Diocese of Cleveland. The report makes two conclusions:

1) That cases *probably* can no longer be processed under Canon 72 of the *Synod of Trullo*. This conclusion is supported by recent Rotal jurisprudence, a decision of the Apostolic Signatura, and most recent canonical literature.

2) That *local* tribunals may handle *by ordinary administrative procedure* cases of "defectus ritus sacri" in the marriage of an Eastern Orthodox with another (non-Catholic) Christian that was not blessed by an Orthodox priest.

† Bernard J. Flanagan, Bishop of Worcester
Chairman: Bishops Committee on Canonical Affairs

11 *Canon Law Digest*, V, 13-14.

12 The terminology "Mixed Religion" was never used in the time of Trullo. Instead, "Disparity of Cult" was used, a term which has a different meaning today. Its continued use is apparent in this letter of the Holy Office dated June 8, 1967 (Prot. N. 1155/67):

Exc.me ac Rev.me Domine:

Litteris die 22 februarii a.d. datis, Excellentia Tua Rev.me postulavit facultatem declarandi nullum matrimonium contractum a Greco-orthodoxa N-N cum lutherano baptizato N-N anno 1942 ob impedimentum *disparitatis cultus*.

Ad rem Tecum communico hanc S. Congregationem decrevisse: "Ordinarius procedere poterit, vi can. 72 Concilii Trullani, ad declarationem nullitatis matrimonii de quo supra ad normam can. 1990.

A. Card. Ottaviani, Pro Pref.

13 Pro No. 2911/59m.

14 *The Jurist*, XXIX, 1969, p. 387.

15 Bassett, *The Jurist*, Vol. XXIX, Oct. 1969, pp. 383-415.

16 Cappello, F., *De Matrimonio*, VI, 1947, pp. 487-488.

17 Herman, Emil, "Adnotationes," *Periodica de Re Morali Canonica Liturgica*, Rome, 1949.

18 *Monitor Eccles.*, 1962, pp. 541-555.

Chapter Four
MATRIMONIAL CONSENT

An Introduction

From the early middle ages, a great debate had existed within the Church regarding the essential factor constituting marriage. Canonists in Bologna maintained that *consummation* was constitutive while the school of Paris maintained that *consent* was essential. This debate was finally settled when Pope Alexander III (1159-1181) using tradition as his basis, stated that consent was, in fact, the essential factor that made a marriage valid. And this remains the authoritative teaching of the Church to this day.

Documents from the Holy See, the decrees of the Second Vatican Council and the ongoing jurisprudence of Rotal decisions since the Code of 1917 show a significant development in the theology of Canon Law regarding the role consent plays in marriage. By de-emphasizing the traditional concept of marriage as a contract and stressing marriage as a covenant (as proposed by Vatican II), a great step forward has indeed been made in the theology underlying our present Canon Law on marriage.

At the Second Vatican Council Christian marriage was redefined as an "intimate partnership of life and love, established by the Creator and qualified by His laws." The Council did not state how the partnership was to be lived or what was necessary for its existence. Completing the teaching of *Gaudium et Spes*, Pope Paul VI clarified the notion in his encyclical letter *Humanae Vitae* when he gave the characteristics of Christian love as found in marriage. The love of the couple for each other must be human, moral, total and fruitful.

Marriage is no longer presented in terms of primary and secondary ends, but rather as a partnership of married life and love. Consequently, matrimonial consent — whose object is necessarily the partnership — is no longer said to consist exclusively in the acceptance and giving of the rights by which both partners join "in one flesh." This approach is not simply the result of a single canonist's theorizing. Indeed, it is re-echoed throughout many important documents of the Church and of its highest tribunals. In his very scholarly study on conjugal love and the juridical structure of Christian marriage, Father W.J. LaDue shows how this teaching was incorporated after the Council into the decisions of the Rota as early as 1969. The famous decision of Msgr. Lucien Anne (February 25, 1969) was probably the very first instance of a case where a marriage was explicitly presented as a *"consortium totius vitae."*

Consent is a multi-faceted reality which reaches into the innermost sectors of every marriage. Without consent, no marriage could exist. The Church teaches that, once given, consent lasts forever, despite the fact that some authors speak of the death of marriage when consent no longer exists.

A. The Nature of Matrimonial Consent

Since marriage is defined as a partnership, the consent to marriage must necessarily include consent to the partnership and to all that it entails. The former Canon 1096, §1 of the Code called for consent to cover those acts apt for the generation of children. The present Code describes consent as that act of the will whereby a man and a woman by means of mutual covenant constitute with one another a communion of conjugal life which is perpetual and exclusive and which by its very nature is ordered to the procreating and education of offspring.

A number of very significant points could be mentioned concerning this new wording. The first is the use of the word "covenant" rather than "contract." Indeed, in his oft-quoted study, "Christian Marriage: Contract or Covenant," Father Paul Palmer analyzed the significance of this change of emphasis, citing "covenant" as a relationship of mutual trust and fidelity as opposed to "contract" which is used of things, of property or of personal belongings. The importance of the change is that we must now take into account the long-range dimensions of marriage and not limit ourselves to the event and the situation occurring at the time of the actual ceremony itself (what could be called the "contract"). Consequently, in the consent to marriage, we must now find this element of lifelong covenant or commitment.

In general, consent is a pact or a covenant, in this case binding to the Christian state of marriage. Juridically it is a pact by which the parties are publicly bound to keep the laws of the Christian institution of marriage.

B. The Object of Matrimonial Consent

Given the new presentation of the nature of matrimonial consent, it was necessary to propose a revision of the canons concerning the object of matrimonial consent. The Code of 1917 (Canon 1086, §2) referred to the exclusion of the conjugal act or of any essential property of marriage as necessary and sufficient for the invalidity of the marriage. Since consent now is said to consist in a mutual covenant for communion of conjugal life, it follows that the willful exclusion of the community of life or of one of its essential elements renders the covenant void. Consequently, if the right to an intimate, lifelong conjugal partnership is not mutually given and accepted, there is no marriage. In positive terms, the parties to a marriage must offer each other: (1) the right to a community of life; (2) the possibility of living this community of life; (3) the right to conjugal acts; (4) the other essential properties of marriage — unity, fidelity, indissolubility.

It must be asked what is the extension of each of these terms. What are, for instance, the essential rights to which a partner in the community must have access? Father G. Lesage has grouped these rights under five headings which could be listed as: (1) the balance and maturity required for a truly human form of conduct; (2) the capacity for interpersonal and heterosexual friendship; (3) the ability to cooperate sufficiently to be of conjugal assistance to one another; (4) mental balance and a sense of responsibility for the material welfare of the home and family; (5) the psychic capacity of both spouses to participate in promoting the welfare of their children.

What is meant by the possibility of living a community of life? This is now generally taken to mean that the partners are able to bind themselves to long-range commitments and fulfill the obligations of the marriage state. This is the counterpart of the rights to which the parties should have access, but here we are dealing with the corresponding duties. By the right to conjugal acts we usually now understand the right to all moral acts without any restriction. In former jurisprudence, it was considered sufficient for any right to be given; today, if any part of the right is reserved, it is understood that the right itself was reserved. A different meaning, therefore, has been given to the expression *"omne ius"* in the Code of 1983.

The other essential properties of marriage — its unity and indissolubility — are to be interpreted as they are now received in the common jurisprudence of the Church.

1. *Qualitative Elements of Consent*

Three particular qualities must be found in matrimonial consent: (1) truth, (2) deliberation and (3) maturity. *Truth* is the cognitive element. The deficiency of truth, or of a correct intellectual apprehension and knowledge, may be rooted in ignorance or error about the actual reality of Christian marriage. *Deliberation* is the volitive element. The act of consent must be fully deliberate, requiring that one proceed with sufficient discretion and act with an enlightened and mature judgment. The consent of the contracting parties, as related to the role of the will, may be defective because of force or fear, or because of a positive refusal of consent or by reason of a condition attached to the contract (cf. Dennis J. Burns, *Matrimonial Indissolubility: Contrary Conditions,* Washington, CUA, 1963, no. 377, pp. 54-67). *Maturity* is the psycho-somatic element. The mental maturity required for valid consent consists in a normal personality and state of mental health with a capacity for adaptation, an aptitude for happiness and an acceptance of one's own sexuality.

2. *Cognitive Elements of Consent*

The knowledge necessary for consent must cover knowledge of the contract, knowledge of the person, knowledge of the object and knowledge of the bond itself.

a. Knowledge of the contract (substantial error)

"For matrimonial consent to be valid it is necessary that the contracting parties at least not be ignorant that marriage is a permanent consortium between a man and a woman which is ordered toward the procreation of offspring by means of some sexual cooperation" (Canon 1096, §1).

Since marriage requires the community of conjugal life and the right to acts apt for the procreation of children, it would be a substantial error to believe that marriage is: (1) a purely friendly society, (2) a work pact for family needs, or (3) a companionship for mutual help. It would be sufficient for validity to know that the parties are obliging themselves to an action or union of the sexual organs.

b. Knowledge of the person (factual error)

"Error concerning a quality of a person, even if such error is the cause of the contract, does not invalidate matrimony unless this quality was directly and principally intended" (Canon 1097, §2).

"Error concerning the person renders marriage invalid" (Canon 1097, §1).

"A person contracts invalidly who enters marriage deceived by fraud, perpetrated to obtain consent, concerning some quality of the other which of its very nature can seriously disturb the partnership of conjugal life" (Canon 1098).

Error, a false or insufficient apprehension of reality, may be either simple (not affecting the will) or prudential (affecting the intention of the party).

Ignorance is a lack of personal information that causes a false apprehension of reality (error).

Deceit is dishonest information that also causes a false apprehension of reality.

Error, caused either by ignorance or by deceit, invalidates a marriage if it affects (1) the physical person or (2) a personality trait which amounts to a substantial condition in the sense that the quality desired and missing in the partner is preferred to the actual physical person. This may occur if recognition of error is seen to deprive the partner of a trait which in the other's mind is the only individualizing note of the partner, or is morally and socially individuating the partner, or introduces in the partner a trait which, because of its nature, precludes the physical presence of the consort.

c. Knowledge of the object (doctrinal error)

"Error concerning the unity, indissolubility or sacramental dignity of matrimony does not vitiate matrimonial consent so long as it does not determine the will" (Canon 1099).

A prudential error can affect the intention of the party to a marriage in three ways: (1) if it takes the form of a mutual pact; (2) if it amounts to a condition for the contract; (3) if it affects the knowledge on which the will power bases its decision or forms its intention, either because of personal reflexive thinking or because of some pervading influence of the surrounding milieu.

d. Knowledge of the bond (juridical error)

If nullity does not really exist, the party involved commits an error either in law or in fact. In both cases, the intention of marrying can subsist either because the party forgets about the invalidity or because he reflexively decides to disregard the law of the Church and marries anyway.

If the nullity does really exist, the marriage is invalid because of the existing cause of nullity, not because of a defect of consent, since consent might be valid if the intention to marry prevails against a known nullity (a very rare case).

3. *Volitive Elements of Consent*

"If either or both parties through a positive act of the will should exclude marriage itself, some essential element or an essential property of marriage, it is invalidly contracted" (Canon 1101, §2).

a. Consent

"The internal consent of the mind is presumed to be in agreement with the words or signs employed in celebrating the matrimony" (Canon 1101, §1).

The object of the consent must be the community of life and the right to sexual relations.

A defect of consent would be present in the case of mental incapacity (lack of human responsibility) or voluntary abstention (total simulation). Likewise consent could be defective because of voluntary distortion (partial simulation), either abstention from consent to an element or an absolute exclusion of that element altogether. Further, consent could be defective because of a lack of mental capacity to perform a true contractual act which could derive from a lack of judgment, of freedom of the will, of firmness of decision or of the capacity to fulfill the obligation connected with the object of the contract.

b. Nullifying intentions

(1) *Against the bond* (total simulation). Simulation is an external manifestation of consent, notwithstanding an internal decision not to really marry. The elements would be an intention to fake the marriage by not really consenting, a determination to follow some concept of marriage in opposition to Christian doctrine by rejecting in practice the consequences of this doctrine, or the overt acceptance of the consequences of the intention (ignoring the invalidity following the simulation).

(2) *Against the community of conjugal life.* Community of conjugal life includes the physical capacity to cohabit in an assiduous way and to perform the conjugal act, and the psychic or mental capacity to realize true heterosexual friendship or conjugal complementarity both morally and psychologically, and to provide for the material welfare of the home and for the good of the children.

(3) *Against fecundity.* An intention against fecundity can be expressed by either a refusal of the object of marriage or a refusal of one of its ends. The refusal of the object of marriage is found in either total refusal of the connatural act (non-consummation) or limitation of the right by following personal fancy (excluding certain periods or using unnatural devices). The refusal of the end of marriage can occur either by denying procreation by birth prevention (abortion), by killing born children, or by denying an education to the children.

(4) *Against fidelity.* An intention against fidelity is a positive prevalent act of the will that excludes the obligation of conjugal fidelity and includes a perverse intention of sharing either the conjugal act or the community of life with a third party.

(5) *Against indissolubility.* An intention against indissolubility is a positive intention to terminate the marriage before death. It may be either an actual intention to divorce that bears on the individual marriage to be contracted, or an habitual belief in divorce.

c. Freedom from external influence (force and fear)

"A marriage is invalid if it is entered into due to force or grave fear inflicted from outside the person, even when inflicted unintentionally, which is of such a type that the person is compelled to choose matrimony in order to be freed from it" (Canon 1103).

The new code adds the expression, "even when inflicted unintentionally."

Force is an external influence used to induce fear in a person. *Fear* is a perturbation of the mind on account of an impending evil. Fear may be either *common* (physical or moral threats) or *reverential* (indignation on the part of parents or superiors).

Force and fear invalidate a marriage if they are grave, unjustly induced from without, and unavoidable except through marriage.

4. *Psychosomatic elements: Elements of Maturity or Psychic Balance*

The new law supplements a deficiency in the old Code by providing for a recognition of the influence of psychosomatic defects on matrimonial consent. The new canon reads as follows: "They are incapable of contracting marriage: (1) who lack the sufficient use of reason; (2) who suffer from grave lack of discretion of judgment concerning essential matrimonial rights and duties which are to be mutually given and accepted; (3) who are not capable of assuming the essential obligations of matrimony due to causes of a psychic nature" (Canon 1095).

They are, therefore, unable to contract marriage who are unable to assume the essential obligations of matrimony because of a serious psycho-sexual anomaly. As Msgr. Lucien Anne states, "The abnormal conditions of the future spouses that radically prevent the establishment of any community of conjugal life in such a way that the principles whereby it may be established are missing — are either a very grave distortion or perversion of the sexual instinct, or an abnormal paranoiac disturbance of the affectivity, or one that is equal to them" (*Ephemerides Iuris Canonici*, 26 (1970), p. 432).

C. Jurisprudence Regarding Matrimonial Consent

Legally speaking a person must be of sound mind to enter into a binding contractual arrangement. Any incapacity for reasonable conduct if it is incurable is the traditional ground of insanity. The lack of due discretion would make one incapable of entering into a valid contract if sufficiently severe. The responsibility essential to the validity of the contract of marriage supposes in the spouses:

(1) an affective maturity that enables them to grasp the deep meaning of the conjugal covenant and to give it a permanent value;

(2) a discernment of judgment proportionate to the importance of the pact being concluded;

(3) an internal free choice of the will, without coercive impulsions or revulsions;

(4) a firmness of character or personality that is capable of effective decision making;

(5) a normal sexuality, without perversions or neuroses that vitiate the perception of values and the attractiveness of marriage.

A physical or psychological incapacity to assume the obligations of the marital contract would render the marriage invalid. Such an incapacity is present when a party is afflicted by a psychic ailment, independent of his or her will, the connatural evolution of which would eventually jeopardize, permanently or even transitorily, the practice of a true community of conjugal life. Being incapable of realizing the essential object of the contract, this person cannot assume the obligations deriving therefrom and consequently cannot conclude a valid covenant.

The Contributions of Psychiatry

As a voluntary and free act, the matrimonial covenant must be exempt from constringent psychosomatic pressures and tensions. Certain pathological defects of the personality render a person "impotent to act indifferently." He or she is impelled by internal dynamics to act beside or against moral rules. The person thus affected cannot reach maturity either psychologically or morally. Mental problems affecting the will include perversion, alienation, obsession, impulsion, depression, phobia, immaturity, etc. Mental problems that may affect marriage come under the general headings of psychoses, neuroses and personality disorders. Church law does not require a specific diagnosis.

(1) *Psychoses.* In general these psychiatric disorders differ from others in one or more of the following ways: (a) *severity* (psychoses are major mental disorders that tend to affect all areas of a person's life); (b) *withdrawal* (objective reality is perceived in a distorted way, causing a person to remove him/herself from social interaction);

(c) *affectivity* (a psychotic's emotions are often qualitatively different from the normal); (d) *intellect* (judgment often fails and hallucinations and delusions may be present); (e) *regression* (there may be a generalized failure to function normally and to fall back to earlier behavioral levels).

(2) *Neuroses.* General symptoms of the neurotic conflict include: (a) *specific avoidances*; (b) *inhibitions of instincts connected with marriage* such as reduced aggressiveness, nervousness associated with sex, reduced affectivity and emotional display; (c) *sexual disturbances* such as impotence, premature ejaculation and frigidity; (d) *lack of interest* in the environment and general impoverishment of the personality; (e) *compulsive behavior* engaged in for the relief of tension; (f) *sleep disturbances.*

(3) *Personality Disorders.* These are deeply ingrained, chronic patterns of reaction that are maladaptive in that they are relatively inflexible. They limit the optional use of potentialities and often provoke unpleasant and unwanted counter reactions from others. The most significant forms of these personality disorders include: (a) abnormal behavior patterns such as a personality that is paranoid, cyclothymic, schizoid, obsessive-compulsive, hysterical, asthenic, antisocial, immature, inadequate or psychopathic; (b) *sexual deviations* such as homosexuality, sadism and hyperaestheaia; (c) *dependency syndromes* such as alcoholism and drug abuse.

1. The Contractual Act

An exchange of consent is required in every contractual act. The parties must be present either in person or by proxy. And the consent must be expressed in words. When a marriage contract is entered into through the mediation of an interpreter, the veracity of the interpretation must be beyond all doubt.

2. Conditional Consent

A condition is a clause or stipulation in the matrimonial contract which provides that the essential obligations of marriage may be qualified or nullified under stated circumstances for certain stipulated reasons.

The new Code (Canon 1102, §1) states that marriage may not be contracted validly if it contains a condition regarding a future event. The ordinary's written permission is required in each case where a condition concerning the past or the present is demanded.

3. *Perseverance of Consent*

"Even if a marriage was entered invalidly by reason of an impediment or lack of form, the consent which was furnished is presumed to continue until its revocation has been proven" (Canon 1107).

The word "impediment" is to be taken in a very broad sense here to mean any obstacle to the marriage itself. This canon is used as a basis for convalidations without renewal of consent (i.e., a *sanatio in radice*).

Canon 1095

They are incapable of contracting marriage:
1° **who lack the sufficient use of reason;**
2° **who suffer from grave lack of discretion of judgment concerning essential matrimonial rights and duties which are to be mutually given and accepted.**
3° **who are not capable of assuming the essential obligations of matrimony due to causes of a psychic nature.**

1. Consensual Capacity

The essential concept of marriage, according to Vatican II, is personalistic in nature. ". . . It is rooted in the contract of the parties, that is, in their irrevocable, personal consent, confirmed by divine law, and receiving its stability from the human act by which the partners surrender themselves to each other in the eyes of society" (*Pastoral Constitution on the Church in the Modern World*, 48).

The validity of marital consent depends upon certain minimal knowledge of what marriage is and the freedom to accept its responsibilities. Validity of consent also depends on the psychological capacity to evaluate the personal choice, elicit the human act of consent and fulfill the corresponding obligations involved.

Canon 1096

§1. For matrimonial consent to be valid it is necessary that the contracting parties at least not be ignorant that marriage is a permanent consortium between a man and a woman which is ordered toward the procreation of offspring by means of some sexual cooperation.

§2. Such ignorance is not presumed after puberty.

2. Ignorance

A person who wishes to enter into marriage validly must be fully aware of the obligations and responsibilities of his or her commitment. Ignorance is a lack of knowledge. If one party to the marriage did not know that marriage was a permanent union or covenant of one man and one woman for the purpose of begetting children, such a marriage would be invalid. In this transaction there cannot be a true and valid marriage without the *real consent* of both parties. Beyond the purpose of rearing children, marriage is also for the purpose of establishing and maintaining a community of shared life between the spouses. The term covenant covers all marriages, whether children will be involved or not, as ever more frequently marriages are contracted between older people who are beyond their childbearing years and who could not validly enter into a marriage whose sole purpose constituted the rearing of children.

Canon 1097

§1. Error concerning the person renders marriage invalid.

§2. Error concerning a quality of a person, even if such error is the cause of the contract, does not invalidate matrimony unless this quality was directly and principally intended.

3. Error of Fact

This canon deals with two types of error of fact: (1) error of person, and (2) error of a quality of the person. The first invalidates marriage; the second invalidates marriage under certain conditions. For instance, if the error concerned the identity of the other party as would be the case if Joseph marries Mary thinking that she is Rose. Today this is hardly possible, but should it happen the marriage would be invalid. An error could involve some quality or characteristic of the other party. Provided that this expected quality or characteristic is such that it amounted to an error concerning the person — e.g., marrying a slave girl thinking she was free — it, too, could invalidate the marriage.

The essence of the marriage contract is the consent. The essential object of the consent is the person, not the qualities of the person. Qualities are something accidental to marriage. But qualities, even though insignificant in themselves, can sometimes be very important to the parties involved. A person may have hoped, wished, thought, believed that his or her spouse possessed this or that quality, and then found out that they didn't. But the consent was given — the contract was made, and the marriage is valid. An error or false judgment was made by the injured party regarding the personal qualifications of the other. The Church could make such an error a nullifying factor, but it does not because human beings are not perfect. Disillusionments and disappointments suffered by one spouse due to the other partner's imperfections would only be equaled by the other partner's similar dissatisfaction. There would be no end to such problems. In practice, it is almost impossible to prove that an error in quality amounts to error of the person. This is possible only when the injured party can give full proof that the quality of the party amounted to a *conditio sine qua non*. In the last few years new interest has arisen in this lack of consent due to error in the wake of two canonical decisions of nullity, one of the appellate court of Sens, dated April 22, 1968 and the other of the Sacred Roman Rota, *coram* Canals, dated April 21, 1970.[1]

Canon 1098

A person contracts invalidly who enters marriage deceived by fraud, perpetrated to obtain consent, concerning some quality of the other party which of its very nature can seriously disturb the partnership of conjugal life.

4. Deception or Fraud

Deception or fraud in which a person is misled into error could happen through behavioral misrepresentation, lies or even silence. It is a quality of the person which is considered in this canon. In civil courts — and now, with the new law of 1983, in ecclesiastical courts as well — fraud, if proven, invalidates a marriage. How is a fraudulent marriage prevented? A lifetime project should always be carefully planned and evaluated. The sexual is only one aspect of married life, yet young people are often so caught up in it, because of their strong physical attraction to one another, that they overlook other even more important areas in their relationship. Too often they marry without knowing enough about one another. During time of war this is a particularly common phenomenon. Prolonged courtship is one way to prevent fraud. If a person fears that he or she is being deceived by the other party, that fact should be made clear in writing or before witnesses. What he or she expects or does not expect of the other party should be clearly spelled out. Only in such a case could fraud be used as the legal basis for invalidating the marriage.

Canon 1099

Error concerning the unity, indissolubility or sacramental dignity of matrimony does not vitiate matrimonial consent so long as it does not determine the will.

5. Error of Law: Simple Error

Whenever a person makes a civil contract, he is bound by all the obligations contained therein, and he cannot be excused from these obligations because they turn out to be different from what he thought them to be. So too, all the principles and characteristics which constitute marriage as instituted by God remain intact and stable regardless what a married person thinks, wishes or believes them to be. Errors, mistakes, judgments or private opinions of persons regarding the principles of marriage cannot be given any consideration in judging marriage cases. While ignorance is a lack of knowledge, error is mistaken knowledge or the making of a false judgment.

1. *Concomitant Error*: An error that has no real influence on the consent, that is, the consent would have been given even though the error existed at the time.

2. *Antecedent Error*: An error which has such influence that, if the truth had been known, consent would not have been given. If a person was in such a frame of mind that he would have refused consent had the condi-

tion been known, this is called an interpretative will. Since refusal did not take place, the marriage is valid. The important factor here is not what would have been done, but what actually did take place.

3. *Simple Error*: Error is simple when it remains in the mind or intellect without passing over into the will. Simple error exists in the mind in a speculative way without actually becoming incorporated into the choice made by the will. For example, a person may have a simple error regarding indissolubility, unity or the sacramental character of a marriage. Nevertheless, the will wishes to contract a marriage that is valid according to the law of nature. Hence, the speculative factor in the intellect did not pass over into the category of the will. The actual fact is that the will selected marriage without any conditions or reservations.

A non-Catholic, wishing to come into the Church as a convert in order to marry a Catholic, asks for a declaration of nullity for his first marriage which he always thought could be terminated by divorce at any time. This is simply an erroneous idea about the indissolubility of marriage which remains speculatively in the intellect. This simple error always carries with it the presumption that one wishes to get married according to God's plan. Therefore, if this non-Catholic merely thinks he could get a divorce or believes he could get a divorce, or wishes he could get a divorce, or hopes that he could get a divorce, this simple speculative error remains in the intellect and never passes over into the will. The marriage is valid. As long as the error remains in the mind, no positive act of the will is placed regarding it. A positive act deriving from this type of error must be proven. It is never presumed! The same is true if a woman marries a man whom she believed or hoped to be temperate and after the marriage found him to be a confirmed alcoholic. Or the same would be true of a man who marries a woman thinking or believing her to be a virgin and then finds out that she is a person of loose morals or even a prostitute.

4. *Qualified Error*: When simple error passes over from the intellect to the will and becomes an intention, this error is called qualified error. Since this process is not easily verifiable, the party entertaining this error must make the process apparent by bringing it into the external forum. This can be done by putting the matter into writing before qualified witnesses. For example, if the above-mentioned convert can prove that he married with the agreement that the marriage could be dissolved by a civil divorce at the will of either party, the marriage would be considered invalid. In this

case the general notion of divorce passes from the intellect to the will. The marriage is thus ruled to have been invalidly contracted because of the presence of two conflicting intentions: one to contract a real marriage, and the other to contract a dissoluble marriage. Further, if a person could prove that he or she comes from a divorce-prone family by citing the same in writing before a qualified witness, then this circumstance could be shown to represent, not only the state of mind but also the will of this person at the time that he or she attempted marriage and the marriage could be declared invalid.

Canon 1100

The knowledge or opinion of the nullity of a marriage does not necessarily exclude matrimonial consent.

4. Knowledge of Nullity

Here again an error concerning one's opinion or belief does not invalidate a marriage contract. For example, John contracts marriage with Anna on June 10, 1950, knowing that he left a wife in Europe. He knows that a diriment impediment exists and that this marriage to Anna is invalid. However, he does everything to contract this marriage, thus giving matrimonial consent. John later learns that his wife died in Europe on May 30, 1950. John and Anna are, therefore, validly married in spite of the fact that John thought that the marriage was invalid. The validity or invalidity of the marriage does not depend on what the parties believe or think at the time of the marriage, but rather on what actually and objectively was the case at the time of the marriage according to the principles of law.

The intention to contract a real marriage is always presumed unless the contrary is proven. When a Catholic contracts a mixed marriage before a civil magistrate, he or she generally knows that the marriage is invalid. However, when a *sanatio in radice* is granted, it presupposes that a natural valid consent was given at the time of this marriage, and that this valid consent is still persevering. Therefore, there is no need for a renewal of consent. If a mere mock marriage took place, valid consent would be absent.

Canon 1101

§1. The internal consent of the mind is presumed to be in agreement with the words or signs employed in celebrating matrimony.

§2. But if either or both parties through a positive act of the will should exclude marriage itself, some essential element or an essential property of marriage, it is invalidly contracted.

7. Simulation

This canon expresses the presumption of law regarding the existence of internal consent when words are expressed and signs are shown externally in the celebration of a marriage. This internal consent must exist in both parties at the same time. If the positive act of the will regarding consent is not given, this fact must be proven in the external forum. We exclude here the simple error of the mind or an interpretative will.

A positive act of the will that stands in opposition to the very nature of the matrimonial contract or opposes the essential properties of marriage makes the marriage null and void. If the parties cannot prove willful opposition in the external forum, the law presumes this marriage to be valid. However, in the forum of conscience, it is not valid, in which case an ecclesiastical court could grant a separation. If it is the case that the couple must live together for some reason, they have an obligation to validate this marriage by giving their consent. If the lack of consent was merely internal, it suffices that the party who refused consent, give this consent now by an internal act. If lack of consent was shown publicly or outwardly, the consent should be given publicly (cf. Canon 1158).

1. *Total Simulation*: when the positive act of the will (the intention) is not to contract a marriage at all. The acts are merely done for show; no internal consent is given. This situation could occur if one marries merely to inherit property or to gain social status, etc. Total simulation occurs when one excludes *all* the essential obligations of marriage.

2. *Partial Simulation*: when one excludes *some* of the essential obligations of marriage, for example, by refusing to participate in the conjugal act which is *per se* suitable for the generation of offspring. In this case, partial simulation makes the marriage invalid.

Simulation is difficult to prove. The testimony of the interested party, taken under oath, is not sufficient proof. Neither is the testimony of the two married parties. Conjectures deriving from the circumstances of the marriage may be revealing. If, for example, a man ran off immediately after the marriage ceremony and made a declaration that he never gave his consent to the marriage, this would constitute a very good and strong presumption that his consent was simulated. When there is a doubt, the presumption of law is in favor of the validity of the marriage (Canon 1060).

A. Conflict Between the Internal and External Forum

Cases may arise in which the parties are certain and the confessor is certain that this particular marriage is null for lack of consent, but it is impossible to prove the matter satisfactorily in court. A second marriage is not permitted. Cohabitation might be obligatory, but conjugal relations would be unlawful. Hence, we have a conflict between the internal and external forums. Such a conflict becomes worse if a person who simulated consent later contracts a valid marriage with another party. In the external forum, his first wife would be his legitimate wife. He would be bound to live with her but could not have marital relations with her. His second wife would be his real wife in the forum of conscience and in the eyes of God. She is the one with whom he could legitimately have marital relations. Since valid marital consent has been given to this second union, there is no possibility of revalidating the first marriage. Much research has been done on this conflict between the internal and the external forum. It is a dilemma recognized by canonists and theologians alike. In the last analyses the "Good Faith Solution," of which we will speak later, must be considered.

B. Homosexuality

Today we find all kinds of people with severe sexual problems. It is the belief of many psychiatrists and canonists along with others that those individuals afflicted with sexual anomalies should not attempt marriage. Unfortunately, such problems often do not show up until after marriage when one of the partners is unable or unwilling to accept the responsibility of an indissoluble union with a resulting separation and divorce. Among these problems is that of homosexuality.

Homosexuality is a strong preferential erotic attraction to members of one's own sex. The *Diagnostic and Statistical Manual of Mental Disorders* (DSMD) does not regard homosexuality in itself as a mental disorder. However, when homosexuality is accompanied by consciously perceived distress resulting from an internal conflict over the fact that homosexual stimuli are incompatible with the person's conscience, then DSMD recognizes this as a disorder. It is called dyshomophilia and is listed among the paraphilias or sexual deviations.

Kinsey and his associates in 1948 suggested the following scale to describe points on a heterosexual-homosexual continuum:

0 exclusively heterosexual
1 predominantly heterosexual, only incidentally homosexual
2 predominantly heterosexual but more than incidentally homosexual
3 equally heterosexual and homosexual
4 predominantly homosexual but more than incidentally heterosexual
5 predominantly homosexual, only incidentally heterosexual
6 exclusively homosexual

People who score 1 and 2 on the scale are sometimes referred to as *facultative* homosexuals; those who rate 3 or 4 are referred to as *bisexual*; and those who rate 5 and 6 on the scale are called *obligatory* homosexuals.

Homosexuality seems to result from a combination of causes, some genetic, others environmental. Genetic causes, the study of which has been aided by the development of modern genetics and endocrinology, would lie in the area of hormonal or chromosonal imbalances. Environmental causes would consist primarily in the psychosexual influence of the parents on the child. Freud held that all heterosexuals have latent homosexual tendencies and that all persons go through a homoerotic phase in childhood as a part of the regular course of development. Normally one outgrows that stage entirely and adult homosexuality is often simply the result of arrested normal development. Bieber takes almost the opposite point of view, holding that all homosexuals are latent heterosexuals. Heterosexuality is the norm in all mammals and the development of homosexuality is, according to Bieber, always a pathological consequence of fears associated with heterosexual functioning that have been produced by unfavorable life experiences. Chief among these experiences for the male homosexual is a parental constellation involving a detached, hostile father and a close-binding seductive mother who dominates and minimizes her husband. Specific environmental causes of female homosexuality are unclear, but generally there is a strong antiheterosexual pattern in the home. There are very strong arguments for and against both of these positions and about all that can be said without fear of contradiction is that a lot has yet to be learned about the genesis of this condition.

In the light of Canons 1095 and 1101, it would seem that the homosexual could not possibly contract a valid marriage if, under the outward appearance of marriage, he retains the desire and intention to continue in a life style incompatible with that of marriage. Proper intention and the will to enter a true marriage are absent. Further, under the same canons, a practicing homosexual would be committing sins against matrimonial fidelity. The fact could be established and substantiated by gathering evidence regarding his life style both before and after the marriage. Again in virtue of Canon 1101, true matrimonial consent would not have been given by an obligatory homosexual since, in that consent, a man and a woman reciprocally hand over and receive perpetual and exclusive right to each other.

According to Canon 1101, any person who externally manifests consent but inwardly does not invoke the corresponding act of the will would simulate consent, since the contract of marriage requires four elements: (1) the intention to make a true contract; (2) the intention to bind oneself to the matrimonial contract; (3) the physical and moral capacity to bind oneself; and (4) the intention and capacity to fulfill the obligations that are undertaken. A homosexual would be unable, physically and morally, to make a contract binding him to the object of the contract. We are certain that a person cannot enter into a valid contract who cannot dispose freely of the object of the same contract. Moreover, this must be an object which is both physically and morally possible since no one is obliged to the impossible.

In his book, *The Homosexual in America*, Donald Webster Cory, himself a homosexual, lists twelve reasons why a homosexual might attempt marriage:

1. Desire for children.
2. Need for a permanent family relationship.

3. Inability to establish a permanent relationship with a male companion or lover.
4. Fear of loneliness in one's later years.
5. Desire to escape a homosexual lifestyle.
6. Deep affection for the girl involved.
7. Latency or repression of homosexuality.
8. Hope of finding companionship in marriage; disappointment at inability to find it outside of marriage with male friends.
9. Desire to create an illusion of married life in the hope that it will protect him from gossip and its concomitant evils.
10. Aspiration for economic and social gain.
11. Desire to please one's family.
12. Inability or unwillingness to take a strong stand that would prevent a drift toward marriage.

The four areas which are normally investigated in incompetence cases merit special observation here:

1. *Severity*: The severity of homosexuality always refers to genuine homosexuals and not to pseudo-homosexuals (heterosexuals who, in circumstances where partners of the opposite sex are not available, turn to persons of the same sex for gratification). While a psychological compulsion to drink in the alcoholic is recognizable by overt acts of drinking, homosexuality is defined apart from any overt acts simply as "a strong preferential erotic attraction." This obviously involves the jurisprudential judgment that the erotic homosexual attraction, even in the absence of overt homosexual acts, is likely to interfere substantially with a person's functioning in an intimate heterosexual relationship. It can be said, as a rule of thumb, that obligatory homosexuals and bisexuals would probably be incapable of those acts which are *per se* apt for engendering children and fostering a community of life with someone of the opposite sex. On the other hand, facultative homosexuals would probably be capable of both. In every case, an attempt must be made to determine the competence of the homosexual to function in a heterosexual relationship.

2. *Antecedence*: When a person is known to be homosexual, the homosexuality may always be presumed to be antecedent to the marriage since a person's psychosexual preference has been found to be fixed at least by the time of early adolescence.

3. *Perpetuity*: Assuming that the homosexual disposition does in fact render a person incompetent for marriage, the question here is whether that disposition could have been reversed at the time of the marriage, whether a genuine shift in preferential sex choice could have been effected. Given a strong motivation to change one's sexual preference, given a youthful age and a history of previous heterosexual responsiveness, given a low rating on the Kinsey continuum, and given no overt acts or a fairly recent onset of infrequent overt homosexual acts, the chances of altering sexual preference do not seem to be entirely out of the question. Given their opposites, the chances are very poor. A court must make a judgment in light of the particular facts in each instance.

4. *Relativity*: The choice of a marriage partner by a homosexual can sometimes be significant. It is always possible that a homosexual condition which is not invalidating in itself could, given the wrong partner, result in an inability of the two parties to relate at all.

Canon 1102

§1. **Marriage based on a condition concerning the future cannot be contracted validly.**

§2. **Marriage based on a condition concerning the past or the present is valid or invalid, insofar as the subject matter of the condition exists or not.**

§3. **The condition mentioned in §2 cannot be placed licitly without the written permission of the local ordinary.**

8. Conditional Consent

A condition is some circumstance which is attached to the consent and upon which the contract of marriage depends. A distinction must be made between a cause and a condition of marriage. Let's say a woman marries a man because she believes or thinks that he is a millionaire. Here we have no condition; it is a cause. This is merely an error and the contract would be valid in spite of the fact that she would not have married the man had she known that he was not a millionaire (*error dans causam contractui*).

Canon 1102 states that when a condition is attached to the marriage contract and not withdrawn before the marriage, the following rules govern the case:

1. If it is a condition concerning a future event which is necessary or impossible or immoral but not contrary to the substance of marriage, it is to be considered as not having been made.
2. If it concerns the future and is contrary to the substance of marriage, it renders the marriage invalid.
3. If it concerns the future and is licit, it suspends the validity of the marriage.
4. If it concerns the past or the present, the marriage will be valid or not depending on whether the matter concerning which the condition is made, exists or not.

We usually do not meet marriages based on conditions. In most cases, conditional marriages remain a secret because it is unlawful to posit conditions to a marriage. If the condition was made prior to the marriage in writing or before two witnesses, whereby it can be proven in the external forum, the marriage would remain valid until contrary proof is obtained by ecclesiastical authorities.

If a pastor discovers that a condition was placed, he must warn the parties not to cohabit. He should then investigate the case and act prudently in the matter in order to avoid any scandal.

A. Illustrations of Future Conditions

   1. Conditions not contrary to the substance of marriage:

     (a) *Necessary Future Conditions*: "I marry you now on condition that the sun rises tomorrow." If this is a serious statement, the marriage is valid only on that condition. If the sun did not rise, it would be invalid. People usually do not make such conditions seriously.

     (b) *Impossible Future Conditions*: "I marry you only on condition that you learn the Russian language within a week." The marriage would never be valid since the condition could never be met.

     (c) *Immoral Future Conditions*: "I marry you only on condition that you have an abortion." The marriage would be valid only when this condition is fulfilled.

     (d) *Licit Future Conditions*: "I marry you only on condition that you pass your Ph.D. examination." The marriage is valid when this condition is fulfilled.

2. Conditions contrary to the substance of marriage: "I marry you only on condition that you agree that I can divorce you any time during the marriage," or, "I marry you only on condition that I will be allowed to sleep with other women." *Note*: If the parties agree to practice birth control, this may be gravely sinful, but it does not invalidate the marriage.

B. Illustration of Past Conditions: "I marry you only on condition that you have had a hysterectomy/vasectomy." If this is not true, the marriage would be invalid.

C. Illustration of a Present Condition: "I marry you only on the condition that you are wealthy." If the party is not, the marriage is invalid.

All these cases are true to the extent that these statements are made seriously. Proof that such conditions were made must be given in writing (*tempore non suspecto*) or before two witnesses; otherwise, such conditions would be valid only in the internal forum (the forum of one's conscience).

Canon 1103

A marriage is invalid if it is entered into due to force or grave fear inflicted from outside the person, even when inflicted unintentionally, which is of such a type that the person is compelled to choose matrimony in order to be free from it.

9. Force and Fear

Force and fear are correlative terms. *Force* is a physical impulse from an external agent which cannot be overcome, as for example when blows or threats are unjustly used. *Fear* is trepidation of mind in the face of an impending evil.

Absolutely grave fear is such that it will overpower the mind and will of a normal, firm and steadfast person because of the real grave injury or loss that is threatened. A loss of life or limb, fortune or freedom, reputation or job, for example, would constitute matter for absolutely grave fear. Internal fear such as that created in one's own imagination, is not an absolutely grave fear.

Relatively grave fear is such that it will overcome the resistance of certain individuals who are not so strong or steadfast. Reverential fear often falls into this category: fear, for example, of being ejected from one's parental home, or fear of offending one's parents or superiors. For overly sensitive persons, this could even constitute an absolutely grave fear.

Fear must be unjustly inflicted from an external agent. Natural causes are excluded. This fear occurs when human justice is violated in forcing a marriage. If, for example, a young man is threatened with bodily harm if he does not go through with a certain marriage, his marriage is considered null. To threaten a seducer with imprisonment if he does not consent to marriage is not considered unjust. This is considered a just penalty, but a better alternative would be to impose a fine or demand support of the child. A principle one should use in evaluating force and fear cases is to judge whether there was any alternative other than marriage.

Whether force and fear is an impediment of the natural or of the ecclesiastical law is debated.

Canon 1104

§1. In order for marriage to be contracted validly, it is necessary that the contracting parties be present together, either in person or by proxy.

§2. Those to be married are to express their matrimonial consent in words; however, if they cannot speak, they are to express it by equivalent signs.

Canon 1105

§1. In order for marriage to be entered validly by proxy, it is required that:
  1° there be a special mandate to contract marriage with a certain person;
  2° the proxy be appointed by the person who gave the mandate and that the proxy fulfill this function in person.

§2. To be valid a mandate must be signed by the person who gave it as well as by the pastor or the local ordinary where the mandate was issued, or by a priest delegated by either of these, or at least by two witnesses, or it must be arranged by means of a document which is authentic according to civil law.

§3. If the person giving the mandate cannot write, this is to be noted in the mandate itself and another witness is to be added who also must sign the document; otherwise, the mandate is invalid.

§4. If the person who gave the mandate revokes it or becomes insane before the proxy has contracted the marriage in that person's name, the marriage is invalid even though either the proxy or the other contracting party was unaware of these developments.

10. Proxy Marriages and Their Requirements

These canons apply to baptized Catholics and non-Catholics as well. Marriage by proxy is not approved except in the most unusual or exceptional circumstances. Most authors agree that the principal party of proxy marriage cannot authorize a proxy to substitute another proxy for himself. One must make out a special mandate for a proxy marriage; it is not proper to give a general mandate to place all the legal acts of the marriage. The mandate must indicate the specific person that will marry by proxy. It would be unlawful to give the proxy a mandate to choose a partner and marry her for him (by proxy). The date and name of the place should be indicated where the proxy marriage is to take place. In the year 1930, the Roman Rota received thirteen such cases; it accepted one and rejected all the rest (AAS XXIII, 1931).

Canon 1106

Marriage can be contracted through an interpreter; however, the pastor is not to assist at such a marriage unless he is convinced of the interpreter's trustworthiness.

11. Marriage Through an Interpreter

All things being equal — and if the pastor is satisfied with the other preliminaries — he may go ahead with a marriage which requires an interpreter. However the pastor must not assist at a marriage which is to be contracted by proxy or through an interpreter unless there is just cause and no doubt regarding the authenticity of the mandate and the veracity of the interpreter.

Canon 1107

Even though a marriage was entered invalidly by reason of an impediment or lack of form, the consent which was furnished is presumed to continue until its revocation has been proven.

12. Perseverance of Consent and Its Presumption

It is arguable whether marriage consent could be present if only one of the parties knew of a diriment impediment that would invalidate the marriage. The marriage consent must be presumed to exist in such a case.

CONSENT — A GENERAL OUTLINE

MARRIAGE CAN BE NULL BY:

1) *An Impediment* (1083-1094)
2) *Lack of Form* (1108)
3) *Lack of Consent* (1095)

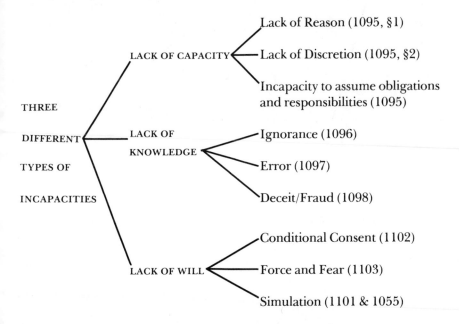

THREE DIFFERENT TYPES OF INCAPACITIES

LACK OF CAPACITY
- Lack of Reason (1095, §1)
- Lack of Discretion (1095, §2)
- Incapacity to assume obligations and responsibilities (1095)

LACK OF KNOWLEDGE
- Ignorance (1096)
- Error (1097)
- Deceit/Fraud (1098)

LACK OF WILL
- Conditional Consent (1102)
- Force and Fear (1103)
- Simulation (1101 & 1055)

THREE TYPES OF SPECIFIC INCAPACITIES

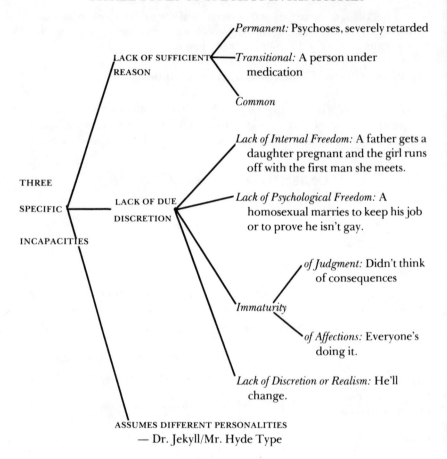

Permanent: Psychoses, severely retarded

LACK OF SUFFICIENT REASON ——— *Transitional:* A person under medication

Common

Lack of Internal Freedom: A father gets a daughter pregnant and the girl runs off with the first man she meets.

Lack of Psychological Freedom: A homosexual marries to keep his job or to prove he isn't gay.

THREE SPECIFIC INCAPACITIES — LACK OF DUE DISCRETION

of Judgment: Didn't think of consequences

Immaturity

of Affections: Everyone's doing it.

Lack of Discretion or Realism: He'll change.

ASSUMES DIFFERENT PERSONALITIES
— Dr. Jekyll/Mr. Hyde Type

---

1   *"Error Qualitatis in Errorem Personae Redundans,"* M.J. Reinhardt, CSLA Proceedings, 1973, pp. 60-63.

Chapter Five

THE FORM OF MARRIAGE

An Historical Summary

As we mentioned elsewhere, whenever a man and a woman contract marriage without any formality and without any witnesses (clandestine marriage) but mutually express matrimonial consent externally, such a marriage is valid according to the natural law. In the early days of the Church, there were no general laws requiring that a marriage be celebrated before an authorized priest for validity, although the Church Fathers did forbid secret marriages and were insistent upon having all marriages contracted publicly and in church.

The Council of Trent (1545-1563): This Council specified the form of marriage contained in the *Tametsi* decree. It stated that all marriages were invalid unless they were contracted before one's own pastor or another priest delegated by the pastor or local ordinary and at least two witnesses.

Before Trent, marriages contracted without a priest were valid but illicit. After Trent, marriages contracted without a priest present were invalid where the *Tametsi* decree was published.[1] In those places where the decree was not promulgated, the marriage was illicit but valid, even without the presence of the priest. All baptized persons, including heretics, who were married in the place where the decree was published were bound by it. Therefore, heretics marrying in such a place married invalidly. The pastor of the domicile or quasi-domicile of the parties to be married had personal jurisdiction over them whereby he was able to assist validly at any marriage of his subjects anywhere and was able to delegate this same power to any other priest. Today the jurisdiction is territorial except in the case of danger of death (Canon 1079).

The Benedictine Declaration (1741): Due to the fact that the *Tametsi* decree caused some hardship upon heretics marrying among themselves or with Catholics, Benedict XIV modified the *Tametsi* decree, exempting heretics from this legislation. In the United States, the *Benedictine Declaration*, like the *Tametsi* decree, was in force only in places where it had been published. Until 1918 when the *Benedictine Declaration* was rescinded, the law stated that a baptized person, Protestant or Catholic, who married a non-baptized person without a dispensation of disparity of cult, married invalidly.

Ne Temere (1908): This decree of Pius X was published and became binding on every Catholic everywhere. Heretics were excluded unless they wished to marry a Catholic. The decree gave the Church the power to prescribe the form of marriage. This power extends to the entire contract which is subject to the natural and divine laws, leaving to the State power over the civil effects alone.[2] This legislation became part of the 1917 Code.

Oriental Law: The form of marriage is precisely the same for the Oriental Church as for the Latin with the exception that in the Eastern Church the marriage must be contracted with the so-called sacred rite, namely the blessing of the priest. Although this sacred rite is only a simple blessing, nevertheless it is required for validity.

The Sacred Congregation of the Council, on March 28, 1908, stated that Orientals were only obliged to the decree *Ne Temere* when they married Latin Catholics. Generally speaking up to May 2, 1949, Oriental Catholics marrying among themselves outside of their patriarchate, or an Oriental marrying a non-Catholic were not held to the form of marriage except in disparity of cult cases. One exception involves Orientals (Ruthenians) of the Byzantine Rite who were bound to the form of marriage prescribed by the *Ne Temere* decree, not from 1908 but from August 17, 1914 when Bishop Ortynsky made a request of the Holy See that, for the sake of uniformity of discipline, the decree *Ne Temere* should be extended to all Uniate Greek Ruthenians in the United States (Decretum, *Cum Episcopo*, AAS VI, 1914, 458-463). From that time on Orientals (Greek Ruthenians) were bound to contract marriage under pain of nullity before a pastor or their ordinary or a delegated priest and two witnesses as called for by the decree *Ne Temere*. This canonical form obliged Ruthenians when they married among themselves and when they married Orientals of the Orthodox churches. The Decree of 1914 refers only to the United

States. Ruthenians of other countries became obligated to *Ne Temere* at different times.[3]

The Second Vatican Council promulgated a new marriage form for Orientals on November 21, 1964. It went into effect in the United States on January 21, 1965.[4] The new form is found in Article 18 of *Orientalium Ecclesiarum*, the Decree on the Eastern Catholic Churches, which states the following: "To obviate invalid marriages when Eastern Catholics marry baptized Eastern non-Catholics, and in order to promote the stability and the sanctity of marriage as well as domestic peace, the Sacred Council determines that the canonical form for the celebration of these marriages obliges only for liceity; for their validity the presence of a sacred minister is sufficient, provided the other prescriptions of law are observed."[5]

The introduction of this new marriage form for Orientals affects the validity of a marriage. Therefore, it is very important that the date *January 21, 1965*, be kept in mind when dealing with cases involving a Byzantine Catholic and a baptized non-Catholic of an Eastern rite.

The liceity of such marriages remains in effect as found in the former law (*Crebrae Allatae*, May 2, 1949) whereby censures and other penalties are incurred if the regular prescriptions of the law are not observed. Neither can ordinaries dispense from this marriage form whereby they would grant permission for a Catholic to contract marriage solely or first before a non-Catholic minister (*communicatio in sacris*). It must be noted that Pospishil makes a fine distinction when he states that although *communicatio in sacris* is forbidden, nevertheless, after such a couple has exchanged the marriage vows before a Catholic priest, thereby becoming recipients of the sacrament of matrimony, the rites performed in the Eastern dissident church cannot lead to a sacrament; therefore this is an extra-sacramental *communicatio in sacris*, which is permissible according to the above-mentioned principle.

Although the Decree *Orientalium Ecclesiarum*, Art. 18, was promulgated only for Orientals, Latin bishops requested the same privilege for their subjects. It was granted three years later and went into effect on March 25, 1967. Therefore this date is important because all marriages between a Latin Catholic and an Orthodox person in the Orthodox Church with or without the Latin ordinary's permission, are considered valid. If no permission were granted, the marriage would be considered illicit.

New Marriage Form for the Maronite Rite Catholics:
DIOCESE OF ST. MARON, DETROIT

Very Reverend and Dear Fr. Siegle,

This is to thank you for your letter of October 15, 1976, regarding the promulgation of the Decree on mixed marriages between Maronite Rite Catholics and Orthodox Church members. The following is the letter that I received from the Maronite Patriarchate. I translated it from the Arabic for your understanding and convenience:

BKERKE, December 16, 1974 — Prot. no. 11/74
Reverend and Dear Msgr. Joseph Abi-Nader,

In reply to your letter, Prot. no. 807/73 dated December 21, 1973, may I inform you that according to the minutes of the Patriarchal Synod held on Friday, April 29, 1966 the Bishops of the Synod and His Eminence Paul Peter Cardinal Meouchi, Patriarch of Antioch and of All the East have decided to promulgate the Decree on mixed marriages on this date (April 29, 1966) and to consider hereafter the marriage of a Maronite to an Orthodox before a non-Catholic priest and in the Orthodox Church, VALID but UNLAWFUL.

With best wishes for health and success,

Bishop Nasral-Lah Sfeir, Patriarchal Vicar

New Marriage Form for the Melkite Rite Catholics:
EXARCHATE FOR THE MELKITES, WESTON, MA.

Dear and Very Reverend Father Siegle,

In reply to your letter of December 17, 1976, I have the pleasure to answer with the following:

1. Until the erection of our own Diocese (1966) we abode with the directives of Rome concerning the "form" in the United States. 2. Consequently the marriage between a Melkite and an Orthodox was always considered valid. 3. However, the Decree effective May 2, 1949, was applied in the United States, but never accepted generally in the Middle East. 4. That is why the Decree on the Catholic Churches of the Eastern Rite of Vatican II was hailed with

enthusiasm in relation to no. 18 by all Melkites (November 21, 1964). In reality we never needed a Decree from Rome to regulate our discipline. The directives of the Synod were more than sufficient.

In summary we can say that the Melkite Synod has always demanded the presence of an ordained priest to make the marriage valid. The non-recognition of a marriage performed by the "Moslem Cheikh" or by a Protestant minister illustrate the idea that the presence of an Orthodox priest to bless a marriage was of a different calibre altogether.

Rt. Rev. Archimandrite Lucien Malouf, Vicar General

Canon 1108

§1. **Only marriages are valid which are contracted in the presence of the local ordinary or the pastor or a priest or deacon delegated by either of them, who assist, and in the presence of two witnesses, according to the rules expressed in the following canons, with due regard for the exceptions mentioned in canons 144, 1112, §1, 1116 and 1127, §2 and §3.**

§2. **The one assisting at a marriage is understood to be only that person who, present at the ceremony, asks for the contractant's manifestation of consent and receives it in the name of the Church.**

1. Form of the Celebration

The pastors mentioned in this canon include all the clerics mentioned in Canon 1108. Canon 1110 must be observed regarding the canonical possession of a parish and the territorial limits. The pastor and local ordinary can validly assist at marriages only from the day on which they take canonical possession of their benefice or enter upon their office. Any priest or deacon delegated by them can validly assist at marriages performed in the presence of two witnesses.

This canon mentions the presence of two witnesses. This presence must simultaneously be both physical and moral. Along with the priest, the two witnesses must be capable of giving testimony to the fact that a marriage was performed. The witnesses may be of the same or different sexes and must understand what is happening in the exchange of consent.

No age limit as such has been established. Usually lay persons are witnesses, but this role may also be filled by clergy or religious. Witnesses need not be Catholic, or even baptized, since their only function is to attest to the fact that a particular marriage took place in their presence. Although it might be customary in some places for witnesses to sign the marriage register, the Code does not specify that this be done. Since witnesses must be fully aware of their role and what is actually happening, witnesses cannot be intoxicated, insane or deaf and dumb.

The priest or deacon is the official witness of a marriage and has an active role in the marriage ceremony. He must ask for and receive the consent of the parties in the name of the Church which he represents. In the new ritual, he asks the couple three questions and then requires them to clearly express their consent so as to be heard by the witnesses.

Whenever other priests or deacons are present, or at a mixed marriage with a non-Catholic minister present, only the official Catholic minister asks for and receives the consent of both parties. Other priests, deacons or non-Catholic ministers merely observe the ceremony at this point, although they may perform other liturgical functions. It is forbidden for a Catholic minister and a non-Catholic minister to share in the eliciting and receiving of consent, e.g., it is forbidden for the Catholic minister to ask and receive consent of the Catholic party and the non-Catholic minister to ask and receive consent of the non-Catholic party.

The official minister must have a subject. Therefore, at least one party to the marriage must be a member of the official minister's rite. A Latin pastor cannot validly witness a marriage between two Oriental Rite Catholics because they are not his subjects. Neither can an Oriental Rite priest marry two Latin Rite Catholics for the same reason. Nor can a Latin priest officiate at the marriage of an Oriental Catholic and a non-Catholic. For such marriages to be valid, the ordinary of at least one of the parties must delegate the faculty to assist at the marriage to the Latin Rite minister. For example, if an Oriental Rite Catholic man wishes to marry a non-Catholic (Methodist) woman, the Latin Rite minister, for validity, must obtain delegation from the Oriental Rite ordinary. He must also receive a delegation from the Apostolic Delegate and faculties from his own ordinary in order to officiate at the wedding of two people, neither of whom is a member of his rite.

It is important to understand the principles of the acquisition of membership in ritual Churches. In the Code of 1917, a person automatically became a member of the rite of his or her parents. Whenever the parents were of different rites, the children were baptized in the rite of the father. If he was Byzantine, the children were baptized in the Byzantine Rite; if Latin, the children were baptized in the Latin Rite. Sometimes children of Byzantine parents were baptized in the Latin rite because there was no priest available in the Byzantine Rite. In the armed forces or in isolated areas where there is no other but a Latin priest, a child can be baptized according to the Latin Rite. This baptism in no way makes the child a member of the Latin Rite. Nor does it give it the privilege of changing to the Latin Rite. The child remains Byzantine. The present Code (1983) clearly states that one's rite is determined by the parents. If the parents are of different rites, they may mutually decide upon the rite of baptism for their child. If they cannot agree, the child is to be baptized in the rite of the father, following the old law (Canon 111, §1).

A conflict may arise whereby the parents decide to baptize some of their children in the Latin Rite and some in the Byzantine Rite. This could easily disrupt the unity of the family, but the present law does not spell out what should be done in such cases. Clarification may come later through the Code Commission.

A person may also transfer from one rite to another for good reasons by apostolic indult (Canon 112, §1). It is very important that records of such transfers be kept. A convert may choose the rite to which he or she wishes to belong provided that he or she has completed the fourteenth year of age.

Canon 1109

> Unless they have been excommunicated, interdicted or suspended from office or declared such, whether by sentence or decree, within the confines of their territory the local ordinary and the pastor, in virtue of their office, validly assist at the marriages of their subjects as well as of non-subjects provided one of the contractants is of the Latin rite.

2. The Official Witness

The local ordinary and all who are included under Canon 543 (vicars general, apostolic administrators, diocesan administrators, vicars apostolic and prefects apostolic) have the power of assisting at the marriages of their subjects as well as of non-subjects of their own rite. This power to witness marriages is given by reason of their office only after they have assumed it canonically and for as long as they hold it. They lose it at retirement or expiration of their term of office. Moreover, a cleric who attempts marriage incurs an automatic suspension *ipso facto* (Canon 1394, §1) and loses any ecclesiastical office he holds at the time (Canon 194, §1.3°). Therefore, clerics who attempt marriage lose the power to assist validly at a marriage and the marriages they perform are invalid. With so many people seeking annulments today, it would be well for pastors to check marriage records to determine the dates when a cleric, who has attempted to marry, may have assisted as official witness at a marriage. A case in point was recently uncovered in which a priest who secretly attempted marriage continued to function as a pastor for a period of four years until a parishioner found his marriage license recorded in the license bureau and reported it. Marriages performed by this priest during those four years were declared invalid because of his *ipso facto* suspension.

In the past when any Oriental Rite Catholic had no ordinary with jurisdiction in the United States or Canada, they came under other jurisdiction. For example, in Birmingham, Alabama, the Melkite Rite was under the Latin ordinary until the Melkites were assigned an ordinary in the U.S.A. Today Eastern Rite Catholics in the States are subject to the jurisdiction of their respective ordinaries and pastors. The following Oriental Rites possess their own U.S. jurisdictions:[6]

1.	Ruthenian	Pittsburgh, Pennsylvania
2.	Ruthenian	Passaic, New Jersey
3.	Ruthenian	Parma, Ohio
4.	Ruthenian	Van Nuys, California
5.	Ukrainian	Philadelphia, Pennsylvania
6.	Ukrainian	Chicago, Illinois
7.	Ukrainian	Stamford, Connecticut
8.	Ukrainian	Parma, Ohio
9.	Maronite	Brooklyn, New York
10.	Chaldean	Southfield, Michigan
11.	Armenian	Paterson, New Jersey
12.	Romanian	Detroit, Michigan
13.	Melkite	West Newton, Massachusetts

Canon 1110

In virtue of their office and within the limits of their jurisdiction, an ordinary and a personal pastor validly assist only at marriages involving at least one of their subjects.

3. National or Personal Parishes

A personal ordinary or pastor is one who has jurisdiction over people of a specific rite, language or nationality. Military ordinaries and chaplains of the armed services would be included here because their jurisdiction is limited to military personnel without regard to territory provided it is on a military base. Sometimes a chaplain is asked to perform a wedding in a parish church off the military base. In this case, he cannot officiate at the wedding without getting delegation from the ordinary of the place or from the pastor of the church. The marriage is recorded in the local parish records.

Canon 1111

§1. **As long as they validly hold office, the local ordinary and the pastor can delegate to priests and deacons the faculty, even a general one, to assist at marriages within the limits of their territory.**

§2. **To be valid the delegation of the faculty to assist at marriages must be given expressly to specified persons; if it is a question of a special delegation, it is to be granted for a specific marriage; however, if it is a question of a general delegation, it is to be granted in writing.**

4. Delegation

General delegation to an assistant may come from (1) diocesan faculties, (2) the pastor, or (3) letters of appointment to a parish from the ordinary. Delegation can be done by (1) a temporary administrator, (2) the vicar substitute, (3) the priest supplying for and appointed by the pastor who for some reason leaves the parish suddenly, even without the approval of the ordinary, as long as notification is sent to the ordinary. All these faculties are given with the power to subdelegate. Further subdelegation, however, is not allowed unless granted by the pastor or local ordinary. Delegated power must be given to a priest. It could also be given to a deacon just before ordination when the marriage is to take place after the ordination because assistance at marriage is merely quasi-jurisdictional. It is not the power of orders as such that is required to assist at marriage. Delegation must be expressed, orally or in writing, or by certain signs or facts surrounding the situation. Presuming delegation or assuming tacit delegation because one is a good friend of the pastor would render the marriage invalid. Oriental law is the same unless a mixed rite is involved.

General delegation means that faculties are given to a specific priest or deacon to assist at all marriages within the territory. The local ordinary or pastor may grant general delegation, but it must be done in writing.

Specific delegation means faculties are given to a specific priest or deacon for a specific marriage. This type of delegation need not be in writing, but it must be indicated in the marriage register (*delegatus*).

Those who have delegated faculties to officiate at a marriage may also subdelegate, that is, empower another priest or deacon to witness the marriage. One who has subdelegated power (e.g., a priest or deacon) has faculties from the pastor to officiate at the wedding but cannot further subdelegate another priest or deacon. To subdelegate another, the faculty must be specifically mentioned when faculties are given and this should be in writing.

By *interritual marriages* are meant marriages between a Latin Catholic and a Byzantine Catholic. The previous requirement of seeking permission from the Apostolic Delegate for such marriages to take place in the rite of the bride has been changed. These cases are provided for by Canon 88:3 of the Oriental Code, *Crebrae Allatae*, and Canon 1117 and 1127 of the new Code. An interpretation from the Cardinal Pro-Prefect for the Sacred Congregation for the Doctrine of the Faith, February 1, 1967, states that the local ordinary can now dispense from these provisions. The local bishop is now competent in interritual marriages to grant permission for the marriage to take place in the rite of the bride. For example, John, a Byzantine Catholic, is going to marry Mary, a Latin Catholic. According to the law, this marriage should take place in the Byzantine Church because the husband is Byzantine. However, the bride prefers to have the marriage in her parish church. The Latin pastor may get permission from his own ordinary to do this. He need not apply to the Apostolic Delegate, as was done in the past, nor need he apply to the Oriental ordinary, since the

Latin ordinary has this faculty. This works both ways, as the Oriental ordinary has the same privileges for a Byzantine bride and Latin groom, should they seek such a privilege.

Canon 1112

§1. With the prior favorable opinion of the conference of bishops and after the permission of the Holy See has been obtained, the diocesan bishop can delegate lay persons to assist at marriages where priests or deacons are lacking.

§2. A suitable lay person is to be chosen who is capable of giving instructions to those to be wed and qualified to perform the marriage liturgy correctly.

5. Lay Persons as Official Witnesses

The delegation of lay persons by the Church to officiate at marriages is a new factor in the Code. It means that the power to act in the name of the Church as an official witness to the exchange of consent can be given to any lay person, man or woman or non-clerical religious, when there is a pastoral need. Hence, official witness of a marriage is an act that does not require sacred orders. Throughout the world there are many places where ordained ministers are lacking. In Brazil, for example, where an ordained minister reaches his missions once a month, it would be feasible to delegate this role to qualified resident lay persons.

Canon 1113

Before special delegation is granted, all the legal requirements for establishing freedom to marry are to have been fulfilled.

6. Obligations of Specially Delegated Persons

Lay persons may be given specific or general delegation after fulfilling the requirements for pre-nuptial investigation and preparations for conducting this special type of wedding liturgy. Lay persons in such a capacity may, for example, preside at the Liturgy of the Word and ask for and receive the consent of the parties. Since they lack orders, however, they cannot give the nuptial blessing, bless the wedding rings, or dispense from impediments. This privilege can be given to lay people only if the local bishop's conference agrees and permission is obtained from the Holy See.

Canon 1114

The person who assists at the celebration of a marriage acts illicitly unless the freedom of the contracting parties has been established in accord with the norm of law and the permission of the pastor has been obtained, if possible, when one is functioning in virtue of general delegation.

7. Responsibilities of the Official Witness

This canon, though repetitious, reinforces the obligation of the one who assists at the marriage to determine the freedom of the parties to marry, according to the norm of law, and to see that the permission of the pastor has been obtained, if possible, when one is acting in virtue of general delegation. Permission should not be confused with delegation here. Failure to obtain permission by one who has general delegation would not affect the validity of the marriage. The permission here reflects a deference to the pastor of the area, whose right it is to witness marriages in his parish (Canon 530.4).

Canon 1115

Marriages are to be celebrated in the parish where either of the contractants has a domicile, quasi-domicile or month-long residence; the marriages of transients are to be celebrated in the parish where they actually reside; marriage can be celebrated with the permission of the proper ordinary or pastor.

8. The Place of Marriage

The pastor or the local ordinary may assist at a marriage: (1) After they have legitimately ascertained the freedom of the parties to marry; (2) After they have ascertained that one of the contracting parties has a domicile or quasi-domicile, or a month's residence; or, in the case of a transient (*vagus*), that he or she is actually staying in the place where the marriage will be contracted; (3) Provided that, if the conditions mentioned in no. 2 are wanting, the permission is had from the local ordinary of the domicile or quasi-domicile or place of a month's residence of one of the contracting parties, unless it is a question of itinerants (*vagi*) who are actually traveling and have no place of sojourn anywhere, or unless some grave necessity occurs which excuses from asking the permission.

In every case it should be taken as the rule that marriages are celebrated before the pastor of the bride-to-be unless a just reason excuses therefrom. Marriages between Catholics of different rites are to be celebrated before the pastor of the groom ordinarily and according to the ceremony of that rite.

This canon deals with the liceity, not the validity, of a marriage. Should permission of the proper ordinary or proper parish priest be lacking, the marriage of those who do not reside in the parish or are transients is valid but illicit. It is the pastor and local ordinary who are obliged to see that the individuals are free to marry. The proper pastor of the investigation is usually the pastor of the bride; the pastor of the groom could do this also, but it belongs to the bride's pastor.

When circumstances warrant it, one month's residence is sufficient for marriage. This brief stay is equivalent to a domicile or quasi-domicile, and this residence need not be made physically for 30 continuous days; a *morally* continuous month suffices before marriage is contracted.

To perform the marriage of a non-subject validly and licitly, a pastor should have the permission of the proper pastor with (1) the pastor of the bride-to-be, or (2) the pastor of the groom.

Permission is not needed for itinerants (*vagi*) who have no domicile or place of permanent residence and no one from whom to get the permission. However, the pastor should consult the local ordinary before assisting at such a marriage.

Permission is not needed in case of necessity. If a businessman, government employee, or soldier is leaving on urgent business and there is not time to get in touch with the proper pastor, and if all the canonical aspects are cleared, the pastor may go ahead with the marriage. Such circumstances constitute cases of necessity.

It must be kept in mind that all pastors can validly assist at all marriages of non-subjects in their own territory (Canon 1111), and they can licitly assist if they have the proper pastor's permission (not delegation).

Conditions for lawful assistance at marriages of Oriental Rite Catholics are the same as in the Latin Code. However, a Latin pastor can assist at the marriage of an Oriental man and a Latin woman validly but not licitly, since the marriage in this case belongs by right and custom to the pastor of the groom. The Latin pastor would have full right if the groom was of the Latin rite and the bride was of an Oriental rite. The marriage must take place in the parish of the groom when there is a marriage between a Latin and an Oriental. In the case of an Oriental woman of the Byzantine Ruthenian rite and a non-baptized person, the Byzantine bishop is the only one competent to grant a dispensation and the marriage must take place in the Byzantine Church. Otherwise, the dispensation would be invalid and the marriage would also be invalid (*Diriment Impediment*).

A. Lack of Form Cases

Since so-called lack of form cases are on the increase — some countries such as Germany and Holland are having high casualty rates in this regard — the Fathers of the Second Vatican Council gave some consideration as to whether a change should be effected regarding the form of marriage. It is the opinion of most canonists that the Church could allow some special means of handling these situations, but that it would not be feasible to oblige the universal Church. The general consensus among canonists, especially those of the United States, is to retain the form of marriage despite the many cases coming to the attention of our tribunals. To do away with the present legislation on the form of marriage would only increase the number of ligamen cases.

Although lack of form cases are ordinarily handled by tribunals, every priest should be acquainted with their essentials. To constitute a lack of form case, a particular marriage must exhibit these three characteristics: (1) At least one of the parties was held to the Catholic form of marriage at the time of marriage; (2) The marriage did not take place before a Catholic priest; (3) The marriage was not later validated or sanated in some church.

The following are, in general, necessary to establish a lack of form case:

1. A petition clearly stating the facts of the case.
2. A recent copy of the baptismal record of the Catholic party.
3. A first communion or confirmation record for a Latin Catholic whose marriage took place before January 11, 1949, or proof of Catholic parentage or training.
4. A certified copy of the marriage certificate.

5. A decree of civil divorce or annulment.
6. Sworn testimony from the Catholic party that the marriage was not validated.
7. Testimonial of character.
8. An investigation into the status of the children of the first marriage to insure that they are provided for by the petitioner and/or the respondent. This is in the 1983 Code.

A Case in Point: On August 14, 1928, John Brown, a Catholic, married Mary White before Rev. George Black of the Christian Alliance Church. John has since become a member of the Evangelical Church in Albany, New York. He and Mary lived together from 1928 until 1932. John claimed that his wife was unfaithful and they were divorced in August of 1950. One child was born of this union. Mary White remarried. John Brown married Jane Green, a parishioner of St. John's Catholic parish since 1943, before a Justice of the Peace and now wants a church wedding (in essence a validation of their marriage). Although these details seem complicated, the pastor of St. John's, in the investigation of this case, merely needs to assemble the lack of form papers.

Canon 1116

§1. If the presence of or access to a person who is competent to assist at marriage in accord with the norm of law is impossible without serious inconvenience, persons intending to enter a true marriage can validly and licitly contract it before witnesses alone:
    1° in danger of death;
    2° outside the danger of death, as long as it is prudently foreseen that such circumstances will continue for a month.

§2. In either case and with due regard for the validity of a marriage celebrated before witnesses alone, if another priest or deacon who can be present is readily available, he must be called upon and must be present at the celebration of the marriage, along with the witnesses.

9. Extraordinary Form of Marriage

When it is well nigh impossible for an appropriate cleric to assist at a marriage in accordance with Canon 1109, then the marriage is valid and licit when, in danger of death (cf. Canons 1079 and 1080), it is celebrated before the witnesses alone. This holds even outside the danger of death provided these circumstances (difficulty in getting an authorized cleric) will last for a month. This rule may be used when there is a reasonable chance that death may occur due to illness, impending surgery or wartime.

In either case, if a priest other than the one properly delegated is available, he must be called and must assist at the marriage, together with the witnesses, without prejudice however to the validity of the marriage contracted before the witnesses alone. *Inconvenience* could be caused by bad highways, rough seas, distance (e.g., in mission territories), too great an expense for either the people or the priest, sickness, bad weather (ice and snow in northern countries), great fear of being apprehended (e.g., living in territory occupied by an enemy), persecutions, floods, disasters, etc. The inconvenience could be either physical or moral and could be on the part of either the priest or the parties wishing to contract marriage. And one is not obliged to use the telephone or telegraph to resolve this inconvenience. There is no provision, if there is any diriment impediment, whereby the impediment could be dispensed, however, without a priest. If any priest were present, he could invoke Canon 1079 and dispense the couple from the impediment.

When it is foreseen that a couple will not be able to approach a priest for a month, the parties may contract marriage before two witnesses. However, if they wish the marriage to be recognized by civil law (because of property rights, etc.), they would be justified in going to a Justice of the Peace or any civil magistrate who is entitled to assist at marriages. Should these be unavailable, the parties would be justified in going to any minister who, not acting as a minister of religion, would perform the ceremony according to the right given him by civil authorities.

In danger of death and outside the danger of death, if another priest or deacon (not authorized as such) can be had, he may assist at a marriage as the official witness. Further, he may use the faculties of Canons 1079 and 1080 as a norm for dispensing from impediments of marriage if necessary. In general, however, either in danger of death or outside the danger of death, a priest should be called if possible; otherwise, two witnesses would suffice for a valid and licit marriage.

The Church recognizes this extraordinary form because there are times when a pastor cannot be reached. The two witnesses for such a marriage can be of the same or different sex, as long as they are capable of attesting to the fact that consent was exchanged. Of course, this extraordinary form presupposes that the parties are free to marry, capable of maintaining a marital covenant, and free of any impediment. This canon does not grant implicit dispensation from impediments. A moral impossibility exists when the proper pastor or minister is forbidden by civil law (as in some communist countries) to perform a religious marriage or when civil sanctions are clearly unjust (as is the case when civil laws forbid inter-racial marriage).

Although Canon 1116 is clear in itself, some canonists point out that in extreme circumstances a marriage would be valid before one witness or before no witnesses at all.[7] The second paragraph of this canon has reference to an undelegated or unauthorized priest or deacon who should be called even though he has no delegation to witness such a marriage. Even though his presence is not required for validity, his knowledge and his presence would add weight to the canonical situation, since he would have the faculty to dispense from certain ecclesiastical impediments if there were any (Canons 1079 and 1080). This canon is most appropriate and useful for missionaries who have catechists supplying for them in their territories.

Canon 1117

With due regard for the prescriptions of Canon 1127, §2, the form stated above is to be observed whenever at least one of the contractants was baptized in the Catholic Church or was received into it and has not left it by a formal act.

10. Persons Bound by the Form

The aforementioned law on the form of marriage obliges (1) all persons baptized in the Catholic Church and those converted to it from heresy or schism, even if the former or latter afterwards fall away, whenever they contract marriage among themselves; (2) these same persons when they contract marriage with non-Catholics, either baptized or non-baptized, even when a dispensation has been obtained from the impediment of mixed religion or disparity of cult; and (3) Orientals who contract marriage with Latins who are bound by this form.

The law is clear in itself. When non-Catholics marry among

themselves, it makes no difference who assists at the marriage: it is considered valid. In the earlier law, certain exemptions were enumerated, among them "persons born of non-Catholic parents, even though they have been baptized in the Catholic Church, who have grown up from infancy in heresy or schism or infidelity, or without any religion, when they contract with a non-Catholic party." This language was abrogated by the *Motu Proprio* of Pope Pius XII, August 1, 1948, and took effect January 1, 1949. Children of non-Catholic parents and those of apostate parents, even though baptized in the Catholic Church were not obliged to the Catholic form of marriage if they grew up from infancy without any religion and married non-Catholics.

What is meant by the phrase, "without any religion"? If one receives instructions for first communion, or if one knows the Our Father and Hail Mary, or if one went to church occasionally, is this sufficient to constitute some religion, some religious training which would oblige one to the form of marriage? This question was argued by canonists from 1918 to 1949. Since January 1, 1949, anyone baptized in the Catholic Church regardless how much or how little religious training he may have had, is bound by the form of marriage. The new Code does not abrogate the *Motu Proprio* of Pius XII. Hence, the importance of this date with reference to the people mentioned in Canon 1117 as the following case illustrates:

John and Mary came to their pastor to see if they could be married. John was married before and was divorced. He and his wife had been baptized in the "Church with the Lighted Cross" (non-Catholic). He knew nothing of his wife's background, but upon investigation it was found that his wife was born in a Catholic hospital and had an emergency baptism. Her mother, a Catholic, died at childbirth. Since the marriage of this baptized Catholic took place after 1949, even though she had no religious instructions in the Catholic religion (she was brought up by her Lutheran grandparents as a Lutheran), her marriage to John was invalid because of lack of form. If the 1949 *Motu Proprio* of Pius XII had not been promulgated, John's marriage would have been valid. The *Motu Proprio* changed the status of John's previous marriage, and Mary and John were permitted to marry after receiving a defect of form decree. In other words, Canon 1117 does not abrogate the mandate of the 1949 *Motu Proprio*, even though it is not mentioned here. It is only since 1949 that "all persons baptized in the Catholic Church are bound by the form." Before that date it depended upon whether or not the baptized person had been brought up in the Catholic faith.

Canon 1118

§1. **Marriage between Catholics or between a Catholic and a baptized non-Catholic party is to be celebrated in a parish church; with the permission of the local ordinary or the pastor, it can be celebrated in another church or oratory.**

§2. **The local ordinary can permit marriage to be celebrated in some other suitable place.**

§3. **Marriage between a Catholic party and a non-baptized party can be celebrated in a church or in some other suitable place.**

11. The Place of Celebration

The proper place for the celebration of marriage is the parish church. Since marriage between a Catholic and a baptized non-Catholic is a sacramental celebration, not a public witnessing of a private commitment between two persons, it should take place in the parish church.

Marriage between two Catholics may take place in the parish of either the bride or the groom. A marriage between a Catholic and a baptized non-Catholic should take place in the parish of the Catholic party, unless a dispensation from canonical form has been granted. Before 1970, marriages between Catholics and non-Catholics were to take place outside the parish church (usually in the rectory) to discourage Catholics from marrying non-Catholics. The *Motu Proprio, Matrimonia Mixta*, March 31, 1970, allows marriages between Catholics and non-Catholics to take place in the parish church.

Canon 1119

Outside of a case of necessity, the rites prescribed in the liturgical books approved by the Church or received through legitimate customs are to be observed in the celebration of marriage.

12. Proper Liturgical Form

The liturgical books[8] contain the Rite of Marriage. They also contain certain options, unlike the 1917 Code that allowed only one rite and no options. The essential element of the Rite of Marriage is the exchange of consent by the parties. The official witness, usually a priest or deacon, must ask for and receive the exchange of consent. Celebration of the Liturgy of the Word is highly recommended, even when the marriage is performed outside of mass. The norms of the nuptial blessing are contained in the Rite of Marriage. Restrictions in the 1917 Code have been deleted. The nuptial blessing may be given to the same person more than once, even outside of mass. In case of necessity, all the prayers of the ritual may be left out, but the exchange of consent can never be omitted.

Canon 1120

The conference of bishops can draw up its own marriage ritual, to be reviewed by the Holy See; such a ritual, in harmony with the usages of the area and its people, adapted to the Christian spirit, must provide that the person assisting at the marriage be present, ask for the manifestation of the contractants' consent and receive it.

13. National Rituals

It is left to the competence of the local conference of bishops to compose and approve a particular ritual for the celebration of marriages. Since every country has its own marriage customs, and since there are one hundred and one (101) conferences of bishops throughout the world, there can be as many different marriage rituals.

Canon 1121

§1. After a marriage has been celebrated, the pastor of the place of celebration or the person who takes his place, even if neither has assisted at the marriage, should as soon as possible note the following in the marriage register: the names of the spouses, the person who assisted and the witnesses, the place and date of the marriage celebration; these notations are to be made in accord with the method prescribed by the conference of bishops or the diocesan bishop.

§2. Whenever a marriage is contracted in accord with Canon 1116, if a priest or deacon was present at the celebration he is bound to inform the pastor or the local ordinary concerning the marriage entered as soon as possible; otherwise, the witnesses jointly with the contractants are bound to do so.

§3. If the marriage has been contracted with a dispensation from canonical form, the local ordinary who granted the dispensation is to see that the dispensation and the celebration are inscribed in the marriage register at the curia and at the parish of the Catholic party whose pastor made the investigation concerning their free state; the Catholic spouse is bound to inform the same ordinary and pastor as soon as possible of the celebration of the marriage, the place of celebration and the public form that was observed.

14. Registration of the Marriage

After the celebration of a marriage, the pastor or one who is taking his place must, as soon as possible, enter the names of the contracting parties and witnesses, the place and date of the celebration of the marriage, and the other items according to the method prescribed in the ritual books and by his local ordinary. This must be done even though another priest, delegated by the pastor or by the ordinary, assisted at the marriage.

Canon 1122

§1. The contracted marriage is also to be noted in the baptismal register in which the baptism of the spouses has been inscribed.

§2. If the marriage was contracted in a parish where a spouse was not baptized, the pastor of the place where it was celebrated is to send a notice of the contracted marriage as soon as possible to the pastor where the baptism was conferred.

15. Notification of Church of Baptism

According to Canon 535, the pastor must also note in the baptismal register that the party has contracted marriage in his parish on a certain date. If the party was baptized elsewhere, the pastor of the marriage shall send notification of this marriage to the pastor of baptism either himself or through the episcopal curia in order that the marriage may be recorded in the baptismal register.

Whenever a marriage is contracted according to Canon 1116, the priest, if he assisted at it, or the witnesses are bound *in solidum* with the contracting parties to take care that the marriage be recorded as soon as possible in the prescribed books.

The Council of Trent (Sess. XXIV, c. 1) commanded that pastors have a book in which to enter marriages which took place in their parishes and that they include the names of the parties and the witnesses along with the day and the place of the contract. The same prescriptions are found in the Roman Ritual giving the forms to be used and stressing that the parish priest should record the marriage as soon as possible. It further prescribed that he put this in his own handwriting, even when another priest took care of the marriage. The 1918 Code had the same prescriptions and added new ones, stressing the gravity of the obligation of parish priests to have marriages registered as soon as possible. It also insisted on the fact that one must be careful to avoid omissions and inaccuracies. The record must contain the names of the contracting parties, place and date of the marriage and other particulars, such as the priest who officiated, if he was delegated, the dispensations that were obtained, the promises that were made in a mixed marriage and so on. If the marriage was declared null later on, this fact had to be recorded also.

A marriage must be entered into the baptismal records of the parties, if any of them were baptized in another parish. The new baptismal record forms provide space for such notations. Notification of marriage can be sent to the parish of baptism either directly or through the chancery office (Instr. 1941). It is best to send it through the chancery or episcopal curia, especially if the marriage was celebrated according to the norms of Canon 1116. If a priest was present at such a marriage, it is his obligation to send in the information. If no priest was present, the obligation rests with the witnesses and the parties themselves.

The recording of all marriages can prevent bigamy and fraudulent unions. By cross-checking, a pastor can very easily find out whether or not a person was previously married. All he has to do is consult the baptismal register or the baptismal certificate, which must be issued at least within the last six months.

Canon 1123

Whenever a marriage is convalidated in the external forum, is declared null or is legitimately dissolved other than by death, the pastor of the place where it was celebrated must be informed so that a notation may be duly made in the marriage and baptismal registers.

16. Additional Data for the Baptismal Register

The baptismal register should contain notations regarding a person's marital status. Whenever a Pauline privilege or privilege of the faith is granted, the date and protocol number is to be noted in the register, as well as the name of the tribunal which declared the nullity. Marriages convalidated in the internal forum are registered in the secret archives of the chancery, noting the fact of simple convalidation or radical sanation (Canons 1156-1165). A similar notification is sent to the parish where the marriage took place.

---

1 The *Tametsi* decree was published in the Provinces of New Orleans, San Francisco, parts of Utah, Vincennes (Indiana) and St. Louis. It was not promulgated in the rest of the USA. Hence, a marriage contracted without a priest in any other place in the States before 1908 was valid.

2 E. Dunderdale, "Anachronism or Pastoral Necessity?" *Studia Canonica*, Vol. 12, 1978, p. 41.

3 Cf. Pospishil, *Law on Marriage*, pp. 185-187, should such information be required on the latter. Also of interest is Marbach, F. Joseph, J.C.D., *Marriage Legislation for Catholics of the Oriental Rites in the U.S. and Canada*, Catholic University Press, Washington, D.C.

4 Cardinal Joseph Slipy, the former Byzantine Archbishop of Lwiw in the Ukraine who possessed quasi-patriarchal power and jurisdiction declared that the Decree would enjoy legal force at a later date, namely April 7, 1965, due most likely to difficulties existing behind the Iron Curtain.

5 This is taken from an unofficial NCWC translation of the Decree.

6 Consult the Kenedy *Catholic Directory* for proper address. Terminology for Oriental and Latin Rites: Eparchy = Diocese; Archeparchy = Archdiocese.

7 Carberry mentions three noted canonists who hold the probable opinion that in extreme circumstances (especially in missionary areas) marriages contracted with no witnesses would be valid. He quotes Gasparri, Vroman and Wouters, and comments further: "In extraordinary circumstances (Canon 1116), if no witnesses are available, marriage would be validly celebrated without them. In such cases a marriage is valid because the natural right (for a man and woman) to marry will prevail over the ecclesiastical law which prescribes the canonical form; in such circumstances validity does not arise from the use of Canon 1098 [1917 law, now Canon 1116]."

8 *The Rite of Marriage*. New York: Catholic Book Publishers, 1969, 1970.

Chapter Six

MIXED MARRIAGE

Canon 1124

Without the express permission of the competent authority, marriage is forbidden between two baptized persons, one of whom was baptized in the Catholic Church or received into it after baptism and has not left it by a formal act, and the other of whom is a member of a church or ecclesial community which is not in full communion with the Catholic Church.

1. Norms for Mixed Marriages (March 31, 1970)

Over the years many different policies have developed with respect to mixed marriages. Norms were given for the performance of such marriages in the rectory or sacristy of the church; later developments found such marriages performed in the church but outside the altar rail, and in some dioceses without flowers on the altar, without music and without lighted candles. As time went on permissions were granted for the wedding to take place inside the altar rail, with music (but no singing) and with flowers on the altar. New norms now permit the celebration of mass and the reception of holy communion on the part of the Catholic.

Today, with the norms of March 18, 1966 supplanted by the *Motu Proprio, Matrimonia Mixta* of Pope Paul VI, dated March 31, 1970, we find very broad privileges regarding mixed marriages. Due to changing times and conditions, the pluralism of society and the rise of mixed marriages worldwide, and in accord with the teaching of Vatican II, Pope Paul VI promulgated these norms of March 31, 1970 which became effective on August 1 of the same year in Canada, and on October 1, 1970 in the United States. The former legislation dealing with mixed marriages did not encourage Christian unity.

Although the principles of mixed marriage remain the same, nevertheless some elements of this canon have been mitigated. For example, we could say that the Church everywhere permits the contracting of marriage between two baptized persons — one Catholic and the other Protestant. Mixed religion in general could mean a marriage between a Catholic and a baptized non-Catholic, or a marriage between a Catholic and a non-baptized person. However, canonically speaking, *mixed religion is restricted to a marriage between a Catholic and a baptized non-Catholic.*

Whenever the baptism of the non-Catholic is doubtful, there exists an impediment either of mixed religion or disparity of cult. Which one it actually is we do not know. After a marriage, the burden of proof rests upon the presumption in favor of the validity of the baptism and of the marriage until it is proven otherwise. Before marriage, when applying for a dispensation, it is granted for mixed religion *and* disparity of cult *ad cautelam.* Thus all possibilities are covered in such a doubtful case. If in the eyes of God the person is baptized validly in a Protestant sect, the mixed religion dispensation would apply. If in the eyes of God, the person is not actually baptized, then the disparity of cult dispensation would take effect. The precautionary phrase *ad cautelam* then prevents any further difficulties. Persons belonging to an atheistic sect require the dispensation of mixed religion or disparity of cult according to whether the person is baptized or not.

Whenever there is danger of perversion of the Catholic party or the children of a mixed marriage, the divine law gravely prohibits such a marriage.

Canon 1124 states that permission is given by the ordinary provided there is a "just and reasonable cause." The *Motu Proprio* of Pope Paul VI takes a more cautious approach by stating that the Church "does not refuse a dispensation. . . provided that a just reason is had." The permission is not to be presumed, even if the conditions are fulfilled. The basic question in determining a grant of permission for mixed marriage is whether such a permission will serve the parties or be a hindrance to the faith of the Catholic. The parties' desire for or insistence upon marriage — especially when the threat of resort to civil marriage or departure from the faith is used — should be closely scrutinized. Maturity and awareness of the great responsibility of marriage, together with serious commitment to each other's churches, should be carefully weighed in the granting of this permission. Prudent judgment is always required.

The canon dealing with mixed marriages should be studied by all parties concerned, not only by the Catholic priest and Catholics in general, but also by non-Catholic ministers, non-Catholic lay people and civil officials. It is essential to know what these norms are, the changes in the law, how they are applied to each individual and all the circumstances surrounding each case. Since mixed marriages are increasing, Pope Paul VI has shown his pastoral concern for them by issuing these new norms which safeguard both the existing principles of divine law and the inherent natural right of men and women to contract marriage. These norms prescribe a twofold obligation upon the Catholic partner: (1) to preserve his or her own faith and avoid any proximate danger of losing it; and (2) to see to it that the children are baptized and brought up in the Catholic faith. These are not merely ecclesiastical mandates but divine commands. The only real dilemma in a mixed marriage is that of the children's upbringing and education. Both parties have equal responsibility in this matter which could pose difficulties when one party is Catholic and the other is not. Hence, Pope Paul VI points out that there cannot be a uniform canonical discipline on mixed marriages as in the past.

The impediment of mixed religion or disparity of cult comes from the divine law to safeguard the danger of perversion of the Catholic party or their offspring. Both of these impediments are prohibitive by the divine law; but in view of ecclesiastical law, mixed religion is merely a prohibitive impediment, while disparity of cult is a diriment impediment, and as such would render a marriage invalid if this dispensation would be lacking.

In issuing these norms, Pope Paul VI was attempting to preserve the divine law obligation of Catholics while at the same time keeping in mind the principles of ecumenism and of religious freedom. Hence, for every Catholic this is a grave obligation: to live his or her faith and to pass it on to the children.

It must be remembered that the obligation is imposed upon the Catholic only in the degree to which this is concretely possible. This obligation is qualified according to this norm: it [the obligation] "is imposed according to the various situations." The Catholic baptism and the education of the children is to be undertaken "as far as possible." In other words, the Catholic promises "to do all in his or her power" because no one is bound to do the impossible. This is a departure from the law of 1917 which stated that no dispensation could be given unless a *guarantee* was given. These norms do not require a guarantee.

A Catholic is asked to respect the sincere conscience of his or her non-Catholic partner just as he or she would want his or her own conscience to be respected. Harmony must be sought in the family, especially when it comes to the education of the children. Here there must be real give and take. A Catholic is asked only to do what is possible, and no more, in a given situation. Therefore, dispensations may be granted even when it is uncertain that the children will actually be brought up as Catholics. The norm seems to imply more the sincerity, the attitude and the intention of the Catholic rather than the actual upbringing of the children. Success in rearing the children as Catholics may vary according to the attitude of the non-Catholic party. Sometimes it will be possible and in other situations it might be impossible, in which case the Catholic is not obliged to do the impossible.

The norm "to do all in his or her power" does not mean that the Catholic must exert pressure or undue strain on the non-Catholic party which would destroy the harmony of the marriage, or contribute to a breaking up of the marriage. Is the promise also a guarantee? These norms do not insist on a guarantee that the children will be baptized and brought up Catholics. It is merely a promise. It simply indicates that the Catholic should be aware of his or her obligation and be ready to fulfill it to the best of his or her ability in the situation. More than this is not demanded. Not even moral certitude is needed that the children will be brought up in the Catholic faith. This drastic change has taken place in respect to the sincere conscience of the non-Catholic party.

Vatican II declared: "All men are to be immune from coercion on the part of individuals or of social groups and of any human power, in such wise that no one is to be forced to act in a manner contrary to his own beliefs, whether privately or publicly, whether alone or in association with others . . . Parents, moreover, have the right to determine, in accordance with their own religious beliefs, the kind of religious education that their children are to receive" (*Declaration on Religious Freedom,* 2-5). Insofar as other Christians are concerned, the Second Vatican Council decreed that "Catholics must gladly acknowledge and esteem the truly Christian endowments from our common heritage which are to be found among our separated brethren . . . nor should we forget that anything wrought by the Holy Spirit in the hearts of our separated brethren can be a help to our own edification. Whatever is truly Christian is never contrary to what genuinely belongs to the faith; indeed it can always bring a deeper realization of the mystery of Christ and the Church" (*Decree on Ecumenism*, No. 4).

Canon 1125

The local ordinary can grant this permission if there is a just and reasonable cause: he is not to grant it unless the following conditions have been fulfilled:

1° the Catholic party declares that he or she is prepared to remove dangers of falling away from the faith and makes a sincere promise to do all in his or her power to have all the children baptized and brought up in the Catholic Church;

2° the other party is to be informed at an appropriate time of these promises which the Catholic party has to make, so that it is clear that the other party is truly aware of the promise and obligation of the Catholic party;

3° both parties are to be instructed on the essential ends and properties of marriage, which are not to be excluded by either party.

Canon 1126

The conference of bishops is to establish the way in which these declarations and promises, which are always required, are to be made, what proof of them there should be in the external forum and how they are to be brought to the attention of the non-Catholic party.

2. Conditions for Granting Permission

The first condition is the promise itself, which is made by the Catholic party. Departing from the Code of 1917, the non-Catholic party is no longer required to make any promises. Although the responsibility rests with the Catholic party, the non-Catholic is obliged to respect the promise made by the Catholic. The Catholic party makes a declaration that he or she will do all in his or her power to remove any danger of departing from the faith and promises to do all in his or her power to see that any children born to the marriage are baptized and brought up as Catholics. The promise applies to children yet to be born of a proposed union, not to children already born to the union. It is not allowed for the couple to baptize and raise their children, some as Catholics and some as non-Catholics. In the Catholic Church there is a continuity between baptism, education and allegiance to the Catholic Church. To baptize children in different denominations seems to solve a problem, but this solution only perpetuates and deepens the disunity that already exists among Christians.

Statistics show that a high percentage of Catholics entering mixed marriages give up their faith. A strong anti-Catholic bias or aversion to regular worship on the part of the non-Catholic is a clear sign of potential danger. Care should also be taken when the partners feel they can no longer worship apart. These concerns should be thoroughly discussed with the priest or pastoral minister during the regular premarital instructions to avoid future problems in the marriage. Annulment cases that come often before tribunals reveal that during the engagement the parties broke up once or several times because of anti-Catholic sentiments. It is a clear danger signal that does not bode well for the future of the marriage.

A frequent misconception on the part of engaged people, especially women, is that they will be able to change their partner's bad habits. This is especially serious when the woman (Catholic or not) plans to reform an alcoholic, drug addict or one who insists on an "open marriage." It never works. Marriage is not an institution for changing or reforming people. To attempt it is to attempt the impossible. At the outset, during premarital instructions, these notions should be thoroughly discussed, whether the party who intends the reforming is non-Catholic or Catholic. Such problems affect people of all religions.

This canon also stresses the practical application of the Catholic's obligation to "do all in his or her power" to see to the Catholic baptism and education of the children. Canon law acknowledges the right and duty of the Catholic party to fulfill this obligation, but it also considers the principles of religious liberty and the rights of the non-Catholic party to practice his or her faith freely and to seek the education of the children in that faith.

After the *Motu Proprio, Matrimonia Mixta* was promulgated, guidelines were issued by various conferences of bishops offering interpretations of the phrase, "to do all in his or her power." Some referred to it as "the good will of the parties" or "absence of unwillingness on the part of the non-Catholic." Some stated that no absolute obligation to baptize and educate the children in the Catholic faith is involved. These are mixed reactions, causing a dilemma. *Matrimonium Sacramentum* of 1966 cited a series of instructions which provide insight into the matter. When the Catholic party could not in conscience promise to bring the children up in the Catholic faith because of the opposition of the non-Catholic party, the dispensation to marry was granted anyway, based upon the sincerity and active faith of the Catholic and on the presumption that, in spite of this situation, the Catholic would do his or her part in bringing the children up in the Catholic faith. In this case, the Church is trying to avoid jeopardizing the marriage itself. This question of bringing up the children must be considered seriously during the pre-nuptial discussions. If a disagreement arises that would cause danger to the marriage itself, the pastoral minister should question the wisdom of the decision to marry. Each situation has to be evaluated on its own merits.

Canon 1127

§1. The prescriptions of Canon 1108 are to be observed concerning the form to be employed in a mixed marriage; if a Catholic party contracts marriage with a non-Catholic of an Oriental Rite, the canonical form of celebration is to be observed only for liceity; for validity, however, the presence of a sacred minister is required along with the observance of the other requirements of law.

§2. If serious difficulties pose an obstacle to the observance of the canonical form, the local ordinary of the Catholic party has the right to dispense from the form in individual cases, but after consulting the ordinary of the place where the marriage is to be celebrated and with due regard, for validity, for some public form of celebration; the conference of bishops is to issue norms by which such a dispensation may be granted in an orderly manner.

§3. Before or after the canonical celebration held in accord with the norm of §1, it is forbidden to have another religious celebration of the same marriage to express or renew matrimonial consent; it is likewise forbidden to have a religious celebration in which a Catholic and a non-Catholic minister, assisting together but following their respective rituals, ask for the consent of the parties.

3. Canonical and Liturgical Form

In discussing ecclesiastical marriage forms of the past, insufficient attention has often been paid to the fact that they cannot always be distinguished by the legal sanctions which were attached. Willful disregard of an obligatory ecclesiastical marriage form, for example, was gravely sinful but the marriage itself may have been valid. In the ancient world, marriage was a public contract as well as an occasion for a religious rite. However, no public official — religious or secular — was commissioned to represent the State. Hence, the Church of the apostolic era had no special interest in strictly demanding that the marriage contract be concluded in the church and in a liturgical rite, particularly when the parties alone were the ministers of the sacramental action. Nonetheless, it was ruled very early that no marriage should be celebrated without the bishop (St. Ignatius, Martyr to St. Polycarp, 107 A.D.). This does not mean the establishment of an ecclesiastical form, but merely that the presence or approval of the bishop should be secured.

Tertullian (160-217) spoke of a liturgical rite of marriage, and ecclesiastical legislators of the following centuries became ever more explicit. Without it, they considered a marriage invalid. In later centuries it was made even clearer. Whoever married without an ecclesiastical rite committed a sinful act, which though sometimes punished by excommunication *latae sententiae*, did not invalidate the marriage. This obligatory ecclesiastical marriage form was not sanctioned with invalidity of the marriage contract. In some of the Oriental Churches, the liturgical marriage form was made obligatory for the nobility or freemen only, while serfs could marry without the ceremony of coronation (blessing). With the Council of Trent (Decree *Tametsi*), the marriage form became obligatory and its neglect invalidated the marriage contract. However, even here a limitation remained, for *Tametsi* was in force only in certain places. It was *Ne Temere* (1907) and the *Codex Iuris Canonicis* (1917) that made the marriage form obligatory with a sanction of invalidity applicable everywhere for Latin Catholics. This obligatory form established for Oriental Catholics by *Crebrae Allatae* (1949).

If a priest of the Latin rite lawfully assists at a marriage of an Oriental Catholic and a non-Catholic (either baptized or non-baptized) he must follow the Latin rite liturgical formula and not the Oriental. Likewise, if a priest of the Oriental rite lawfully assists at a marriage of a Latin Rite Catholic and a non-Catholic (baptized or non-baptized), he must follow the Oriental ritual according to Canon 85 of the Oriental law.

If the religious form (blessing or crowning) is required for validity of a marriage, it must be proven that such legislative authority had been granted by the Church, either by specific enactment or by tacit recognition of a legal custom. Neither of these has ever been done. The argument has been brought forward that the obligatory marriage form among dissident Orientals may have been in existence before the schism and therefore continues its legal force which it acquired then. However the studies of E. Herman, S.J., on the historical evolution of the marriage form within the many Oriental groups shows that, in the Byzantine rite, the act of exchanging consent accompanied by a religious, liturgical rite was not customary all the time, nor did it apply to all classes of the faithful or even become a general practice in all Byzantine territories. The same may be said, but more strongly, for the other Oriental rites.[1]

"It might be advanced," Pospishil states, "that the Oriental dissidents by themselves could evolve a legal custom introducing an obligatory marriage form sanctioning that marriage contracted in defiance of it void, but this would have to be proven in each single community. The argument can never be more than a mere hypothesis. It was never adopted or followed by any office of the Catholic Church, and will not contribute to the solution of problems in practice, that is, will not overcome the presumption enunciated in Canon 6 of *Crebrae Allatae* (Canon 1016): *in dubio standum est pro valore matrimonii*, 'in cases of doubt, the validity of the marriage must be upheld.' "

As to the nuptial blessing itself, required by Canon 85:2 as an essential part of the Oriental marriage form, the Pontifical Commission for the Redaction of the Oriental Code resolved that *any* blessing suffices as far as the validity is in question and no specific liturgical act is required. For lawful assistance at marriage, the respective liturgical formularies must be followed. Many dissident Orientals consider the solemn coronation of the spouses, which consists in an imposition of wreaths or crowns on their heads by the priest, the essential form of marriage, an assumption not substantiated by historical documentation, even though the coronation ceremony belongs to the age-old custom of the marriage rite.[2] The Oriental law requires a simple blessing given by a priest assisting at the marriage. It is essential, but only for liceity; without it, the marriage would still be valid.[3]

A. Dispensation from the Form for Special Cases

The Instruction, *Matrimonii Sacramentum*, of March 18, 1966 from the Sacred Congregation of the Doctrine of the Faith established a new discipline for mixed marriages and provided for recourse to Rome in cases where dispensation from the form or from the *"cautiones"* were necessary in certain cases. The Diocese of Montreal, for example, has obtained various dispensations from Rome in particular cases as described below:

(a) *Dispensation from the Form*
  (1) For a Catholic and an Orthodox
      with Catholic baptism and education of children
      with Orthodox baptism and Catholic schooling of children
      with Orthodox baptism and Orthodox education of children
  (2) For a Catholic and an Anglican
      with Catholic baptism and education of children
      with Anglican baptism and Anglican education of children
  (3) For a Catholic and a Presbyterian
      with Catholic baptism and Catholic education of children
  (4) For a Catholic and a member of the Dutch Reformed Church
      with Reformed Church baptism and Catholic education of children
  (5) For a Catholic and a Jew
      with Catholic baptism and Catholic education of children
      with Jewish circumcision and Jewish education of children

(b) *Marriage Permitted in Spite of Refusal of* Cautiones
  (1) As above with Orthodox, Anglican, Presbyterian, United Church, Dutch Reformed, Jew
  (2) *Cautiones* refusal
      of baptism only, of Catholic baptism and education with acceptance of Catholic schooling
      of Catholic baptism and education
      of Catholic education
  (3) Minimal condition for granting dispensation: that the Catholic party do his or her best to see to the Catholic baptism and education of the children

(c) *Place of Celebration*
  (1) In several cases the ordinary has permitted, in special circumstances that a mixed marriage take place in a non-Catholic church or chapel with a Catholic priest officiating and the non-Catholic doing only what is allowed in the Instruction, *Matrimonii Sacramentum* (congratulate, exhort, pray with the assembly for the happiness of the couple) after the marriage has been solemnized by the Catholic priest alone.
  (2) Conditions: (a) least possible publicity; (b) that the non-Catholic minister and higher authorities of his Church agree to the arrangement.

(d) *Sanatio*
  (1) Permission was granted for a *sanatio* in a case where the non-Catholic party refused to agree to the Catholic baptism and education of future children on condition that the Catholic party do his best.

(e) *Double Ceremonies*
  (1) Permission to be married in both Churches granted in the U.S.A. In two cases, exchange of matrimonial consent in both Churches.
  (2) Has not been granted here yet where two ceremonies permitted: Catholic marriage first, followed by ceremony in non-Catholic Church where renewal of consent had to be omitted. Reason: Impractical, not applicable.

(f) *Catholic Priest with non-Catholic Minister*
  (1) Catholic priest officiating with non-Catholic minister in non-Catholic (Orthodox) Church. Requested once; permission refused.

Canon 1128

Local ordinaries and other pastors of souls are to see to it that the Catholic spouse and the children born of a mixed marriage do not lack spiritual assistance in fulfilling their obligations and are to aid the spouses in fostering the unity of conjugal and family life.

Canon 1129

The prescriptions of Canons 1127 and 1128 are also to be applied to marriage involving the impediment of disparity of cult mentioned in Canon 1086, §1.

4. Mixed Marriages and Pastoral Care

Canon 1128 mandates pastors to provide the surveillance and help that mixed marriages might need by way of moral support to fulfill their obligations.

---

1 Herman, E., S.J., "De Benedictione nuptiali quid statuerit ius Byzantium sive ecclesiasticum sive civile," found in *Orientalia Christiana Periodica*, 1938, pp. 189-234.
2 *Ibid.*
3 Pospishil, *loc. cit.*

Chapter Seven

SECRET MARRIAGES

Canon 1130

For a serious and urgent reason the local ordinary can permit a marriage to be celebrated secretly.

Canon 1131

The permission to celebrate a marriage secretly also includes:

1° permission that the pre-matrimonial investigation be made secretly;
2° the obligation that secrecy concerning the marriage be observed by the local ordinary, the assisting minister, the witnesses and the spouses.

Canon 1132

The obligation to observe secrecy mentioned in Canon 1131, §2, ceases on the part of the local ordinary if serious scandal or serious harm to the sanctity of marriage is threatened by observing the secret and this is to be made known to the parties before the celebration of the marriage.

Canon 1133

A marriage celebrated secretly is to be noted only in the special register which is to be kept in the secret archives of the curia.

1. Marriages Secretly Celebrated

The Code of 1917 referred to secret marriages as marriages of conscience. "Secret marriage" is a better terminology, because "marriage of conscience" used to be mistakenly interpreted as allowing marriage merely because the conscience of the parties compelled them to marry.

A secret marriage is one in which a marriage is contracted without the publication of banns, and in which the priest and witnesses who assist at the ceremony are bound to strict secrecy. Cases occur infrequently, but after careful investigation the local ordinary may permit a secret marriage. In each instance the information regarding the parties must be gathered secretly without revealing their identities. Secret marriages might be requested for many reasons. For example, a widow may have a number of children to bring up while her business forbids her to marry. If it were known that she were married, it would put the business in jeopardy and, hence, her children. Or perhaps a person in the army is forbidden to marry while he holds a certain position, and yet he has a grave reason to get married. There may be cases in which people are living in concubinage or are involved in marriages contrary to civil law — especially if the prohibition is contrary to nature or to ecclesiastical law, as is the case with inter-racial marriages in some countries, marriages where the Church is persecuted, and so on. Conditions such as these would warrant granting permission for a secret marriage, but would not exempt the parties from pre-nuptial investigations and instructions.

There must be a serious and urgent reason to request that a marriage be performed in secret, and the seriousness must be weighed insofar as the public good is offset by the good achieved through secret celebration. The permission of the local ordinary is necessary, and it can be granted to those who have a domicile, quasi-domicile or temporary residence in the place of marriage. Permission to celebrate a secret marriage imposes a promise and grave obligation on the assisting priest, the witnesses, the ordinary and his successors as well as on the contracting parties not to divulge the existence of the marriage. This promise also applies to anyone else who is aware of it. If both parties agree to divulge the fact of their marriage later, the obligation of secrecy ceases for all involved.

Regarding the permission for a secret marriage, the local ordinary must insist on the obligation of secrecy about this marriage and all those connected with its celebration. He is also bound implicitly to the secret in such a way that it is a conditional promise, for if there is some danger to the common good, or if some evil should follow from such a marriage, he would be bound to reveal the secret. This is the local ordinary's prerogative. Canon 1132 states that the obligation of the ordinary does not extend to cases in which scandal or grave injury to the sanctity of the marriage is imminent as a result of the observance of secrecy. The local ordinary may cease to observe secrecy without the consent of the parties if he judges that the continual secrecy will be a source of scandal. This may happen when it is publicly known that the parties are living together and participating in the sacraments of the Church.

Secret marriages should not be recorded in the usual matrimonial and baptismal register but in a special book kept in the secret archives of the chancery (Canon 489). If some kind of notification should be made in the church of baptism, this should be put in the secret archives of the respective chancery, but this is left up to the discretion of the local ordinary. Children who are born of secret marriages must at times be given fictitious names. Precautions must be taken that the names of the parents do not appear on the baptismal register, nor on the proof of the legitimacy of the children. Whenever the ordinary permits a secret marriage to a couple who are forbidden by civil law to marry, all the necessary precautions and care must be taken that the marriage does not become known publicly, because the State can press charges against both the couple and the priest who assists at the marriage. Some marriages, permissible under the laws of the Church, can be forbidden by civil law; therefore, it is necessary to handle these matters with utmost caution. In the final analysis, marriage is governed objectively by the divine law and the Church who is the custodian of that law.

If, as in other cases, one or both parties is a minor, the parents should be consulted unless a serious reason or prudence determines otherwise, as for example, if parental objections are clearly unjust and a grave harm would befall the minor if the proposed marriage were discovered. Consultation with the parents may be omitted only after discussing the matter with the local ordinary (cf. our commentary on Canon 1071).

Chapter Eight

CONSEQUENCES OF MARRIAGE

Canon 1134

From a valid marriage arises a bond between the spouses which by its very nature is perpetual and exclusive; furthermore, in a Christian marriage the spouses are strengthened and, as it were, consecrated for the duties and the dignity of their state by a special sacrament.

Canon 1135

Each of the spouses has equal obligations and rights to those things which pertain to the partnership of conjugal life.

Canon 1136

Parents have the most serious duty and the primary right to do all in their power to see to the physical, social, cultural, moral and religious upbringing of their children.

1. The Effects of Marriage

A valid marriage bond is established by the sincere and outward sign of consent by the two parties entering marriage. *Gaudium et Spes* expresses this clearly: "Once a valid consent is given, the parties to the marriage enter into a covenant. The human and divine are intertwined, as it were. It was God who established marriage for male and female for the propagation of the human race."

Despite the fact that ancient Jewish law and Roman civil law traditionally sanctioned marital dissolubility by the spouses themselves, the Church nevertheless has constantly taught that Christians were forbidden to remarry after obtaining a divorce.[1] Once marriage has taken place, the bond is perpetual, and the property of unity must be maintained regarding one man and one woman and excluding all others. The natural bond and sacramental bond are explained in our commentary on Canon 1061. This canon, and Canon 1135, expresses the fact that a marriage covenant imposes certain fundamental obligations and rights on the spouses. Christ raised the dignity of women, even though it was contrary to the Jewish law; so we might say that Christianity has, as a whole, introduced and furthered the equality between the spouses in marriage, despite other cultural forces. In the early Church, the position of the wife was culturally inferior to that of the husband. Also absolute fidelity was usually demanded of the wife but not of the husband. Today, regardless of social and cultural inequalities imposed from without, Christian marriage demands equal obligations of the spouses toward one another. Even though expressions of love, partnership, sharing and commitment vary from one culture to another, nevertheless there are certain basic obligations which the spouses have a right to expect from one another.

Canon 1136 stresses parents' duties toward their offspring. Their primary duty and right require them to do all in their power to see to the physical, social, cultural, moral and religious upbringing of their children. Marriage has a twofold dimension: the relationship of the spouses with one another, and their relationship with their children which, while it begins with the act of procreation, extends also to their education. The religious formation of children starts with baptism, continues with sharing the practice of the faith and providing for their Christian education.

Canon 1137

Children conceived or born of a valid or putative marriage are legitimate.

Canon 1138

§1. The father is he whom a lawful marriage indicates unless evident arguments prove otherwise.

§2. Children are presumed to be legitimate if they are born at least 180 days after the celebration of the marriage or within 300 days from the date when conjugal life was terminated.

Canon 1139

Illegitimate children are rendered legitimate through the subsequent valid or putative marriage of their parents, or through a rescript of the Holy See.

Canon 1140

Insofar as canonical effects are concerned, legitimized children are equivalent in everything to legitimate children unless the law expressly states otherwise.

2. Legitimation

In both civil and Canon Law, legitimate children are defined as those conceived or born of a valid or putative marriage. The 1917 Code has been changed insofar as legitimacy is concerned as a requirement for nomination as a candidate for Church office (old Canon 232, §2.1°), for appointment as a prelate or abbot nullius (old Canon 320, §2), for nomination to the episcopate (old Canon 331, §1.1°) and for the reception of sacred orders (old Canon 938, §1). However, we may be sure that the Church will continue to scrutinize the background of illegitimate individuals who are promoted to higher offices in order to avoid scandal.

Canon 1138 is self-evident. With regard to Canon 1139, children born of an invalid (not putative) marriage become legitimate upon the validation or radical sanation of the marriage, especially if invalidating impediments are removed. Legitimacy is also attained by rescript of the Holy See. A rescript does not validate an invalid marriage; it is independent of the marriage itself. Foundlings and adopted children are presumed legitimate until the contrary is proven.

According to Canon 1140, children who are illegitimate and later legitimized are equal in law to those born or conceived of a valid marriage.

---

1 A. Bevilaqua, *A History of Indissolubility of Marriage*, 1972, pp. 253-308.

Chapter Nine

SEPARATION, ANNULMENT AND REMARRIAGE

Canon 1141

A ratified and consummated marriage cannot be dissolved by any human power or for any reason other than death.

1. Dissolution of the Bond

When two baptized persons (Catholic, Protestant or Orthodox) get married, we call it a ratified marriage. When this ratified marriage is consummated by sexual intercourse (Canon 1061), the union becomes absolutely indissoluble and, according to law, no human power, civil or ecclesiastical, is capable of dissolving it. Death alone can dissolve such a bond. Theologically speaking, the argument for such indissolubility is based on Christ's own words: "What God has joined together, let no man put asunder." But Christ does not deal with degrees of indissolubility, the nature of sacramentality or the effect of consummation. It was left to the Church to determine the limits of indissolubility.

Some canonists and theologians argue that a ratified, consummated marriage could theoretically be dissolved by the Supreme Pontiff. The new Code, however, upholds the historical position of the Church on the matter, despite arguments for or against this proposition. This controversy has, nonetheless, shed light on some questionable texts (Mk 10:9, 11, 12; Mt 5:32, 19:9; Lk 16:18) which have been set forth in support of the argument that the Church has, in fact, allowed remarriage after divorce (cf. "Select Bibliography on the Sacrament of Marriage" by T. Doyle in *Marriage Studies* 1, 83-85).

This canon is precise and clear in its statement that marriage cannot be dissolved by the parties themselves (*intrinsic indissolubility*). Neither can a marriage be dissolved by any human power, secular or religious (*extrinsic indissolubility*). Natural law would seem to be the basis for indissolubility as an essential property of marriage whereby every marriage is indissoluble but not absolutely. Extrinsic dissolubility is possible when the marriage is not consummated.[1] A ratified marriage is one which is sacramental (between two validly baptized persons, not necessarily Catholic). A ratified and consummated marriage is one in which two baptized persons (Catholic or non-Catholic) performed the human act of copulation whereby there is penetration of the vagina by the male organ and emission of true semen therein. Thereafter, such a marriage is indissoluble, even beyond the power of the Supreme Pontiff to undo.

The ultimate reason for this inflexibility may be found in the mystical signification of Christian marriage. According to St. Paul (Ep 5:32), marriage symbolizes the bond between Christ and his Church. This likeness is achieved in its perfection in a consummated marriage between baptized persons. Common sense teaches us that by use of the conjugal right, marriage receives a sort of completion; something irreparable has taken place; the affective and verbal self-surrender has been supplemented by an actual physical one which justifies the significant expressions, "the two shall become one flesh" and "the marriage was consummated." The consummation of the marriage in the symbolical and mystical orders represents the indefectible union between Christ and his Church. In a perfect representation of this union, the indefectibility of the union must have its own symbol and it has it in the absolutely indissoluble marriage.[2]

The indissolubility of marriage is not a question of fact, but rather a question of law, and from time to time authors boldly step forward with their opinions. We find one such opinion in *Ephemerides Theologicae Lovanienses*.[3] "Does it follow then that what the Church has bound today she can loose tomorrow through the exercise of the same power of the keys . . . ? Inasmuch as all marriages are contracts, even though some of them are sacramental and consummated, they all come under the power of the keys . . . In *actu primo*, therefore, even ratified consummated marriages form no exception to this unlimited power of the Church. In *actu secundo*, however, these marriages are extrinsically indissoluble *de iure divino* simply because the Church has used her divinely given binding power upon them instead of her loosing power . . . Having once committed herself to its intrinsic indissolubility, there need be no fear that at some future time she may reverse herself and dissolve a marriage of this kind." Other authors hold that in virtue of the same ministerial power with which the Church declares ratified and consummated marriages *indissoluble*, she can at some future time change her mind and allow their dissolution.[4] Although in recent years the Church has granted dissolution of the matrimonial bond in cases where, in the past, she never conceded a dispensation, we should not make or formulate categorical assertions in this regard. It is only after some practical experience with actual cases that we know the precise limits of the ministerial power of the Church which is derived from divine law. That does not mean that it is unreasonable to assume that at some future date the Church may intervene in a ratified and consummated marriage, dissolving it, not by extending its power but by revising the notion of non-consummation to cover where conjugal copulation, though having taken place, has, e.g., because of permanent sterility, never attained one of the ends of marriage, namely, the generation of offspring.

It is certain that consummation, like sacramentality, does not add any fuller perfection to the indissolubility of the validly contracted bond. What it does is to actuate in a more adequate manner, the symbolism existing in a marriage between the baptized. The marriage that is solely sacramental represents the union of Christ with the soul through grace, a union which can be destroyed by mortal sin. The marriage crowned by consummation, however, represents the unbreakable union with Christ and human nature. It is only on account of this element that the ratified and consummated marriage is asserted to be absolutely indissoluble, both extrinsically and intrinsically.

Essential Facts in Dealing With non-Consummated Marriages

1. There is no consummation of marriage unless there is actual penetration of the vagina by the male organ and emission of true semen in it.

2. True consummation cannot take place under circumstances of physical or moral force which is of such a degree as to remove the freedom of one of the parties. Hence, marriage is not considered consummated through rape.

3. There is no true consummation if contraceptive devices are used. However, each case must be thoroughly investigated and studied before making a decision.

4. A marriage is considered non-consummated if intercourse took place only before the marriage.

5. In the past, the investigation of non-consummation of marriage cases and of the existence of a just cause for granting a dispensation belonged solely to the Sacred Congregation of the Sacraments. No ordinary was able to constitute a tribunal and conduct a test trial with the questioning of the parties and witnesses until he had received express authorization to do so from this Sacred Congregation. This permission is no longer necessary.

6. Since marriage is naturally indissoluble by the parties themselves or by any other human power, by what right does the Church, then, occasionally dissolve them? Theologians have long discussed whether the dissolution of the marriage bond is based upon the natural law, the ecclesiastical law or the positive divine law. The Church has never given an official pronouncement on this matter. The Council of Trent condemned anyone who claimed that the Church has no power to dispense from the marriage bond. Theological discussion tends toward the notion that, since marriage and its indissolubility have reference to Christian morality, and since the Supreme Pontiff cannot err in matters of faith and morals, we can reasonably conclude that the Pope has this power.

Canon 1142

A non-consummated marriage between baptized persons or between a baptized party and non-baptized party can be dissolved by the Roman Pontiff for a just cause, at the request of both parties or of one of the parties, even if the other party is unwilling.

2. Dissolution of a Ratified, Non-Consummated Marriage

If it can be proven to a matrimonial court that a marriage was not consummated, the Pope can, by dispensation, dissolve a ratified unconsummated marriage of Christians. A just cause is required for the validity of the dispensation. Such cases are long and very involved. The 1917 Code held that such marriages were dissolved also by solemn religious profession. The new Code makes no mention of this.

Canon 1143

§1. A marriage entered by two non-baptized persons is dissolved by means of the pauline privilege in favor of the faith of a party who has received baptism by the very fact that a new marriage is contracted by the party who has been baptized, provided the non-baptized party departs.

§2. The non-baptized party is considered to have departed if he or she does not wish to cohabit with the baptized party or does not wish to cohabit in peace without insult to the Creator unless, after receiving baptism, the baptized party gave the other party a just cause for departure.

3. The Pauline Privilege

Canons 1144-1149 deal with the pauline privilege and Canon 1150 deals with the privilege of the faith when a doubt arises in connection with invoking the pauline privilege. When we speak of the privilege of the faith, we do so in generic terms, for the privilege of the faith is a genus, whereas the pauline privilege and the petrine privilege are the species of this genus.

The petrine privilege is one whereby the Roman Pontiff dissolves a legitimate consummated marriage between a baptized person and an unbaptized person in favor of the faith. Regarding the valid baptism of heretics, it is morally certain that heretical baptism would be a sufficient foundation to use the petrine privilege but the Church does *not* use it. It is a difficult procedure to handle such a case.

The pauline privilege is one whereby a legitimate marriage between two unbaptized persons, even though it is consummated, is dissolved in favor of the faith. To utilize this privilege it is required that: (1) the two persons be unbaptized at the time of their marriage; (2) that one of these persons be validly baptized after that marriage; (3) that the unbaptized party be questioned according to the norms of Canon 1145. When a new marriage is contracted the former marriage is automatically (*ipso facto*) dissolved.

Strictly speaking the pauline privilege allows the dissolution only of "legitimate marriage between *non-baptized* persons." Yet, as long as both remain infidels, the Church will take no jurisdiction over the marriage. The use of the privilege supposes that one of the parties, and only one, after the marriage receives valid baptism. Since heretical baptism may be valid, it is now morally certain that valid baptism even in an heretical sect is a sufficient foundation for the Church to make use of the pauline privilege. There would be practical difficulties in the procedure, though, unless the person became a Catholic.

The departure of the unbaptized party must be proven by interpellations (Canons 1144-1146). Departure of the unbaptized party is understood if he or she causes offense to the Creator by giving scandal (moral departure), or threatens the party with physical harm or causes life to be miserable, e.g., by quarrelsome outbursts of anger, perversion, etc. The departure of the unbaptized party must not be the fault of the convert after the baptism has taken place. The pauline privilege gives the new convert the right to marry a Catholic. However, in recent years, the Holy See has granted permission under the pauline privilege to marry another unbaptized person or a baptized non-Catholic. When the unbaptized party wishes baptism but not cohabitation with the baptized convert, it is considered a physical departure. It would be best for the convert to use the pauline privilege before the other spouse is baptized, otherwise a ratified marriage would result causing complications and another intervention by the Holy See. Sometimes it happens that the unbaptized party (who separated and married) receives baptism in an heretical sect while the pauline privilege case is being expedited but the heretical baptism is unknown to the newly baptized convert. When the interpellations are made and this is discovered, the case becomes a ratified marriage and is referred to the Holy See. Physical departure is also said to occur when the unbaptized party is already married for the second time.

Canon 1144

§1. In order for the baptized party to contract a new marriage validly, the non-baptized party must always be interrogated on the following points:

1° whether he or she also wishes to receive baptism;
2° whether he or she at least wishes to cohabit in peace with the baptized party without insult to the Creator.

§2. This interrogation must take place after baptism; for a serious reason, however, the local ordinary can permit this interrogation to take place before the baptism, or even dispense from this interrogation either before or after the baptism, provided it is evident in light of at least a summary and extra-judicial process, that it cannot take place or that it would be useless.

Canon 1145

§1. As a rule, the interrogation is to take place on the authority of the local ordinary of the converted party; if the other spouse asks for a period of time during which to answer, the same ordinary is to grant it while warning the party that after this period has elapsed without any answer, the person's silence will be considered to be a negative answer.

§2. An interrogation carried out privately by the converted party is also valid and is indeed licit if the form prescribed above cannot be observed.

§3. In either case the fact that the interrogation took place and its outcome must legitimately be evident in the external forum.

Canon 1146

The baptized party has the right to contract a new marriage with a Catholic party:

1° if the other party answered negatively to the interrogation or if the interrogation has been legitimately omitted;

2° if the non-baptized party, interrogated or not, at first peacefully cohabited without insult to the Creator but afterwards departed without a just cause, with due regard for the prescriptions of Canons 1144 and 1145.

Canon 1147

For a serious cause the local ordinary can permit the baptized party who employs the pauline privilege to contract marriage with a non-Catholic party, whether baptized or not, while observing the prescriptions of the canons on mixed marriage.

Canon 1148

§1. After he has received baptism in the Catholic Church, a previously non-baptized man who simultaneously has several non-baptized wives can keep one of them as his wife while dismissing the others if it is difficult for him to remain with the first. The same is true for a non-baptized woman who simultaneously has several non-baptized husbands.

§2. In the situations mentioned in §1, marriage is to be contracted according to the legitimate form after the reception of baptism, while observing the prescriptions on mixed marriages necessary, as well as the other requirements of law.

§3. After considering the moral, social and economic situation of the area and of the persons, the local ordinary is to take care that sufficient provision is made in accord with the norms of justice, Christian charity and natural equity for the needs of the first wife and of the other wives who are dismissed.

Canon 1149

A non-baptized person who, once having received baptism in the Catholic Church, cannot restore cohabitation with a non-baptized spouse due to captivity or persecution can contract another marriage even if the other party received baptism in the meantime, with due regard for the prescription of Canon 1141.

4. The Interpellations

The interpellations should take place after the baptism and before the conversion of the other party. If the interpellations were made before the baptism, the action would be valid provided that the non-baptized party did not change his or her mind. Moreover, in a summary or extra-judicial form, the ordinary must give an extension of time if the unbaptized party asks for it according to Canon 1145, §1.

If the unbaptized person gives the necessary guarantees allowing the newly baptized convert to practice his or her religion freely and later violates them, the Catholic party is not obliged to live with that party and may get a divorce provided the interpellations are made or a dispensation is obtained.

It must be kept in mind that a legitimate marriage is not dissolved at the time of the baptism of the convert but only at the moment of the convert's new marriage.

If the case is such that the interpellations cannot be made because it would be useless to make them or because the party cannot be found, or because the party is already married again, nevertheless Canon Law would still render the new marriage invalid if the interpellations are not made. Canon 1145 is clear: ". . . the fact that the interrogation took place and its outcome must legitimately be evident in the external forum." Responsibility for the interrogation lies with the local ordinary of the convert. When an unbaptized party is already married again or cannot be found, practically speaking, the interpellations are useless. Nevertheless, the law requires that only the ordinary and the Holy See are competent to dispense with them.

Investigating Both Parties' Lack of Baptism

In dealing with a pauline privilege case, conclusive evidence of the lack of baptism on the part of both parties of the legitimate marriage must be obtained. Proving negative facts is difficult but by a process of elimination it can be done as follows:

1. Check the religious affiliation and background of the parents or guardians. A very good and strong presumption of non-baptism exists if the parents belong to a sect which rejects baptism, or believes only in adult baptism, or have no religious affiliations whatsoever.

2. If a person's siblings were baptized but the party under investigation claims no baptism, inquiry should be made as to why baptism did not take place. A check should also be made of the beliefs or practices of the parents regarding the baptism of their children. A search should be made for possible records of baptism in the church or churches in the place of domicile.

3. Besides asking the parents, a check should be made with the sisters, brothers, relatives and friends.

Canon 1150

In a doubtful matter the privilege of the faith enjoys the favor of the law.

5. The Privilege of the Faith

Strictly speaking, the privilege of the faith signifies a faculty granted to a convert from infidelity by the Roman Pontiff whereby, after the reception of baptism, the convert may contract a second marriage if the unbelieving party departs. In this sense, the privilege of the faith is synonymous with the pauline privilege. Non-sacramental marriages can be dissolved according to Canon 1143, as we saw in our discussion of the pauline privilege. Contrary to the widespread misconception, Canon 1150 cannot be applied to marriages between one party who is certainly unbaptized and one who is certainly baptized in heresy. This canon deals only with questions of doubt. In the case just cited, the validity of the marriage as well as the baptism of one party is certain. The privilege of the faith has been broadened, however, to include the vicarious power of the Pope over such consummated, legitimate marriages. For instance, in the Helena, Montana case (1924), a non-baptized man contracted marriage with a baptized non-Catholic woman before a non-Catholic minister. The Holy Office petitioned the Holy Father to dissolve the *natural bond* of this marriage in favor of the faith. The marriage was dissolved. The pauline privilege was not applicable because the pauline privilege deals with valid marriages between non-baptized persons. This case also cannot be adjudicated according to Canon 1150 which deals in doubtful cases in favor of the faith. It is clear that the dissolution of the Helena case was one in which the Holy Father, acting with the supreme power which is his, dispensed from a marriage which was valid. He did so because the marriage was not ratified, or in other words, because the marriage was not a sacrament. Since a ratified (sacramental) marriage which has been consummated cannot be dissolved by any human power (Canon 1141), an otherwise valid marriage can be dissolved for a grave reason by virtue of its lack of ratification.

In a Fresno, California case, the Roman Pontiff dissolved a valid marriage contracted by a baptized Catholic and a non-baptized person with a dispensation from disparity of cult. Since it was not a sacramental marriage but a natural contract, there was no intrinsic difference between it and one of a baptized non-Catholic and a non-baptized person. In the hierarchy of values, a sacramental union is to be preferred to a non-sacramental union. *Salus animarum* is the principle involved. The marriage of a Catholic and a non-baptized person with a dispensation given by the Church for disparity of cult is no more a sacrament than a marriage contracted by two non-baptized persons since we cannot have half a sacrament. Moreover, it is no more a sacrament than a marriage between a baptized non-Catholic and an un-baptized person. The granting of a dispensation by the Church for such a marriage does not render it intrinsically different. It is understood that some who are concerned with such problems do not look with favor upon the granting of such dispensations for reason of scandal, laxity on the part of Catholics and so on. However, the meaning of the phrase *in favorem fidei* is sometimes misunderstood.

Documentation Required for Privilege of the Faith Cases

1. A history of the case. This history should set forth all the facts: who the baptized party is and who the unbaptized; the date of the marriage; the history of their marital difficulties; the time, place and petitioner of the divorce; the certificate of marriage and divorce (if the parties desire to keep the original certificates, certified copies should be obtained from the County Clerk). The complete history should be written out on separate sheets of paper.

2. The full name and address of the petitioner.

3. The names and addresses of the parents of the petitioner.

4. The name and address of the unconverted party.

5. Names and addresses of the parents of the unconverted party.

6. The names and addresses of people who can give testimony about the baptism or absence of baptism of either party, specifying for which party each witness appears. Witnesses for the unbaptized party should be parents and relatives who lived with or in the vicinity of the person from infancy on and who are knowledgeable about the whole life of the person. If an authentic baptismal record can be furnished, no witnesses need be brought forward to substantiate the baptism.

7. Names and addresses of several people, preferably Catholics, who can testify concerning the truthfulness of the above-mentioned witnesses, especially concerning those who testify to the non-baptism of one of the principals.

8. The Catholic baptismal record of the convert.

9. The names and addresses of at least seven witnesses who can testify that the couple had no marital relations after the baptism of the spouse who had never been baptized. This is very important when the convert is the one who had not been baptized previously.

10. The name of the pastor.

11. The name or names of the priest who instructed the convert.

The Non-Catholic as Plaintiff

The Instruction, *Provida Mater*, August 15, 1936 (35, 3) states that non-Catholics, whether baptized or not, cannot act as plaintiffs in marriage cases without recourse in each case to the Congregation of the Holy Office. However on January 20, 1970, a letter from the Apostolic Pro-Nuncio to Archbishop Plourde of Canada expressed the opinion of the Signatura that marriage cases initiated by non-Catholic plaintiffs may be heard by diocesan tribunals since non-Catholics, whether baptized or not, no longer need to request the ability to act as a plaintiff in marriage cases because of the promulgation of the apostolic constitution *Regimini Ecclesiae Universae.*

In a letter from the Congregation of the Doctrine of the Faith to the bishop of Portland, Oregon, dated October 15, 1968, it was stated that the ordinary who is competent to process a case in the first instance can allow a non-Catholic the faculty to stand in court. A similar letter is found under Canon 1646 of the old Code in Volume VI of the *Canon Law Digest* (New York: Bruce, 1969, p. 827). Dated February 12, 1966, it is a private reply from the Congregation of the Doctrine of the Faith that "the ordinary who is competent to draw up the process in the first instance can grant to the petitioner the faculty to sue in court even though the person is a non-Catholic, and this is true also in a case of nullity."

Canon 1151

Spouses have the duty and the right to preserve conjugal living unless a legitimate cause excuses them.

6. Separation While the Bond Endures

Spouses have the right and duty to common life by actually living together in order to attain the purpose of marriage. The common life (*convictus conjugalis*) is a fundamental obligation of marriage. Marriage is a mutual covenant whereby each one is to help the other and thus provide for the welfare of any children born to the marriage. This obligation stems from the nature of marriage itself. However, given human nature, some marital discord is inevitable. In cases where the extent of the discord makes married life impossible, separation may be the prudent (or only) way to deal with a relationship that has deteriorated to a point of no return.

The 1917 Code contained no norms on marital separation. The matter was discussed in 1976 among Code Commission members. Since separation is not a universal practice, it was at first to be omitted from the new code. But since separation was found to be the practice in those dioceses where such cases come to the attention of the Church court, it was decided to retain this canon.

Byzantine tribunals declare that separation has proved helpful, as it makes the spouses realize the many problems they would have to face alone. Separation is often a sort of therapy, a "halfway house" between marriage and divorce, and many marriages have been saved through its use. Canons 1692-1696 give procedural norms on marital separation and the means of determining if a case warrants it.

Due to the indissoluble nature of marriage and its larger ecclesial role, the Church respects the seriousness of the marital covenant by requiring the parties to submit their case of discord to the Church when they plan to separate. The Church also asks for the charitable forgiveness of the spouses, a forgiveness which is embedded in the nature of the conjugal covenant. Further, the Church may ask the spouses to seek the aid of professional counselors or some other appropriate means that could help restore marital life. The Code wisely stresses that pastoral care must be provided for married couples (Canon 1063, §4). It is one of the important duties of the pastor. A priest who had been giving such pastoral care would have a better idea of a couple's marital situation, would know how far deterioration had set in, and could better evaluate the case for the chancery. He, as well as the spouses, should realize that separation will have manifold psychological, social, familial and economic effects, especially upon the children.

Separation can be made on a party's own initiative if the legal cause is certain and there is danger in delay. As soon as possible, the separating party should take the case to a priest and all priests should make themselves available for such cases and situations. Ultimately separation cases should be handled through the local chancery where experts can evaluate each situation. Here the parties are interrogated separately with reconciliation as the objective, especially if there are children involved. In too many instances, however, these cases of marital conflict have been going on for a long time. A pastor who knows his people can and should enter into these conflicts and try to settle them. As the pastor of souls, this is his obligation. If he gets the case in its early stages, chances are good that a resolution will be found.

Canon 1152

§1. Although it is earnestly recommended that a spouse, moved by Christian charity and a concern for the good of the family, not refuse pardon to an adulterous partner and not break up conjugal life, nevertheless, if the spouse has not expressly or tacitly condoned the misdeed of the other spouse, the former does have the right to sever conjugal living unless he or she consented to the adultery, gave cause for it, or likewise committed adultery.

§2. Tacit condonation exists if the innocent spouse, after having become aware of the adultery, continued voluntarily to live with the other spouse in marital affection. Tacit condonation is presumed if the innocent spouse continued conjugal living for a period of six months and has not had recourse to ecclesiastical or civil authority.

§3. If the innocent spouse spontaneously severed conjugal living, that spouse within six months is to bring a suit for separation before the competent ecclesiastical authority; this authority, after having investigated all the circumstances is to decide whether the innocent spouse can be induced to forgive the misdeed and not to prolong the separation permanently.

7. Adultery

To separate because of adultery the act must be formal, complete, morally certain and not in any way whatsoever attributable to the other party. Presumption or suspicion of adultery is ruled out.

Whenever one party is guilty of adultery, the other party — the bond remaining intact — has a right to terminate, even permanently, the community of life unless he or she consented to the crime, was the cause of it, condoned it expressly or tacitly, or had committed the same crime themselves. Tacit condonation is present if the innocent party, after learning of the adultery, of his or her own accord receives the other with conjugal affection. This tacit condonation must be spontaneous. It must not rise from fear or danger of grave inconvenience. If after six months the party does not separate or bring legal action, condonation is presumed unless the contrary is proven.

The innocent party who has separated legally, whether by judicial decree or on his or her own authority, is never bound to admit the adulterous partner again to conjugal life but may either receive or recall the party, unless the latter, with the consent of the innocent party has in the meantime embraced a state of life incompatible with the married state.

Canon 1153

§1. If either of the spouses causes serious danger of spirit or body to the other spouse or to the children, or otherwise renders common life too hard, that spouse gives the other a legitimate cause for separating in virtue of a decree of the local ordinary, or even on his or her own authority if there is danger in delay.

§2. In all cases, when the reason for the separation ceases to exist, conjugal living is to be restored unless ecclesiastical authority decides otherwise.

8. Separation for Other Causes

Although these two canons (Canons 1152 and 1153) refer to guilt and innocence, nevertheless, marital discord with need for separation could result from other than acts of adultery which are morally culpable. Separation can be called for if the other party has joined a non-Catholic sect or is educating the children as non-Catholics, if he or she is leading an ignominious and criminal life, is causing grave spiritual or corporal danger to the other, is making the common life too difficult by cruelty of one kind or another, not necessarily physical. These and other things of this kind are lawful reasons for a party to depart on the authority of the local ordinary.

The ecclesiastical authority mentioned here is either the local bishop or the competent judge of the local tribunal; the bishop may grant a separation by decree; the judge would issue a decree of separation at the conclusion of a judicial court session. One party of the marriage may start a temporary separation on his or her own authority, but to make the separation permanent, the party or parties must be authorized to do so by the competent ecclesiastical authority.

In all cases where the cause of separation has ceased to exist, the common life is to be restored. But if the separation was decreed by the ordinary for a definite or indefinite time, the innocent party is not bound to the common life unless by decree of the ordinary or upon expiration of the time.

Canon 1154

After the separation of the spouses, suitable provision is to be made for the adequate support and education of the children.

9. Children of Separated Parents

In cases where the parents are separated, the children are to be brought up by the innocent party. If one of the parties is not Catholic, the children should be brought up if at all possible by the Catholic party, unless in either case the local ordinary has declared otherwise for the benefit of the children.

In some dioceses there is no established procedure for handling separation cases and it is usually left up to the pastor. If the pastor is indifferent, little is done and disaster follows. It is the prerogative of every ordinary in his administrative and judicial capacity to adjudicate marriage cases, and this includes cases of separation. When separation is sought, the party or parties usually resort to a civil action for legal separation, which process normally outlines the rules regarding support of the children, terms of custody, visitation rights and so forth. The Church, if possible, should insure that there be no factions whereby one party works against the other through the children which can do irreparable harm to them in the long run. There are civil as well as ecclesiastical agencies which offer help specifically to separated parents in dealing with their children.

Canon 1155

The innocent spouse can laudably readmit the other spouse to conjugal life, in which case the former renounces the right to separate.

10. Resumption of Common Life

Despite the fact that the innocent party sought and obtained a permanent separation from the ecclesiastical courts, the situation remains open and the innocent party can recall or readmit the other party to resume normal married life together. Should the parties again encounter difficulties in their marriage, they must again go through the canonical separation process, all things being equal. It must be stressed that during a separation period the parties may not be deprived of the sacraments. Here again, the Church is attempting to promote the principles of a stable Catholic marriage.

In recent years divorce has risen at an alarming rate and threatens to undermine society. Our pastors and pastoral ministers *must* provide thorough instructions to people contemplating marriage. The marriage cases examined in our tribunals indicate that pastors have been negligent in this regard. The Holy See has periodically emphasized the importance of thorough premarital instruction.

To better understand and appreciate the critical need for premarital guidance in the face of what amounts to a "divorce epidemic," the following books and articles are highly recommended: M. Durkin and J. Hitchcock, *Catholic Perspectives: Divorce* (Chicago: Thomas More, 1979); J. Rue and L. Shanahan, *The Divorced Catholic* (New York: Paulist Press, 1972); T. Doyle, "Marital Breakdown: The Experience of the Tribunal," *Priest*, 38 (1981), pp. 16-20; T. Young, *Ministering to the Divorced Catholic* (New York: Paulist Press, 1979).

---

1 The existence of this power was clearly and explicitly taught only in the 13th century and, with the exception of cases of solemn religious profession only in the 15th century was the power knowingly used, by Pope Martin V (1417-31) and Pope Eugene IV (1431-47). Solemn religious profession has been deleted from the 1983 Code.
2 Vermeersch, *What Is Marriage?*, no. 68, p. 26.
3 O'Connor, W.R., *The Indissolubility of a Ratified, Consummated Marriage*, XII, 1936, pp. 720-722.
4 Abate, Antonius, O.P., "The Dissolution of the Matrimonial Bond," in *Ecclesiastical Jurisprudence*, Desclee, New York, pp. 25-29. Cf. also, Bride, A., "Le Pouvoir du Souverain Pontif sur Le Marriage des infideles," *Revue de Droit Canonique*, X-XI, 1960-61, pp. 98-99.

Chapter   Ten

CONVALIDATION AND SANATION
OF A MARRIAGE

Canon 1156

§1. To convalidate a marriage which is invalid due to a diriment impediment, it is required that the impediment cease or that it be dispensed and that at least the party who is aware of the impediment renew consent.

§2. This renewal of consent is required by ecclesiastical law for the validity of the convalidation even if both parties furnished consent at the beginning and have not revoked it later.

1. Simple Convalidation of Marriage

A diriment impediment must first cease or be dispensed before convalidation takes place by renewal of consent. This renewal is required by ecclesiastical law, not by the natural law. If a non-baptized person marries and later is divorced, but marries again, this person has a ligamen (bond) impediment and his second marriage is considered invalid while he is living with his second wife. If his first wife dies and he continues to live with his second wife, since his marriage is governed by the natural law, he need not renew consent. But if he were a Catholic, he would have to renew his consent since it is required by Canon Law. When it is impossible to get a non-Catholic party to renew consent, and the children are being brought up Catholic, one can apply for a *sanatio*, as will be explained later on.

A pastor should never be too hasty in getting a marriage validated and should never be too quick to tell the parties that their marriage is invalid. When it is discovered that it is impossible to validate the marriage, the couple theoretically should separate, but if they are in good faith, in extraordinary circumstances, they should be allowed to remain together.

Canon 1157

The renewal of consent must be a new act of the will concerning a marriage which the person who is renewing consent knows or thinks was null from the beginning.

Canon 1158

§1. If the impediment is a public one, the consent is to be renewed by both parties according to the canonical form, with due regard for the prescription of Canon 1127, §3.

§2. If the impediment cannot be proven to exist, it is sufficient that the consent be renewed privately and in secret by the party who is aware of the impediment, provided the other party perseveres in the consent already given, or by both parties when each of them knows about the impediment.

2. Renewal of Consent

When the impediment is occult and known to both parties, they need not go before the priest (Canon 1108) but should renew their consent explicitly, externally and through a mutual act. The conjugal act would not necessarily supply this: however, if they agreed to this way of giving mutual consent, this act would suffice.

If the impediment is occult and known to only one of the parties, all that is required is to make an internal act of the will. The confessor handling the case would simply ask the party to express his or her consent explicitly.

Canon 1159

§1. A marriage which is invalid due to a defect of consent is convalidated when the party who had not consented now gives consent, provided the consent given by the other party still exists.

§2. If the defect of consent cannot be proven it is sufficient that the party who did not consent gives consent privately and in secret.

§3. If the defect of consent can be proven it is necessary that the consent be given according to the canonical form.

3. Lack of Consent Cases

Here we have three types of lack of consent cases: (1) internal, (2) external and occult, and (3) external and public. If one party withheld his or her consent by a positive act of the will regarding, for example, the conjugal right, the marriage would be null, but its nullity could never be proven in the external forum. However, when this fact comes up in the confessional, the confessor should have the party consent then and there explicitly.

If, on the other hand, the party withheld consent by an external act, impossible to prove in the external forum, he or she need merely express consent externally, not necessarily publicly.

If, however, the lack of consent were both public and external, consent must be renewed publicly and externally, otherwise the marriage would be invalid.

Canon 1160

With due regard for the prescription of Canon 1127, §3 [apparently should read 1127, §2], marriage which is invalid due to a defect of form must be contracted anew according to canonical form in order to become valid.

4. Canonical Form Required

The canon is self-explanatory. If serious difficulties pose an obstacle to the observance of the canonical form, the local ordinary of the Catholic party has the right to dispense from the form in individual cases (cf. Canon 1127, §2).

Canon 1161

§1. The radical sanation of an invalid marriage is its convalidation without the renewal of consent, granted by competent authority and including a dispensation from an impediment, if there was one, and from the canonical form, if it was not observed, and the retroactivity into the past of canonical effects.

§2. The convalidation occurs at the moment the favor is granted; it is understood to be retroactive, however, to the moment the marriage was celebrated unless something else is expressly stated.

§3. A radical sanation is not to be granted unless it is probable that the parties intend to persevere in conjugal life.

5. Radical Sanation

A radical sanation implies (1) a dispensation from or cessation of an impediment; (2) a dispensation from the law (Canon 1156) which requires the renewal of consent; and (3) retroactivity.

When a marriage has been contracted invalidly due to some impediment or for lack of the proper form, the consent which was given in the invalid marriage must continue or persevere. The dispensation removes the impediment, if any, and the necessity of observing the form of marriage, or of renewing consent. The original consent, which had no effect canonically, is now canonically made effective. When the sanation is given, by fiction of law, the marriage is considered as retroactively valid from the very beginning. The dispensation *sanates* it. Children who were born illegitimately to such an invalid marriage are fully legitimated canonically.

Sanations commonly occur in connection with mixed marriages in which the non-Catholic party refuses to have his marriage validated in a Catholic Church because he or she claims the first marriage ceremony to be valid (even though it may have taken place before a Justice of the Peace). Nevertheless, the Catholic party is allowed the practice of his or her religion and the children are permitted to be brought up Catholic. The non-Catholic simply will not go before a Catholic priest to renew consent. Since this creates a problem, the Church allows this dispensation in favor of the Catholic party so the Catholic may receive the sacraments.

There are two kinds of sanations: (1) *Perfect*, when both parties are dispensed from renewal of consent. All effects are retroactive. (2) *Imperfect*, when only one party renews consent, or when a sanation is given after the death of the other party. The bond of marriage is not present in this latter case, but effects such as legitimation of the children take place retroactively by fiction of the law. Sanation is also imperfect when the retroactive effects are only partially so.

With the *Motu Proprio, Pastorale Munus*, of Pope Paul VI, November 30, 1963, "all bishops, both resident and titular, have the special privilege to grant this sanation, provided that the consent perseveres, in marriages that are invalid because of minor impediments, or defect of form, even if there is a question of mixed marriage, but in this last case, Canon 1061 [Canon 1125 of the new Code] of the Code must be observed." They can also grant "the sanation *in radice* provided that the consent perseveres in a marriage that is invalid because of the impediment of disparity of cult, even if they are invalid because of the lack of form, as long as Canon 1061 [again, Canon 1125 of the new Code] of the Code is observed." Canon 1125 deals with the necessary promises.

Canon 1162

§1. A marriage cannot be radically sanated if consent is lacking in either or both of the parties, whether the consent was lacking from the beginning or was given in the beginning but afterwards revoked.

§2. If, however, consent was indeed lacking in the beginning but afterwards was given, a sanation can be granted from the moment the consent was given.

Canon 1163

§1. A marriage which is invalid due to an impediment or due to defect of legitimate form can be sanated provided the consent of each party continues to exist.

§2. A marriage which is invalid due to an impediment of the natural law or of divine positive law can be sanated only after the impediment has ceased to exist.

6. Perseverance of Consent

Any marriage which was contracted with the consent of both parties which was naturally sufficient but juridically ineffective because of a diriment impediment of ecclesiastical law or because of defect of form can be sanated provided that the consent perseveres.

A marriage, however, that was contracted with an impediment of divine or natural law, even if the impediment has since ceased to exist, cannot be sanated by the Church, even from the time of the cessation of the impediment. According to this canon, whenever an impediment ceases, the consent must be given again. Gasparri claims that the sanation could be given up to the time that the impediment ceased, but the Church ordinarily does not do so. The Code does not deny this power, and indeed we have evidence of such cases being granted by the Holy See.[1]

Canon 1164

A sanation can be granted validly even when one or both of the parties are unaware of it, but it is not to be granted except for serious reason.

7. Awareness of the Parties of the Sanation

A sanation depends primarily on the persevering consent of the parties. Once consent is given and continues, it is enough to grant a sanation and it is not necessary for either of the parties to know of it. If, for example, a husband refuses to have the marriage validated in the Catholic Church because he claims that "one celebration is enough," the wife for reasons of conscience, can obtain the sanation without the husband's knowledge. A sanation can be granted even if neither party is aware of it, as would be the case if the children of a marriage know that consent is persevering and want the marriage validated for reasons of legitimacy. They can have this done without their parents' knowledge.

Canon 1165

§1. Radical sanation can be granted by the Apostolic See.

§2. In individual cases radical sanation can be granted by the diocesan bishop, even if several reasons for nullity exist in the same marriage, provided the conditions mentioned in Canon 1125 concerning the sanation of a mixed marriage are fulfilled. The diocesan bishop cannot grant radical sanation, however, if there is present an impediment whose dispensation is reserved to the Apostolic See in accord with Canon 1078, §2, or if it is a question of an impediment of the natural law or of the divine positive law which has ceased to exist.

8. Those Authorized to Grant a Radical Sanation

The Holy See and the local ordinary can grant the radical sanation of a marriage. If there are impediments of the natural or divine positive law which have ceased to exist or an impediment arising from sacred orders or from a public perpetual vow of chastity in a religious institute of pontifical right, the local ordinary must have recourse to Rome for dispensation and sanation.

---

1 Gasparri, *De Matrimonio*, II, nos. 1215-19; Cappello, *De Matrimonio*, no. 854.

APPENDICES

I. Internal Forum Cases

1. Intolerable Marriage Situations

Conflict Between the External and the Internal Forum. The Code of Canon Law has numerous laws that govern and protect the institution of Christian marriage. The procedure for handling informal and formal marriage cases are all found in the laws on marriage in Canons 1400 to 1716 and in the Instruction *Provida Mater Ecclesia* (1936). The purpose of this legislation is to protect and promote the value of Christian marriage. As members of the Catholic Church, these laws must be upheld if we are to be faithful to Christ and his Church, at least in our present understanding of what Christian marriage is.

Since the codification of Canon Law in 1917, drastic changes have taken place throughout the world, especially societal changes that have affected the institution of marriage. Changes have occurred in the development of the jurisprudence dealing with grounds for annulment of marriage, such as psychic incapacity, alcoholism, sociopathy, homosexuality, etc. Annulments on such grounds are granted today, while years ago this was an impossibility.

No law is ever perfect because Church lawmakers are subject to imperfection. We must admit that we live in an imperfect and a changeable world. Even St. Thomas admitted this when he stated that "because the human acts with which law deals are surrounded with particular circumstances which are infinitely variable, it is impossible to establish any law that suffers no exception; lawmakers observe what generally happens, and legislate accordingly; in some instances, to observe the law would violate the equality of justice and hurt the very welfare which law is meant to serve." This is also the reason why we have such things as *epikeia*, rescripts and dispensations of all sorts. We must look to new insights from theological and scriptural sources and from the secular sciences, such as sociology, psychology, anthropology, etc., which are so intimately connected with human beings.

Everyone is aware of the changes that have come about and are continuing since Vatican Council II. To cite only one example of these changes as they apply to the canons associated with marriage, resolutions of intolerable marriage situations are being provided to a hungry and large segment of our Catholic population through the "good faith solution."

Before venturing into this category, for the sake of the would-be critic who will claim that the private good must suffer to preserve the common good, we reply that a balance must be maintained between the common good of society and the justice and rights due to any individual within that society. Even Christ, who had a great respect for Jewish law and order as well as for the common good, made many exceptions to the Law when human beings were suffering. For example, he healed the sick on the Sabbath, which was directly opposed to the Jewish law and thus caused great scandal among the people. In reference to the common good, did he not suggest that we leave the ninety-nine and go in search of the one that was lost? The woman who was caught in adultery was to be stoned to death according to the Law, but Christ stepped in and opposed the Law. And instead of reprimanding the Samaritan woman for adultery, he accepted a drink from her, in contravention of the Jewish law.

Pope John XXIII also spoke clearly on this issue of the common good, the ultimate concern for which must be the welfare of the person, namely "the sum total of those conditions of social living whereby men are able to achieve their own integral perfection more fully and more easily."

Marriage as we know it is indissoluble, but there must be a marriage first in order to speak of indissolubility. We cannot take apart something that has not been molded together. We have seen many marriages that have failed because they were not true marriages to begin with (cf. Appendix II, "What God Has Joined Together"). According to our laws, marriage is a public act, not a private one. Marriage enjoys the favor of the law by legal presumption, and is therefore considered valid until someone can prove it to be invalid. If an ecclesiastical annulment could be obtained more reasonably than the present Code permits, the problem of private versus public good would be lessened. The following illustration shows the conflict which can arise between a just law and the private good of an individual conscience.

Mary Jones was abandoned by her husband shortly after their marriage. He left telling her that he only married her to give the baby a name and that he never intended to remain with her permanently. In this case, Mary would have good grounds for an ecclesiastical annulment, but she must first prove these facts in an ecclesiastical court. According to the law, she would have to bring two or more witnesses to establish conclusively that her husband lied to the priest before the marriage when he was asked: "Do you intend a permanent union?" The difficult burden of proving that he lied at the time of the marriage falls on her. Mary was deceived by her husband, but she is not able to produce the necessary evidence to convince the Church officials of the invalidity of her marriage. She can find no witnesses; she can offer no legal proof. Tribunal officials are satisfied that they have done all they can under the circumstances. Mary finds herself faced with the frightening alternatives of living alone for the rest of her life, according to the law, or of marrying again outside the Church. She wants neither. Later on, when Mary falls in love and is married outside the Church, she is denied the sacraments because she is considered to be "living in sin." Is she really? Is this second marriage invalid?

Ayrinhac and Lydon give their version of this dilemma in the following example, which fits our case: "The conflict would be more serious if the man who simulated consent had afterwards, being really free, contracted a valid marriage with another woman. In the external forum the first woman would be considered his legitimate wife; he would be bound to live with her and forbidden to have relations with the second one. In conscience, before God, the second woman would be his real wife, and there would be no possibility of revalidating the first marriage."[1]

The dilemma is self-evident. Our attempt is to maintain a healthy attitude towards the laws governing marriage and to look into the possibilities that would allow for a just and reasonable way of handling these situations where we find the legal system of the Church inadequate, unprepared or incapable of handling them. In past years, the Canon Law Society of America and Canada, theologians and other canonists have looked elsewhere in their search for an answer. The solution was obtained through the internal forum. At first only a few priests knew about the "internal forum solution." Today it is referred to as the canonico-moral solution, or pastoral solution, and is being used in many dioceses throughout the United States. The Chicago tribunal has made use of the internal forum solution under several different Cardinal Archbishops.

The problem illustrated by the case of Mary Jones concerns the adjudication of a situation where there is a conflict between truth internally known and truth externally unknown. It concerns the difficulty that arises from apparently genuine irregularity on the one hand, and a desire to be in line with the community on the other. The problem concerns primarily the conflicting situation that arises when a marriage is invalid before God, but the invalidity cannot be proven before a human tribunal. Secondarily it concerns situations in which a sacramental marriage was broken and an individual, now remarried, desires to receive the sacraments while remaining faithful to a second marital union. This is the case of those who are divorced and remarried and who are now anxious to return to full communion with the Church but cannot do so either because their first marriage, invalid as it was, ended in divorce and there is now another marital union.

The "internal forum solution" recommended by the Holy See is the only possible means for settling this conflict. In years past, solutions were offered by the Sacred Penitentiary. Such cases have appeared in the Canon Law Digest. The bibliography below is offered for those interested in this matter. Because of the controversy that existed in the United States, the Holy See intervened in 1975 with the following instruction regarding "internal forum" cases.

Letter of the Sacred Congregation of the
Doctrine of the Faith: Prot. No. 1284 66
March 21, 1975

Dear Archbishop Bernardin,
    As you reminded us in your recent letter of December 31, 1974, and also during your recent visit of March 11, Cardinal Krol, when he was President of the National Conference of Catholic Bishops, wrote to this Sacred Congregation requesting an official interpretation of the phrase used in the circular letter of April 11, 1973, *"probata praxis Ecclesiae."* This phrase referred to Catholics living in irregular marital unions.
    I would like to state now that this phrase must be understood in the context of traditional moral theology. These couples may be allowed to receive the sacraments on two conditions, that they try to live according to the demands of Christian moral principles and that they receive the sacraments in churches in which they are not known so that they will not create any scandal.

Sincerely yours in Christ,
(signed) Archbishop Hamer

Bibliography of Books and Articles on Internal Forum

Basset, William. *The Bond of Marriage*, University of Notre Dame Press, 1968.
Bresnahan, James F., "Problems of Marriage and Divorce," *America*, May 25, 1968, pp. 706-709.
Carey, Raymond G., "The Good Faith Solution," *The Jurist*, Vol. XXIX, Oct. 1969.
Catoir, John T., "Church and Second Marriages," *Commonweal*, April 14, 1967, p. 113. "What is the Marriage Contract?" *America*, Vol. 118, no. 7, p. 229.
Constitution on the Church in the Modern World, nos. 12, 17.
Council Daybook, Vatican II Session 4, pp. 71-72. An Address by Archbishop Elie Zoghbi.
Doherty, Denis, "Problem of Divorce and Remarriage," *Marriage* 28, 1966, pp. 12-18.
Haring, Bernard, *The Law of Christ*, Newman Press, 1966. Vol. III, p. 327.
Hertel, James R., O.D.M., *When Marriage Fails*, Paulist Press, Paramus, N.J.
Hertel, James, "Save the Bond or Save the Person," *America*, Vol. 118, no. 7, Feb. 17, 1968, pp. 217-220.
Hurley, M., S.J., "Christ and Divorce," *Irish Theol. Quarterly* 35, 1968, pp. 56-72.
"Indissolubility of Marriage, The," *The Theological Tradition of the East*, pp. 97-116.
Kelleher, S.J., "The Problem of the Intolerable Marriage," *America*, Sept. 14, 1968, pp. 178-182.
Krebs, A.V., "American Catholic Marriage and the Church," *America*, Feb. 1969, p. 228.
Mahoney, John, "Do They Intend Marriage," HPR, 67, 1966.
Monden, Louis, S.J., *Sin, Liberty and Law*, Sheed & Ward, New York, 1965, pp. 135-136.
Montserrat, J. Torrents. *The Abandoned Spouse*, Bruce, 1969.
Pope John XXIII. *Pacem in Terris*, no. 58.

Pospishil, Victor J., *Divorce and Remarriage*, Herder and Herder, New York, 1967, pp. 40-73.

"The Damned Millions: The Problem of Divorced Catholics," HPR, 1968, pp. 95-104.

"Sacraments: An Ecumenical Dilemma, The," *Concilium* 24, Paulist Press, New York, 1967, pp. 113-138.

Shaner, Donal, *A Christian View on Divorce*, E.J. Brill, 1969, Leiden, pp. 14-25.

Sullivan, Jos. Deuel, "Divorce and Psychological Change," *Catholic Theological Society of America Proceedings*, Vol. 22, 1967, pp. 245-252.

The Jurist, January 1970 contains these excellent articles:
(1) "Intolerable Marriage Situations: The Conflict between the External and Internal Forum," by Ladislas Orsy, S.J.
(2) "Law, Conscience and Marriage," by Peter Huizing.
(3) "Internal Forum Solutions to Insoluble Marriage Cases," by Bernard Haring.
(4) "The Pastoral Care of Those Involved in Canonically Invalid Marriages," by Anthony Kosnik.
(5) "Toward 'An Immediate Forum Solution' For Deserving Couples in Canonically Insoluble Marriage Cases," by Leo C. Farley and Warren T. Reich, S.J.

"The Tragedy of Broken Marriages," *Jubilee*, March 1966, p. 48.

Cf. *Chicago Studies*, Vol. 15, no. 3, 1976, pp. 300-303.

---

1 Ayrinhac, Henry, *Marriage Legislation in the New Code*, 4th rev. ed., rev. & enl. by P.J. Lydon, N.Y., Benziger, 1959.

II. What God Has Joined Together

An elderly priest met a young priest engaged in tribunal work and said, "Why are your people undermining God's command in dissolving so many marriages today? You seem to have no respect for the Scriptures or the law as we studied it in the seminary in my days. A dispensation or nullity in marriage was practically unheard of then. I do remember in the 1920's when our bishop got his first petrine privilege from Rome. It meant so much that he felt this was an occasion for rejoicing. So he invited all the clergy in the diocese for a *gaudeamus*. I could understand this when it happens occasionally, but we were taught that our faith is unchangeable and the numerous nullities granted today disturb me very much. I think you tribunal people have forgotten the real meaning of Scripture: *'What God hath joined together, let no man put asunder.'* What right do you people have to interfere with this divine mandate?"

This challenging question is amusing, yet very sad. It is a question brought up from time to time by priests at Forty Hours celebrations, which are held in some dioceses, and at other priests' gatherings. This question clearly reveals the lack of knowledge of some of our clergy, especially the older ones. They feel that the seminary gave them all the knowledge and education that was necessary for a successful priestly life. Once they left the seminary their books were closed.

1. Continuing Education

The priest who came out of the seminary three or four decades ago was imbued with the idea that the Church had a monopoly on truth. We knew everything, shunned non-Catholics and were reprimanded if we associated with them. The priest of that era had the feeling that only Catholics knew the truth. Truth was wrapped up in a nice package, as it were, and God help anyone who dared to disturb that package. Do you remember how some Vatican officials were disturbed when Pope John XXIII announced that he was going to call a Council? Do you recall how some churchmen went so far as to say that "outside the Church there is no salvation," and meant the Roman Catholic Church quite literally? That attitude still prevails to a certain degree among some of our clergy who think that we alone have a monopoly on truth. It is a sure sign that they have not read the decrees of the Second Vatican Council.

I was fortunate to have a professor in the seminary who constantly reminded us that "a little knowledge is a dangerous thing." But the one which most of my colleagues will remember is, "You must study until you are buried." In the 30's and 40's, before the Second Vatican Council, we were exhorted to participate in continuing education. But unfortunately we have priests in our midst who couldn't care less. Statistics regarding continuing education in our seminaries show that the Protestant clergy are more interested many times in continuing education than are our Catholic clergy.

Despite prevailing attitudes, it is the obligation of every priest to accept and study the decrees of the Council. Each one who is negligent in this respect should open up the window of his "shut in" life and let in some of good Pope John's invigorating fresh air. They may be in for a surprise; the Holy Spirit may come right in with it. The Second Vatican Council has renewed the face of the earth more than we actually realize. It was Vatican II that gave the big boost and sustains the momentum that accounts for the present expertise of tribunal officials throughout the world. The idea that our contemporary tribunal officials are interfering with God's command not to put asunder what He has joined together is absurd. All God-fearing and open-minded tribunal officials *do* uphold the divine command. They would not dare to challenge this great mandate.

A response to our elder priest can be given clearly by asking another question, "Does God *really* (in every instance of marriage) join people together in matrimony so that 'no man can put them asunder'?" The answers we get to this question from some priests—and this is no exaggeration—are: 'I'm the one who baptized them and saw them grow up. They were educated by our good Sisters. Both parties were good Catholics. I know their parents well. I officiated at the marriage of this couple in my church with a big wedding, and everybody present knew that this was a real marriage—a valid marriage. If I ever saw a sacramental marriage it was theirs. So how dare you tribunal men put such a marriage asunder! This was a perfect marriage in my estimation and God help those who dare to dissolve it!"

At one of our Canon Law Society's meetings one member told me that he was warned by such and such a pastor that if a nullity were ever granted on a marriage that he performed—it happened at the time that one case in which he was involved was being processed by the tribunal—he definitely would report the matter to Rome for an explanation because he was firmly convinced that this particular marriage was perfect, valid and sacramental. No one had any right to tamper with it. The tribunal official reported that the nullity was in order and was granted despite these threats, and the parties entered into a new marriage. The pastor never carried out his threat for obvious reasons.

Since challenges of this kind come to tribunal personnel from time to time, we might ask ourselves, "Does God *really* join together *all* marriages that take place in church with all the required legality and solemnity?" The answer is definitely, "No."

Do we have a perfect rendition of a violin concerto, if the violin is missing? Do we have a perfect mosaic, if some of the essential pieces are missing? A mosaic on the ceiling of St. Peter's basilica in Rome might appear perfect when seen from the floor, but upon closer examination by experts some pieces will be found lacking. It cannot be called a perfect mosaic. A jig-saw puzzle is not complete or perfect unless we have all the pieces in place. One cannot call a portrait perfect, or complete, if it lacks the face of the model. There is something missing in all of these examples. So, too, in marriage. All the essential factors for a perfect marriage must be present and in place at the time of the marriage. It would be a contradiction to claim that God would take part in joining a couple in matrimony when one or several essential elements are missing. Even if the Pope or a bishop performs the marriage, it would not be considered valid if essential factors are not there.

2. Missing Pieces

What are some of these essential pieces that we find missing in a seemingly "perfect" marriage? All priests are familiar with some of them but are unaware of others. We all know that the pre-nuptial investigation papers list diriment impediments which prevent a valid marriage if any of them are present in one of the parties to a marriage. Should one of the parties conceal the impediment, or the priest examiner overlook it, and the marriage takes place anyway, this would be one of the missing pieces to a perfect marriage. (This, of course, presumes that a dispensation was not obtained for the said impediment). The existence of a diriment impediment would disqualify a person from entering into a valid marriage.

Some of the other essential pieces that are occasionally missing from an otherwise "perfect marriage" can be found by reading the current Canon Law periodicals such as the *Jurist, Studia Canonica*, the *Tribunal Reporter, Annulments* (Wrenn), *Matrimonial Jurisprudence in the United States* (CLSA), etc. Priests can also enhance their ongoing formation in this field by attending meetings of the Canon Law Society and reading their extracts. Those members of the clergy who are critical of Canon Law and tribunal activities are probably unaware that, since about 1960, Rome has become more lenient and more pastoral in handling all marriage cases, something which has set a precedent for marriage tribunals throughout the world. The new Code of Canon Law reflects many of these changes. Canonical jurisprudence—the art of applying, interpreting and supplying for the codified law through rescript and by judicial sentences—has likewise changed in keeping with the times. For example, an example of an *application* would be utilizing or fitting

Canon 1057 regarding capability of matrimonial consent to a severe case of schizophrenia; of an *interpretation*, fitting the same canon to a case of sociopathy; and an example of *supplementation* would be adjudicating marriages on the grounds of a sexual anomaly.

"The approach of canonical jurisprudence is made by studying the recent contributions of related sciences like medicine and psychiatry, which sifts them through juridic principles and thus like the sea, gradually modifies the coastline of law. This may seem to make the tribunal judge a dilettante in the sciences, an incompetent intruder in the professional fields. But if the judge is careful not to make medical judgments but only legal ones he can make genuine contributions to the field of jurisprudence. The alternative is to reject scientific progress" (Wrenn, *Annulments*).

The zealous pastor who wants to do everything possible in preparing young people for a perfect, valid marriage, could be unaware of some of these missing pieces. These only come to light after much scrutiny and careful study by the experts. For example, some of these missing pieces might be the following:

1. Force and/or fear
2. Ignorance
3. Total simulation
4. Partial simulation
   a) Intention against fidelity (*Bonum fidei*)
   b) Intention against children (*Bonum prolis*)
   c) Intention against permanence (*Bonum sacramenti*)
5. Various conditions
6. Psychic irregularities
   a) Epilepsy
   b) Alcoholism
   c) Psychoses
   d) Depressive neurosis
   e) Obsessive-compulsive behavior
   f) Sociopathy
   g) Immaturity
   h) Homosexuality
   i) Hyperaesthesia

We could go on and on enumerating the possible missing pieces in the seemingly perfect marriage. Therefore, to answer the query of the old priest: "What God hath joined together . . ." is self-evident; but we cannot attribute to God a marriage that lacks the essential qualifications. All things being equal—all qualifications being present—God does join couples in marriages which no man can put asunder. By this we mean that the minds of the parties are in complete accord with the words expressed and that the spouses are willing and capable of fulfilling all the qualifications necessary to make a lifelong commitment.

Therefore, to uphold the mandate—"What God hath joined together, let no man put asunder"—and to examine the ship-wrecked marriages that come to the attention of the bishop's chancery, the tribunal experts, those so-called "canonical scientists," are employed to scrutinize the case to seek out any missing pieces and then to adjudicate the case. Once missing pieces are found, a nullity is declared. Otherwise, *"quod ergo Deus coniunxit, homo non separet."*

III. Brother and Sister Arrangement: The Last Resort

We find very little written about the brother and sister arrangement among authors. Yet such arrangements have been in existence for almost two thousand years, since the early years of Christianity. Only within recent times has this arrangement been adopted on a wider scale which allows the external forum better control. Although some clergy still frown upon this arrangement, nevertheless it is a viable solution to many unfortunate marriage cases. It requires very little reasoning to understand that such an arrangement is possible and sometimes feasible. To illustrate a case. A woman lived in an invalid marriage for years and, after ceasing marital relations for some ten years, asked a priest why she could not receive the sacraments. She explained that she was married by a Justice of the Peace; there were no children of the marriage; and she lived in a large city where no one knew of her status. She further stated that for the past ten years she had been living as any housekeeper does. She wondered why she could not go to the sacraments under these conditions, and after reasoning the matter out, she asked for the priest's advice. Her case was none other than those we handle now as brother and sister cases. It did not require much reasoning for this simple woman to draw the practical conclusions.

More and more cases of these kinds are coming to our attention, and we must be prepared to meet them. With the necessary and proper precautions we can be of immense assistance to many souls who are in an invalid marriage, but for some reason or other, cannot separate. The best method, in handling such cases, is through the diocesan chancery or tribunal. Here the experts can scrutinize the case with care and with greater success than could the parish priest who might not be fully aware of the dangers in handling such a case. Scandal is the great factor that must always be considered here.

Some chanceries are not too anxious to handle these case through diocesan channels, which leaves the parish priest at a loss about what to do. In 1950, when this kind of case was first being discussed, we found that some bishops frowned upon this arrangement. Today we have thousands who have found their salvation through this particular channel. A few years ago, a Catholic woman published a book with an *imprimatur* in which she explained the brother and sister arrangement that solved a marital problem of her own which was of long standing. The brother and sister solution is no longer the secret it once was. Priests who cannot handle these cases through their diocesan chanceries or tribunals and are forced to take care of these matters themselves could use the following formula:

After careful investigation of the case one must be sure that:

1. Validation of the marriage is impossible.
2. Separation of the parties is extremely difficult for reasons of children and property.
3. Scandal will not result from this arrangement.
4. Danger of incontinence is removed (advanced age, illness or serious operation).

A. *Questionnaire*

1. Name?
2. Address?
3. Date and place of birth?
4. Religion? If Catholic, when did you go to the sacraments the last time? If non-Catholic, what church do you attend?
5. Did you ever ask for such permission before? If so, when? Were you ever refused? Explain.
6. Where were you married? When? Before whom?
7. Did many people know at that time your marriage was invalid? How many?
8. How many children were born of this marriage?
9. How long have you lived in this town?
10. How many neighbors and friends know your marriage is invalid? List them on a separate sheet.
11. How many relatives and friends know your marriage is invalid? List them in the same way.
12. How many know that your marriage cannot be validated? List them.
13. Is it at all possible for you to separate? If not, why?
14. What type of illnesses, if any, do you have?
15. How many times were you married before?
16. What is the date and place of your wife's (husband's) death?
17. Her (his) name (if living)? Religion?
18. When were you married? Where? By whom?
19. How many children were born of this marriage? List them.
20. Why did you separate?
21. Where did you get your divorce? When? Where? By whom?
22. Did she (he) remarry? When? Where?
23. If you had more than one wife (husband), list them.

24. Give the names and addresses.
25. Are you sure that you can keep your promise to live as brother and sister? Why are you so sure?
26. Have you ever tried to live in such a manner? For how long a period of time?
27. Would you be able to support your wife if she would separate from you?
28. Would there be scandal if she (he) separated from you (do people consider you married)?
29. If the answer is no, check on the financial standing.
30. Where will you go for confession and communion? [Here the priest may advise the party where they might go without causing any scandal.]
31. Do you realize that you will have to forfeit your right to Christian burial?

B. *Promises*

We, the undersigned, knowing full well that our marriage is invalid in the sight of God, and realizing that it is sinful to live in the manner of husband and wife, and realizing that it would be difficult for us to separate, hereby beg for permission to live together as brother and sister and to be readmitted to the sacraments of the Church. [Leave out this part if one party is non-Catholic.]

C. *Oath*

[Each party recites the entire oath in the presence of the other]

I, _____, realizing full well the sacredness of an oath, and my obligation before God, touching the Holy Gospels, solemnly swear:

1. That I will not attempt to live as husband and wife with my present consort.
2. That I will not separate, and refer the matter to the (bishop, priest) before I receive the sacraments again.
3. That I will receive the sacraments only in the churches where my marital status is unknown to the parishioners.
4. That I will explain my status to my regular confessor and will report to him regularly.
5. That I will take every precautionary measure to avoid scandal in using this privilege, so help me God and these Holy Gospels which I touch.

Signatures _____(Man)
_____(Woman)
_____(Priest)

Date: _____
Seal:

IV. The Role of Judges and Lawyers in Divorce

1. The Judge

Every judge before entering upon the duties of his office usually takes an oath or affirmation, swearing (or affirming as the case may be) in some such terms as these that he will support the Constitution of the United States and the Constitution of the State in which he will preside, and will faithfully discharge the duties of judge in the particular court to which he is assigned, according to "the best of his ability." *Could a judge in conscience take such an oath if he knows that he cannot grant a divorce decree in the manner in which the State understands it?* We can assuredly answer in the affirmative that he could take such an oath. This is so because every oath taken by any man is understood in such a way that there is no intention to violate the law of God. It would be blasphemy to think otherwise. Moreover, there is no civil law which requires that the judge must share the intention of the legislator—the lawgiver. Consequently, when he grants a divorce he is not coerced or forced in any way *to intend* to dissolve the bond of marriage in any way. He must stress the civil effects, however, either in the decree or in the admonishment. Despite all this, the State, the public and the divorced parties will look upon the divorce decree as a means of breaking the bond of marriage. Even so, the judge has the right to grant the divorce, if statutory evidence warrants it and there are *grave reasons* for his action and cooperation.

What would be considered a grave reason for a judge to cooperate in such a case? Judges are public officials who are working for the common good. In looking further, what does a judge do but hear the case presented to him in court? He weighs it on the "scale of justice" and then pronounces the verdict according to all the evidence which is presented to him. It would be wrong to ask all upright and conscientious judges to give up their offices in order to prevent them from granting a divorce decree. The judge on the bench holds a very important position. In this position he can offer his advice, counsel and possibly the ways and means for proper reconciliation. It is a known fact that many such judges have been very successful in this way. The judge is doing a service for the common good and at the same time is preventing a greater evil which is a justifying reason for permitting the judge to cooperate *materially* in granting a decree of divorce.

It must always be kept in mind, though, that a judge should never be guilty of *formal* cooperation in granting a separation or divorce decree. He must never act as if the case really pertains solely to the competency of the civil court. Otherwise, he would be considered as formally cooperating and really usurping the power of the Church. This would be true in cases where a complete divorce, annulment, or separation maintenance are concerned, or even if he were to be denying such petitions. It would also be true even if the Church had already declared the marriage in question to be null and void on account of some impediment of the natural or divine law. Every judge, Catholic or non-Catholic, should endeavor to persuade and assist the parties in becoming reconciled for the common good and the lessening of evil in the world.

2. The lawyer

The lawyer is in a category different from that of the judge. A lawyer is called a private attorney because he is just that. As a private professional individual he has an option to accept or refuse a case that comes to his or her attention, whereas a judge, as a public official in a public office, has no choice in the matter. He must act on the cases that are presented to him.

According to Canon 31 of the Statutes of Professional Ethics issued by the American Bar Association, we find: "No lawyer is obliged to act either as advisor or advocate for every person who may wish to become his client. He has the right to decline employment. Every lawyer upon his own responsibility must decide what business he will accept as counsel, what cases he will bring into court for plaintiffs, what cases he will contest in court for defendants. The responsibility for advising as to questionable transactions, for bringing questionable suits, for urging questionable defense, is the lawyer's responsibility. He cannot escape it by urging as an excuse that he is only following his client's instructions." The ecclesiastical norm of moral conduct is the same regarding divorce and separation cases. *By the very fact that the lawyer represents and speaks for his client, he may licitly do only what his client may licitly do in regard to divorce and separation.* The lawyer is considered by the public as the "alter ego" of the client. Moreover, he is the necessary cooperator with the client in the case which he petitions or defends. As a result, in these divorce and separation cases, he is the cooperator, at least materially, in all the evil that would follow from the divorce, as for example, the unjust usurpation of competency in marriage cases on the part of the State, and in the violation of the divine law on the indissolubility of a valid marriage. However, just as the judge may be morally justified in cooperating materially with such evils, so also may the lawyer if he has a proportionately grave reason for such cooperation in the case. This will be determined on what the *client* may licitly do in regard to seeking a civil divorce or separation.

A Catholic may licitly seek a civil divorce in the following circumstances: (1) when the Church declares a marriage null and void. In this case nothing more is done than dissolving the civil effects of an invalid contract; (2) when the Church decides that there is sufficient reason for a permanent or indefinite separation in a valid marriage and merely permits the civil divorce to protect the civil rights of the party. Two conditions must be verified by the client: (a) that there is a just cause for the separation; and (b) that the party obtain the permission of the ordinary of the place to bring the matter to the civil court to obtain separate maintenance. If all of these conditions are fulfilled, the lawyer may licitly represent his client. If the client is seeking a real dissolution of a *valid* marriage in order to remarry, the lawyer cannot represent him or her. Neither could he take it because another lawyer will take the case anyway. The lawyer must be objective in dealing with his clients. Subjectivism has no place for the good lawyer. He must obey his own conscience, not that of his client.

V. Canonical Bases for Deferral of Marriage [1]

Anthony J. Bevilacqua

Two major problem areas:

1. Lack of faith commitment: Though baptized Catholics, couples at times seem to bring no spiritual dimension to the marriage. Frequently they are either grossly ignorant of Catholic teaching or have rejected important doctrines or hold them in contempt. Except for the absence of the religious dimension, they often possess sufficient psychological maturity to give otherwise adequate consent. Motives for their request for a Catholic marriage run the gamut from wanting to please parents or grandparents to a nostalgia for the interior artistic design of the church. Priests instinctively find it difficult to accept such couples as worthy candidates for Catholic marriage. Yet it is equally difficult for such priests to find and articulate the legal grounds for denying or deferring marriage in these instances.

2. Immaturity with consequent inability to fulfill the obligations of marriage: Priests frequently intuit that one or both prospective marriage partners are so immature that the prognosis for a lasting marriage is very poor. This intuition of the priests is one derived from the behavior, age, remarks, background, etc. of the couple, the product of the knowledge and experience of the priest, and can approach moral certitude. Usually this evaluation of the priest involves teenagers, though not limited to them. The blatant immaturity can or cannot be accompanied by lack of faith commitment. Though instinctively certain of the eventual failure of the marriage in such cases, the priest often cannot support with canonical authority his judgment to refuse or postpone the marriage.

Cautions

A. In prescribing and utilizing canonical bases for the denial or deferral of marriage, we must be aware that there are various tensions to be considered.

B. The tensions arise primarily from the following rights and interests which must be protected and balanced: Rights and interests of parties themselves, natural right of all to marry, interests of institution of marriage, rights and interests of the Church, rights and interests of society, and rights and interests of children either born or to be born.

C. The major tension seems to be between the natural right to marry and the preservation of the institution of marriage.

D. In all problems of deferral or refusal of marriage, the major concern should be pastoral not canonical. Opportunity should be used to instruct persons, retain pastoral contacts even in denials or postponements, explain reasons for the refusal or deferral.

E. A priest cannot canonically "forbid" marriages. He can declare that parties do not have a present right to marry.

F. Where dioceses have established marriage guidelines such as "Teenage Marriage Policies": Policies should provide some sort of recourse for parties if they feel that the decision of the priest is arbitrary, whimsical, capricious or unreasonable. Policies should not set down such absolute, rigid prohibitions that in effect they are establishing impediments or permanent barriers to marriage in contravention of C. 1038:2 and C. 1039, e.g., "No one under 18 can give valid consent." The purpose of policy should not be solely to prevent invalid marriages but it should provide the couple with reasonable opportunity to seek expert aid in achieving the required maturity and faith commitment.

G. Note that in most cases of possible deferral of marriage, the law prescribes that the bishop must be consulted before priest can make the decision.

Required Certitude of Freedom of Parties

A. Before a priest can officiate at a marriage, he must be certain that there are no legal obstacles to its valid and licit celebration. If there are reasonable doubts about either the valid or the licit celebration, then he cannot proceed until the doubts are removed. What degree of certitude for freedom must the priest acquire?

B. Authorities indicate that moral certitude is required: C. 1019: — "Before a marriage is celebrated it must be *certain* that nothing stands in the way of its valid and licit celebration."

a. Latin is "debet constare." "Constare" is generally used by tribunals to mean "moral certitude."
Instructions of S.C. Sacraments in 1921 and 1941 make it very clear that the freedom to marry must be established beyond all reasonable doubt. This is equivalent to reaching moral certitude.
Bouscaren-Ellis-Korth commenting on C. 1019:1: "Before a marriage is celebrated it must appear with *moral certainty* from a careful investigation, that there is no obstacle to its valid and licit celebration."

Canonical Bases

  A. General Canonical Bases—The legal grounds on which a marriage can be
deferred or denied fall generally into the following three areas: Impediments, religious instruction or commitment and consent. A few bases cannot
be fit into any of the above categories, such as C. 1034 on marriage of
minors; C 1067:2 on customary age.

  B. List of specific canonical bases with brief evaluation. This list will attempt to
give all the possible grounds even though some are tenuous and without
much force.

    1. Religious Instruction C. 1020:

    1. The pastor who has the right to assist at the marriage shall, a suitable
time beforehand, carefully investigate whether there is any obstacle to the
celebration of the marriage.

    2. He must ask the man and woman, even separately and cautiously,
whether they are under any impediment, whether they are giving their
consent freely, especially the woman, and whether they are sufficiently
instructed in Christian doctrine, unless in view of the quality of the
persons this last question should seem unnecessary.

    3. It is the province of the Ordinary of the place to lay down special rules
for this investigation by the pastor.

    According to this canon, a marriage can be deferred until the couple
receive sufficient instruction in Christian doctrine if the priest determines
such is needed. According to 3 of this same canon, the Ordinary can set
down regulations on the number and content of instructions. If parties
lack sufficient knowledge of Christian doctrine and refuse to take instructions, what can be done? This question was asked of the Code Commission on June 3, 1918:

Question: "If either of the parties to a prospective marriage be found ignorant of
Christian doctrine, should the priest refuse to marry them, or postpone the
marriage until he has instructed them?"

Reply: "The Pastor should observe the prescription of C. 1020:2, and while he does
what the Code prescribes, he should carefully teach the ignorant parties at least the
first elements of Christian doctrine. If, however, they refuse, he should not refuse
to marry them as is prescribed for other cases in C. 1066."

    This same policy is repeated in the Instruction of the S.C. Sacraments of June
29, 1941 (N° 8): "If he finds them ignorant of Christian doctrine, he must carefully
instruct them at least in its first elements; in case they refuse, however, there is no
reason for refusing to marry them, as is prescribed for other cases in Canon 1066."

Evaluation—This basis can frequently be used to delay a marriage for as long as the priest wants to give them sufficient instruction. If the couple happen to have knowledge of the Code Commission reply or happen to be defiant in this regard and refuse instructions, the basis loses all of its force in virtue of the 1918 reply and 1941 instruction.

2. *Reception of Confirmation*

C. 1021: 2. "Catholics who have not yet received the sacrament of confirmation should receive it before being married, if they can do so without grave inconvenience."

Evaluation—One does not ordinarily resort to this canon as a basis for deferral. However, it can be utilized if a priest is looking for a peg to hang on his postponement of marriage especially in cases where a person lacks a faith commitment or is inadequately instructed. The priest must determine according to the circumstances what constitutes "grave inconvenience."

3. *Instruction on Marriage*

C. 1033. "The pastor must not fail, with due regard to the condition of the persons concerned, to instruct the parties on the sanctity of the sacrament of matrimony, the mutual obligations of husband and wife, and the duties of parents toward their children; and he must earnestly exhort them to make a careful confession of their sins before the marriage, and to receive with devotion the Most Blessed Eucharist."

Evaluation—This would not be a very strong support for refusal or deferral. However, it can be used indirectly if the priest senses in the parties an ignorance of the responsibilities and nature of marriage. It can serve as a basis for delaying the marriage especially if the bishop, in virtue of C. 1020.3, has set down regulations on such instructions as part of the investigation.

4. *Minors*

C. 1034. "The pastor must seriously dissuade minor sons and daughters from contracting marriage without the knowledge or against the reasonable wishes of their parents; in case they refuse to obey, he should not assist at their marriage without having first consulted the Ordinary." Minors include both male and female under 21 years of age.

C. 1034 does not require consent of parents. It requires that they be aware of the marriage or that it not take place against their reasonable objections. Note the need for consultation with the Ordinary in the event they refuse to abide by the directives of the canon.

Evaluation—This canon could serve as a formidable basis for deferral of marriage until the age of 21 if the parents would cooperate. Unfortunately its strength is frequently depleted since, in spite of objectively good reasons against the marriage, the parents acquiesce in the wishes of the children to marry.

5. *Vetitum of Ordinary*

C. 1039:1—"Only Ordinaries of places can forbid marriage in a particular case, but only temporarily, for just cause, and as long as such cause continues, to all persons actually stopping in their territory, and to their subjects even outside their territory."

This canon can serve as one of the strongest supports for postponement of marriage since the required "just cause" covers a multitude of possibilities. The "just cause" includes all the other canonical bases for deferral such as possible presence of impediments, possible defect of consent, lack of knowledge of faith or marriage. But it is not limited to these grounds. The Ordinary may in accordance with the nature of his diocese consider other circumstances as a "just cause" for a temporary ban.

Waterhouse, in his thesis, enumerates "scandal" in the broad sense as a "just cause" within C. 1039. Thus it would include "notions of enmities, quarrels, and dissensions among the faithful, and even bewilderment, shock and wonderment when these are detrimental to the welfare of the Church." Waterhouse seems to be saying that the obligation of the Ordinary to seek the common good and preserve public order justifies him in individual circumstances to use C. 1039 to restrict the rights of certain individuals in regard to marriage.

Evaluation—One of the most formidable and inclusive bases if properly used.

6. *Attempted Marital Consent Before Non-Catholic Minister*

C. 1063:1. "Even though a dispensation from the impediment of mixed religion has been obtained from the Church, the parties may not, either before or after the celebration of the marriage before the Church, apply also, either in person or by proxy, to a non-Catholic minister in his religious capacity, in order to express or renew matrimonial consent."

C. 1063:2. "If the pastor knows for certain that the parties intend to violate or that they have violated this law, he must not assist at their marriage except for the gravest reasons, on condition that scandal be removed, and after consulting the Ordinary."

Evaluation—In mixed marriages, this can serve as a strong basis for delaying a marriage in Church should the priest judge this necessary. The strength of this basis can be seen in the three conditions set down for assisting at such a marriage: gravest reasons, removal of scandal, consultation of Ordinary. However, the force of the canon has waned in recent years because of the growing desire for "ecumenical marriages." Today marriage outside the Church before a non-Catholic minister is not seen in the same forbidden light as in yesteryear. Much less would there be opposition voiced against a second ceremony. Nevertheless, the canon still remains in force to be used when needed.

7. Notorious Abandonment of Faith; Members of Condemned Societies

C. 1065:1. "The faithful must also be deterred from contracting marriage with persons who have either notoriously abandoned the Catholic faith, even without having gone over to a non-Catholic sect, or have notoriously become members of societies which are condemned by the Church."

C. 1065:2. "The pastor must not assist at the above-mentioned marriages without having consulted the Ordinary, who may in view of all the circumstances of the case permit him to assist at the marriage, provided that there be a grave reason and the Ordinary judges that adequate measures have been taken to insure the Catholic education of all the children and the removal of danger of perversion from the other party."

There would not be too much call for use of this canon in the case of members of condemned societies.

It is not neglect in the practice of the Faith which is grounds for the prohibition of this canon. Rather it is a public profession by a person that he no longer considers himself a member of the Church or publicly and habitually derides or rejects Catholic teaching.

Evaluation—In the case of parties without a Faith commitment, this canon is a strong support for postponement of the marriage provided the definition of "notorious abandonment of the faith" is fulfilled. The severity of the prohibition can be gleaned from the conditions set down for assistance at the marriage: grave reasons, consultation and permission of Ordinary; guarantees for Catholic education of children; removal of danger of perversion.

8. Public Sinner; Notoriously Under Censure

C. 1066. "If a public sinner or one who is notoriously under censure refused to go to sacramental confession or to be reconciled to the Church before marriage, the pastor must not assist at his marriage unless there be a grave reason regarding which he should if possible consult the Ordinary."

Ordinarily, there would be little occasion to resort to this canon for anyone "notoriously under censure." Some canonists consider a public sinner one who is publicly known to have been away from the sacraments for years. Cappello, for example, lists among public sinners one who is publicly known not to have made his Easter duty.

Evaluation—A priest can use this canon to delay a marriage until the party reforms his way of life. At first sight, this canon seems to be a strong basis since it calls for a grave reason and consultation with the Ordinary before a priest can assist at the marriage. However, the effectiveness of the canon is diminished by the response of June 3, 1918 given above on the question of religious instruction. The reply states that if the parties refuse to take religious instructions, the pastor "should not refuse to marry them as *is prescribed for other cases in C. 1066.*"

9. Customary Age

C. 1067:2. "Although a marriage contracted after the aforesaid age is valid, yet pastors of souls should try to deter young people from marrying before the age at which, according to the received customs of the country, marriage is usually contracted." The first paragraph of C. 1067 states the age for validity, i.e., 16 for boys and 14 for girls.

Evaluation—The force of the canon itself is weak since it can only exhort pastors to "try to deter" young people. Teenage marriage guidelines in various dioceses have proved much more effective and acceptable.

10. Impediments

The impeding and diriment impediments are enumerated in Cs. 1058-1080. If there is certitude of the existence of an impediment, a priest cannot officiate at the marriage until the impediment is dispensed from or ceases. If there is reasonable suspicion of the presence of an impediment, a priest cannot officiate at the marriage until the investigation removes the suspicion.

Evaluation—All the force of law prevents the performance of a marriage when an impediment exists or is reasonably thought to exist.

11. Defect of Consent

—The following is an enumeration of various defects of consent, which if there is reasonable suspicion of their existence, would be a canonical basis for refusal or deferral of marriage.

a. *Amentia*—This would be a total lack of required consent. In effect, there would be no human act. The total absence of consent in amentia would stem either from a psychological or pathological ailment or from a temporary incapacity, such as intoxication. The present legislative articulation of the consent which is required for validity is contained in C. 1081:

1. "Marriage is effected by the consent of the parties lawfully expressed between persons who are capable according to law; and this consent no human power can supply."

2. "Matrimonial consent is an act of the will by which each party gives and accepts a perpetual and exclusive right over the body, for acts which are of themselves suitable for the generation of children."

b. Ignorance that marriage is a permanent society of man and woman for procreation of children.

C. 1082: 1. "In order that matrimonial consent may be possible it is necessary that the contracting parties be at least not ignorant that marriage is a permanent society between man and woman for the procreation of children."

2. "This ignorance is not presumed after puberty."

3. Exclusion of marriage itself, or of the right to the conjugal act, or of any of the essential properties of marriage.

C. 1086: 2. "But if either party or both parties by a positive act of the will exclude marriage itself, or all right to the conjugal act, or any essential property of marriage, the marriage contract is invalid."

c. Consent obtained through force or fear.

C. 1087: 1. "Likewise invalid is a marriage entered into through force or grave fear unjustly inspired from without, such that in order to escape from it a party is compelled to choose marriage."

2. "No other fear, even if it furnish the cause for the contract, entails the nullity of the marriage."

d. Lack of Due Discretion—

Involves a defective judgmental appreciation concerning the rights and obligations exchanged in marriage. Because of this judgmental impairment affecting consent, a party is incapable of marital consent.

e. Inability to fulfill the obligations of marriage:

Exclusion of right to community life. This category will be considered separately in the next section.

Fuller examination of the two major problem areas

A. Lack of Faith Commitment, Though Otherwise Mature

1. This is becoming more and more an occasion of frustration for parish priests. It is also injurious to the law which seems anachronistic in this problem. It is very difficult for priests to see how a couple, often without any comprehension of or regard for the Catholic Faith, can be said to be entering

Christian marriage and receiving the sacrament. If it were not for the fact of their baptism, they would be labeled pagans.

2. In these cases, priests instinctively feel that they should deny marriage, presuming all pastoral means were in vain. Yet they often feel a sense of guilt since they know the couple will marry invalidly outside the Church. They are more reluctant to give the couple a positive directive to marry before a civil official since they feel they would be cooperating in a sinful act and would be advocating trial marriage.

3. The problem has been largely complicated by two legislative norms: That all baptized Catholics are subject to the canonical form of marriage. For Catholics, either the marriage takes place before the Church, or it is invalid. This must not be construed to be a suggestion to abrogate the canonical form but merely a statement of reality.

Even more by C. 1012:2 which states: "Therefore it is impossible for a valid contract of marriage between baptized persons to exist without being by that very fact a sacrament." In other words the marriage between two baptized persons is automatically a sacrament even though the parties do not intend to receive the sacrament, even though they are indifferent to the sacrament, even though they are not even aware they are baptized. For baptized persons, the only condition seems to be that they do not positively exclude the sacrament.

How a marriage between baptized parties is automatically a sacrament becomes more difficult to comprehend when we recall our theology that to receive a sacrament one must have at least a virtual intention to receive the sacrament. The Church teaches that in infant baptism, the faith and intention of the parents and godparents supplies. But one may ask where is the requisite minimal intention for the sacrament of baptism in persons who do not even know that marriage is a sacrament and could not care less.

Some have suggested that the Church consider the possibility that marriages between baptized without a faith commitment be considered valid but not sacramental. In present legislation, this is not possible. In these cases of couples without faith commitment, it is often possible to delay the marriage on the basis of lack of knowledge of marriage, lack of religious instruction, public sinner prohibition of C. 1066, use of just cause vetitum of C. 1039:1. It may be even possible to deny the marriage because of a reasonable suspicion of the exclusion of one of the essential properties of marriage.

But in the long run, presuming all other requirements are present, it is difficult to see how one can refuse marriage to a couple solely on the lack of faith commitment. In virtue of the 1918 response and 1941 Instruction that a priest may not refuse marriage when a couple refused to take instructions in the teachings of the Faith, the Church does not seem to consider this a formidable obstacle to marriage. In this instance, the Church seems to favor the natural right to marry over the need for a faith commitment.

B. Immaturity which renders parties incapable of fulfilling obligations of marriage: Exclusion of right to community life.

1. *General Observations*: The experience of priests has underlined the widespread immaturity which exists among couples, especially teenagers, who want to be married. By their words, actions, attitudes, background, style of life and in many other ways, these parties reveal almost a certitude that they are incapable of carrying out the heavy obligations and responsibilities of life involved in marriage.

If a priest has a reasonable suspicion that a couple is so immature that they are incapable of fulfilling the obligations of marriage and therefore, incapable of giving and receiving the right to community of life which is an essential element of marital consent, then he has a legitimate basis to postpone the marriage. It should be emphasized that when the essential element of the right to community of life seems to be clearly lacking in the consent that a couple is required to make, the priest should provide the opportunity for the parties to receive expert counseling. In other words, the priest's main function is not to prevent marriage but to assist persons to become capable of happy and successful marriages.

When a couple requests marriage, it is not their burden to prove that they are capable of fulfilling the obligations of community of life in marriage. To refuse marriage in the case of this immaturity, the priest would have to see positive signs that they lack the minimal maturity needed for the responsibilities of community life. This is in conformity with the prescription of C. 1035 that: "All persons who are not prohibited by law can contract marriage."

2. Authority that marriage is a communion of life and that the right to this communion of life is an essential element of marital consent.

a. Vatican Council II

Gaudium et Spes, No. 48: "The *intimate partnership of married life and love* has been established by the Creator and qualified by His laws. It is rooted in the conjugal covenant of *irrevocable personal consent*" "... By their very nature, the institution of marriage itself and conjugal love are ordained for the procreation and education of children and find in them their ultimate crown."

Gaudium et Spes, No. 50: "Marriage to be sure is not instituted solely for procreation. Rather, its very nature as an *unbreakable compact between persons*, and the welfare of the children, both demand that the mutual love of the spouses, too, be embodied in a rightly ordered manner, that it grow and ripen. Therefore, *marriage persists as a whole manner and communion of life*, and maintains its value and indissolubility, even when offspring are lacking."

b. *Humanae Vitae*, No. 8:

"Marriage is not, then, the effect of chance or the product of evolution of unconscious natural forces; it is the wise institution of the Creator to realize in mankind His design of love. By means of the reciprocal personal gift of self, proper and exclusive to them, husband and wife tend towards *the communion of their beings* in view of mutual personal perfection, to collaborate with God in the generation and education of new lives."

c. *Pope Paul VI's Address to the Sacred Roman Rota* (February 9, 1976)

". . . marriage has become better known and understood in its *true nature as a community of love* . . ."

d. *Pope Paul's Address to the Equipes Notre-Dame* (September 26, 1976)

"Marriage—let us constantly recall—is a *communion founded on love* and made stable and definitive by an irrevocable covenant and commitment."

"Understood in this way, this interpersonal communion, widened by the birth of children, is a mark of God's love and goodness."

e. *Sacred Roman Rota Decisions*: Coram Anne, February 25, 1964

"The formal substantial object of matrimonial consent is not only the exclusive and perpetual bodily right to acts suitable for the generation of children but also embraces a right to a *community of life* which is properly called marriage together with its correlative obligations."

Coram Anne, July 22, 1969 (unpublished)

"Marriage consists in an *interpersonal relationship* underlying which there is a healthy orientation of two persons toward each other. If from the history of the common life, in the opinion of experts even before the marriage there was seriously lacking that necessary internal and interpersonal integrity, such a person must be considered incapable to undertake that *community of life* for the procreation and education of children, and incapable likewise, of judging and reasoning correctly, about instituting a *community of life* with another person. There is lacking that discretion of judgment which would be necessary for a valid judgment about marriage."

Coram Serrano, April 15, 1973: "Thus, one can understand that, in dealing with individual cases, to claim or to deny ability to marry, it is not enough to establish either the absence of any mental abnormality taken in its restricted sense or a lack of freedom, if these two are viewed in themselves in isolation from any *specific relationship to the other person* just as he must be accepted in marriage. For though the *intimate interpersonal relationship* depends on the powers mentioned, still the personality can be seriously disturbed precisely in that it ought to accept him as he is so that in some way he makes him master of himself in some matters. Thus, in no way is it impossible to imagine a person who not only sees marriage as a complexity of rights and duties which intrinsically carry an obligation, but obliged himself only objectively without any reference to his partner as a person with independent existence. In such a case, whether this happens consciously or not, I do not know whether there would arise a juridical 'bilateral personality' relationship: *it certainly would not be an interpersonal marriage covenant.*"

"Though it must be granted that the *interpersonal relationship* can reach greater or lesser perfection in different couples, yet in no way can it be said that this relationship completely belongs to the 'more perfect' or 'desirable' ideal marriage, since, in fact, according to what has been said, it *constitutes an essential property of any marriage consent. If this relationship is completely lacking, the consent itself is missing.*"

"Therefore, the question arises about the radical incapacity of people in whom one encounters all these personality disorders which, according to psychiatrists, are not so serious as to be classified as illnesses, and yet cause a psychopathic abnormality which can influence the very power which the subject should have to enter into an *interpersonal relationship* by which the rights of another over him and his rights over the other are correctly understood, deliberately pursued, and exchanged by mutual giving and accepting."

f. Draft of Proposed Code: C. 295 (revision of C. 1081)

1. "Marriage is effected by the consent of the parties lawfully expressed between persons who are capable according to law; and this consent no human power can supply."

2. "Matrimonial consent is an act of the will by which a man and a woman, by means of a mutual covenant constitute with one another a *communion of conjugal life* which is perpetual and exclusive and which by its very nature is ordered to the procreation and education of children." C. 303:2 (revision of C. 1086:2)

"But if either party or both parties by a positive act of the will exclude marriage itself or the *right to the community of life*, or the right to the conjugal act, or any essential property of marriage, the marriage is invalid."

3. Some argue that the "right to community of life" may be an essential element of marital consent in the new code, but it is not yet the law and therefore cannot be considered part of marital consent until the new code goes into effect. The answer to this lies in the fact that community of life as a constitutive element of marital consent is not a creation of ecclesiastical law but a product of the natural law. There are many authorities to corroborate this conclusion but the following Rotal decision is reflective of the accepted

position that even now a marriage would be invalid if the parties were incapable of giving and accepting the right to communion of life.

Coram Fagiolo, January 23, 1970: "There are some today who think that there should be included explicitly in the new code a new matrimonial impediment which should be called moral impotency. This new impediment would declare as incapable of contracting marriage one who suffers from a mental debility such that he is not capable of assuming the burdens and responsibilities of marriage."

"*Whatever the status of the new code, it can no longer be doubted that anyone who is incapable of assuming the essential burdens of marriage is likewise incapable of contracting marriage, and the basis for this is the natural law itself* . . . This capacity is not only that which is spelled out in positive law but primarily is that which the natural law determines. According to this natural law, those parties are certainly incapable of marriage who are not capable of perceiving, accepting and giving the right to that intimate community of life which by its very nature is ordained to the procreation of children and which is correctly termed matrimony."

"We do not have to wait for a new and explicit statute of the Code since we already know from our traditional principles and from our jurisprudence that all habitual mental defects and mental disturbances can cause serious defects in the use of reason which can relate to defects of consent or to lack of discretionary judgment . . . Among the defects of consent can be included all classes of inability to assume the essential burdens of marriage."

"In weighing the evidence of the exclusion of the bonum prolis, the judge should not waste time solely on the statements of the parties and witnesses concerning the words spoken by the one who simulated if it is seen that the exclusion stemmed from some incapacity of the party to assume the essential burdens, such as the duty of intimate community of life which is ordered to the procreation of children."

---

1. The canons cited throughout this article refer to the 1917 Code.

VI. Documents of the Holy See

The Second Vatican Council is an historical event of major proportions and several years have elapsed since it was completed. A special Synod was celebrated from November 24 to December 8, 1985 to commemorate its twentieth anniversary. In the interim between the Council and the promulgation of a new Code of Canon Law, laws and directives have been promulgated as need required via Decrees, *Motu Proprios*, Instructions, etc. Because the proposed new Code of Canon Law was found inadequate by members of the hierarchy, canonists and others, it was suggested that the new law be tested in the manner of a *Motu Proprio* whereby the laws would prove their worth or be abrogated. For example, the Norms of Procedure for the United States of 1970 were issued in such a manner and have proven to be very successful in justice and for the salvation of souls. This, however, was not done.

Included in this part of the Appendices are various important documents from the Holy See which respond to many of the questions that arose during this time. Many of the norms outlined in these documents have been incorporated into the new Code of 1983 which was promulgated on January 25 of that year. Many of these *Motu Proprios* originated through requests from various countries who were seeking authoritative interpretations and adjudications with respect to special circumstances existing in those countries. The Holy See decided it was necessary to standardize these laws. One such law was that on procedure. Thus came about in 1971 a special document, the *Motu Proprio, Causas Matrimoniales* for the entire world. Variations from this procedure were allowed for the United States and Canada (Norms 1970). Both of these documents will be found in these appendices. The Holy See also standardized the procedure on non-consummation cases on March 7, 1972.

Besides these, a special Instruction was issued by the Holy See for natural bond petitions. About 1968, the Sacred Congregation of the Doctrine of the Faith began examining the procedures being used which examination created a doubt as to whether the Holy Father even had the power to grant such favors. For example, a Catholic party who was married to a non-baptized party with a dispensation from disparity of cult, after a dissolution of this natural bond, now wanted to marry another unbaptized person. This meant the Catholic party was entering into a series of dissoluble unions. This procedure was suspended and a special commission of theologians was established to study the matter. On December 6, 1973, the same Congregation issued an Instruction on the proper procedure now required for natural bond cases. This document is also to be found in the Appendices. The most important documents relating to marriage are incorporated here for the convenience of the reader.

Document I

Special Faculties & Privileges to Local Ordinaries

The Motu Proprio, *Pastorale Munus* of Pope Paul VI, given December 3, 1963 grants special faculties and privileges to all local ordinaries on a permanent basis.

The bishops, though hindered by many obstacles, have nonetheless given an example of special charity in all times and dedicated themselves to the pastoral office to which Jesus Christ assigned the very important task of teaching, of leading to holiness, of binding and loosing.

With the increase through the centuries of the Church's concerns and labors, the Apostolic See has always replied promptly and eagerly to the requests of the bishops regarding pastoral care and not only has it added to the extraordinary authority and jurisdiction of the heads of dioceses but also endowed them with singular faculties and privileges which appropriately met current needs.

Now, moreover, while the second session of the Second Vatican Ecumenical Council approaches its end and since we wish nothing more dearly than to express to the council Fathers the very great esteem we have for all the venerable brothers in the episcopacy, it seemed good to us to accept their requests willingly and grant them things which may place their episcopal dignity in the proper light and at the same time render their pastoral function freer and more effective. We think this is very fitting to our office as universal Shepherd. In bestowing these things most willingly on the bishops, we at the same time request that they all, moved by the breadth of flaming charity and joined closely with Christ and with us, His vicar on earth, should seek through their collaboration to lighten *that care for all the churches* (cf. 2 Cor 11:28) which weighs upon our shoulders.

Since it is a matter of faculties of the utmost importance, we grant them in such a way that they cannot be delegated by the bishops except to a coadjutor, auxiliaries and vicar general, unless expressly noted in the concession of an individual faculty.

According to the prevailing norm of law, however, such faculties, which we declare belong by law to residential bishops, also belong by law to vicars and prefects apostolic, permanent apostolic administrators, abbots and prelates *nullius*, who in their territory enjoy the same rights and faculties that residential bishops have in their own dioceses, and although vicar general, they nevertheless can legitimately delegate to their vicar delegate the faculties treated here.

Having maturely considered everything from our reverence and charity toward each bishop of the Catholic Church, of our own initiative (motu proprio) and by our apostolic authority we decree and establish that from the eighth of December of this year 1963, the bishops may immediately and legitimately use and enjoy the following faculties and privileges:

I. *Faculties* which by right belong to a residential bishop from the moment that he takes canonical possession of the diocese. Unless it is expressly stated in the faculties, he may not delegate them to others except to coadjutor and auxiliary bishops and a vicar general.

1. Proroguing for a just cause, but not beyond a month, the lawful use of rescripts or indults which were granted by the Holy See and have expired, without a request for their renewal having been sent at the proper time to the Holy See. There is an obligation to apply at once to the Holy See for the favor, or to seek a reply if the petition has already been submitted.

2. Permitting priests, because of scarcity of clergy and for a just cause, to celebrate Mass twice on weekdays, and even three times on Sundays and Holy Days of obligation, provided genuine pastoral necessities so demand.

3. Permitting priests, when celebrating two or three Masses, to take liquids even though there be not an interval of an hour before the next Mass.

4. Permitting priests, for a just cause, to celebrate Mass at any hour of the day and to distribute Communion in the evening, with due observance of the other prescriptions of law.

5. Granting the faculty to priests who suffer from poor eyesight or are afflicted with some other infirmity, to offer daily the votive Mass of the Blessed Virgin or the Mass of the dead with the assistance, according to their needs, of a priest or deacon and with due observance of the Instruction of the Sacred Congregation of Rites of April 15, 1961.

6. Granting the same permission to priests who are totally blind provided they are always assisted by another priest or deacon.

7. Granting priests the faculty to celebrate Mass outside a sacred place, but in a reputable and decent place, never in a bedroom, on an altar stone: in an individual case for a just cause but habitually only for a graver cause.

8. Granting also the faculty to celebrate Mass for a just cause at sea and on rivers, with observance of the required precautions.

9. Granting the faculty to priests, who enjoy the privilege of the portable altar, that, for a just and grave cause, they may use instead of an altar stone, the Greek antimension, or the cloth blessed by the bishop, in the right corner of

which are placed relics of the holy martyrs authenticated by the bishop, with due observance of other requirements of the rubrics, particularly regarding altar cloths and the corporal.

10. Granting to infirm or elderly priests the faculty of celebrating Mass at home, but not in a bedroom, daily and even on the more solemn feasts, observing the liturgical laws, but with the permission of sitting if they are unable to stand.

11. Reducing because of a decrease in income, as long as the cause obtains, Masses from a legacy (which per se remain fixed) at the rate of the stipend lawfully in effect in the diocese, provided that there is none who is obliged and can rightfully be expected to increase the stipend; likewise, of reducing the obligations or legacies of Masses which burden benefices or other ecclesiastical institutes, if the income of the benefice or institute becomes insufficient for the suitable sustenance of the beneficiary and for fulfilling the works of the sacred ministry attached to the benefice or for attaining in a fitting manner the proper end of the ecclesiastical institute.

12. Granting the chaplains of all hospitals, orphanages and prisons the faculty, in the absence of the pastor, to administer the sacrament of Confirmation to the faithful in danger of death, with due observance of the norms of the Sacred Congregation of the Discipline of the Sacraments established by the decree, "Spiritus Sancti munera" of September 14, 1946, for priests administering the sacrament of Confirmation.

13. Granting to confessors the faculty, in individual cases, of absolving any of the faithful in the act of sacramental confession from all reserved sins, with the exception however of the sin of false denunciation in which an innocent priest is accused of the crime of solicitation before ecclesiastical judges.

14. Granting confessors distinguished for knowledge and prudence the faculty, in individual cases, of absolving any of the faithful in the act of sacramental confession from all censures even reserved, with the following exceptions: (a) "ab homine" censures; (b) censures reserved in a most special way to the Holy See; (c) censures which are attached to disclosure of the secret of the Holy Office; (d) the excommunication incurred by clerics in sacred orders and all presuming to contract marriage with them, even only civilly, and actually living together.

15. Dispensing for a just cause from the defect of age for ordination provided that it does not exceed six full months.

16. Dispensing from the impediment to orders by which the sons of non-Catholics are bound as long as the parents remain in error.

17. Dispensing those already ordained, for the purposes both of celebrating Mass and obtaining and retaining ecclesiastical benefices, from any of the irregularities, whether ex dilicto or ex defectu, provided that scandal does not arise

thereby and provided that the ministry of the altar is correctly performed, with the exception of those mentioned in Canon 985:3 and 4 of the Code of Canon Law. In the case of the crime of heresy or schism, there must be a prior abjuration in the hands of the one absolving.

18. Conferring sacred orders outside the cathedral church and "extra tempora," including weekdays, if this is useful from a pastoral point of view.

19. Dispensing for a just and reasonable cause from all the minor matrimonial impediments, even if there is question of mixed marriages, but with observance in this latter case of the prescriptions of Canons 1061-1064 of the Code of Canon Law.[1]

20. Dispensing when a just and grave cause urges, from the impediments of mixed religion and disparity of worship, even in the case of use of the Pauline Privilege, with observance of the prescriptions of Canons 1061-1064 of the Code of Canon Law.

21. "Sanandi in radice," provided the consent perdures, marriages that are invalid because of a minor impediment or defect of form, even if there is a question of mixed marriages, but in this case there must be observance of Canon 1061 of the Code of Canon Law.

22. "Sanandi in radice," provided consent perdures, marriages that are invalid because of the impediment of disparity of worship, even if they are also invalid because of a defect of form, with observance of prescriptions of Canon 1061 of the Code of Canon Law.[2]

23. Permitting for a grave cause, that the interpellation of an infidel spouse may be done before the baptism of the party who is being converted to the faith; and dispensing, also for a grave cause, from the same interpellation before the baptism of the party who is being converted: provided, in this case that it is clear from a summary and extra-judicial process that the interpellation cannot be made or it would be useless.

24. Reducing, for a just cause, the obligation by which cathedral chapters and colleges of canons are obliged to perform ritually the daily Divine Office in Choir, by granting that choral service may be satisfied either only on certain days or merely by a certain determined part.

25. Entrusting where necessary, certain canons with the tasks of the sacred ministry, of teaching or of the apostolate, with a dispensation from choir, while preserving the right of receiving the fruits of the prebend, but not the distributions, whether *inter praesentes*, as they are called, or daily.

26. Commuting for reason of weak eyesight or other cause, as long as the condition persists, the Divine Office into daily recitation of at least a third part of the Rosary of the Blessed Virgin Mary or other prayers.

27. Deputing in particular cases, or for a time, the vicar general or another priest

with ecclesiastical dignity, to consecrate portable altars, chalices and patens, according to the rite prescribed in the Pontifical and using the Holy Oils blessed by the bishop.

28. Allowing minor clerics, lay Religious and also pious women to wash with the first ablution, palls, corporals and purificators.

29. Using the faculties and privileges, while observing their extent and intent, which religious communities having a house in the diocese enjoy for the good of the faithful.

30. Granting to priests the faculty by which, with the rites prescribed by the Church, they may erect the Stations of the Cross, even in the open air, with all the indulgences that have been granted to those who make this pious exercise. The faculty cannot be exercised in parochial territory where there is a house of religious who by apostolic grant enjoy the privilege of erecting the Stations of the Cross.

31. Admitting illegitimate sons into the seminary if they show the qualities required for admission into the seminary, provided it is not a question of offspring of an adulterous or sacrilegious union.

32. Granting permission that, for a legitimate cause, ecclesiastical goods may be alienated, pledged, mortgaged, leased, redeemed from a long-term lease, and that ecclesiastical moral persons may contract on indebtedness to an amount proposed by the national or regional conference of bishops and approved by the Holy See.

33. Confirming even to a fifth triennium the ordinary confessor of Religious women if another provision cannot be made because of the scarcity of priests suitable for this office, or if the majority of the Religious, even those who in other matters do have the right to vote, agree in secret ballot to the confirmation of the same confessor. Another provision must be made for those who disagree, if they so desire.

34. Entering, for a just cause, into a pontifical cloister of monasteries of nuns situated in his diocese, and permitting for a just and grave cause, that others be admitted into the cloister, and that the nuns go out from it, for a truly necessary period of time.

35. Dispensing, on the petition of the competent superior, from the impediments which prevent those who have adhered to a non-Catholic sect from being admitted into Religion.

36. Dispensing, on the petition of the competent superior, from illegitimacy of birth, those to be admitted into Religion who are destined for the priesthood, and also others who are forbidden admission into Religion by a prescription of the Constitutions. In neither case can adulterous or sacrilegious offspring be dispensed.

37. Waiving in whole or in part, on the petition of the competent superior, the dowry which postulants should bring to be admitted to a monastery of nuns or another religious community, even of pontifical right.
38. Permitting religious to transfer from one to another community of diocesan right.
39. Dismissing from the diocese, in the presence of a most serious cause, individual Religious, if their major superior has been warned and has failed to provide; moreover, the matter is to be referred immediately to the Holy See.
40. Granting, also through other prudent and capable men, to the individual faithful subject to himself, the permission to read and retain, with care however less they fall into the hands of others, prohibited books and periodicals, not excepting those which purposely defend heresy or schism, or attempt to overturn the very foundations of religion. However, this permission can be granted only to those who need to read the forbidden books and periodicals either to attack them, or to meet properly their own obligations or to follow lawfully a course of studies.

II. *Privileges*, which besides those enumerated in their titles in the Code of Canon Law, belong to all bishops, residential or titular, as soon as they have received the authentic notification of canonical election.

1. Preaching the word of God—everywhere in the world, unless the Ordinary of the place expressly denies it.
2. Hearing the confessions of the faithful and of Religious women anywhere in the world, unless the Ordinary of the place expressly denies it.
3. Absolving any of the faithful anywhere in the act of sacramental confession, from all reserved sins, except however the sin of false denunciation in which an innocent priest is accused of the crime of solicitation before ecclesiastical judges.
4. Absolving any of the faithful anywhere in the act of sacramental confession from all censures, even reserved, except however: (a) censures "ab homine"; (b) censures reserved in a most special way to the Holy See; (c) censures which are attached to disclosure of the secret of the Holy Office; (d) the excommunication incurred by clerics in sacred orders and all presuming to contract marriage with them, even only civilly, and actually living together. Residential bishops can also use this faculty for their subjects in the external forum.
5. Reserving the Blessed Sacrament in their private oratory provided that the prescriptions of the liturgical laws are fully observed.
6. Celebrating Mass at any hour of the day, for a serious reason, and distributing Holy Communion even in the evening, observing all norms enjoined.
7. Blessing anywhere by a single sign of the Cross, with all the indulgences usually

granted by the Holy See, rosaries and other beads used for prayers, crosses, medals, scapulars approved by the Holy See and imposing them without the obligation of inscription.

8. Blessing for the faithful, who because of infirmity or other lawful impediments cannot visit the sacred Stations of the Cross, images of the Crucified with an application of all the indulgences attached by the Roman Pontiffs to the devout exercise of the Way of the Cross.

We with pleasure grant these faculties and privileges to Our Brothers in the Episcopacy with the intention and purpose we have noted above: that all these may particularly be for the glory and advantage of the Church of Christ to whom We and Ours are indebted for all things.

Notwithstanding anything to the contrary, even worthy of special mention.
Given at Rome, at St. Peter's on November 30, 1963.

PAUL PP. VI

1. Cf. C. 1063, New Decree on Mixed Marriage.
2. Cf. C. 1063.

Document II

NORMS FOR MIXED MARRIAGES
Matrimonia Mixta
Apostolic Letter Issued "Motu Proprio"
Determining Norms For Mixed Marriages
Pope Paul VI

Mixed marriages, that is to say marriages in which one party is Catholic and the other is non-Catholic, whether baptized or not, have always been given careful attention by the Church in pursuance of her duty. Today the Church is constrained to give even greater attention to them, owing to the conditions of present times. In the past Catholics were separated from members of other Christian confessions and from non-Christians, by their situation in their community or even by physical boundaries. In more recent times, however, not only has this separation been reduced, but communication between men of different regions and religions has greatly developed, and as a result there has been a great increase in the number of mixed marriages. Also a great influence in this regard has been exercised by the growth and spread of civilization and industry, urbanization and consequent rural depopulation, migrations in great numbers and the increase of exiles of every kind.

The Church is indeed aware that mixed marriages, precisely because they admit differences of religion and are a consequence of the division among Christians, do not, except in some cases, help in re-establishing unity among Christians. There are many difficulties inherent in a mixed marriage, since a certain division is introduced into the living cell of the Church, as the Christian family is rightly called, and in the family itself the fulfillment of the gospel teachings is more difficult because of diversities in matters of religion, especially with regard to those matters which concern Christian worship and the education of the children.

For these reasons the Church, conscious of her duty, discourages the contracting of mixed marriages, for she is most desirous that Catholics be able in matrimony to attain to perfect union of mind and full communion of life. However, since man has the natural right to marry and beget children, the Church, by her laws, which clearly show her pastoral concern, makes such arrangements that on the one hand the principles of Divine Law be scrupulously observed and that on the other the said right to contract marriage be respected.

The Church vigilantly concerns itself with the education of the young and their fitness to undertake their duties with a sense of responsibility and to perform their obligations as members of the Church, and she shows this both in preparing for marriage those who intend to contract a mixed marriage and in caring for those who have already contracted such a marriage. Although in the case of baptized persons of different religious confessions, there is less risk of religious indifferentism, it can be more easily avoided if both husband and wife have a sound knowledge of the Christian nature of marital partnership, and if they are properly helped by their respective Church authorities. Even difficulties arising in marriage between a Catholic and an unbaptized person can be overcome through pastoral watchfulness and skill.

Neither in doctrine nor in law does the Church place on the same level a marriage between a Catholic and a baptized non-Catholic, and one between a Catholic and an unbaptized person; for, as the Second Vatican Council declared, men, who, though they are not Catholics "believe in Christ and have been properly baptized are brought into a certain, though imperfect, communion with the Catholic Church."[1] Moreover, although Eastern Christians who have been baptized outside the Catholic Church are separated from communion with us, they possess true sacraments, above all the Priesthood and the Eucharist, whereby they are joined to us in a very close relationship.[2] Undoubtedly there exists in a marriage between baptized persons, since such a marriage is a true sacrament, a certain communion of spiritual benefits which is lacking in a marriage entered into by a baptized person and one who is not baptized.

Nevertheless, one cannot ignore the difficulties inherent even in mixed marriages between baptized persons. There is often a difference of opinion on the sacramental nature of matrimony, on the special significance of marriage celebrated within the Church, on the interpretation of certain moral principles pertaining to marriage and the family, on the extent to which obedience is due to the Catholic Church, and on the competence that belongs to ecclesiastical authority. From this it is clear that difficult questions of this kind can only be fully resolved when Christian unity is restored.

The faithful must therefore be taught that, although the Church somewhat relaxes ecclesiastical discipline in particular cases, she can never remove the obligation of the Catholic party, which, by divine law, namely by the plan of salvation instituted through Christ, is imposed according to the various situations.

The faithful should therefore be reminded that the Catholic party to a marriage has the duty of preserving his or her own faith; nor is it ever permitted to expose oneself to a proximate danger of losing it.

Furthermore, the Catholic partner in a mixed marriage is obliged, not only to remain steadfast in the faith, but also, as far as possible, to see to it that the children be baptized and brought up in that same faith and receive all those aids to eternal salvation which the Catholic Church provides for her sons and daughters.

The problem of the children's education is a particularly difficult one, in view of the fact that both husband and wife are bound by that responsibility and may by no means ignore it or any of the obligations connected with it. However the Church endeavors to meet this problem, just as she does the others, by her legislation and pastoral care.

With all this in mind, no one will be really surprised to find that even the canonical discipline on mixed marriages cannot be uniform and that it must be adapted to the various cases in what pertains to the juridical form of contracting marriage, its liturgical celebration, and, finally the pastoral care to be given to the married people, and the children of the marriage, according to the distinct circumstances of the married couple and the differing degrees of their ecclesiastical communion.

It was altogether fitting that so important a question should receive the attention of the Second Vatican Council. This occurred several times as occasion arose. Indeed, in the third session the Council Fathers voted to entrust the question to us in its entirety.

To meet their desire, the Sacred Congregation for the Doctrine of the Faith, on the 18th of March, 1966, promulgated an Instruction on mixed marriages, entitled *Matrimonii Sacramentum*,[3] which provided that, if the norms laid down therein stood the test of experience, they should be introduced in a definite and precise form into the Code of Canon Law which is now being revised.[4]

When certain questions on mixed marriages were raised in the first General Meeting of the Synod of Bishops, held in October 1965 [5] and many useful observations had been made upon them by the Fathers, we decided to submit those questions to examination by a special commission of Cardinals which after diligent consideration, presented us with its conclusions.

At the outset we state that Eastern Catholics contracting marriage with baptized non-Catholics or with unbaptized persons are not subject to the norms established by this Letter. With regard to the marriage of Catholics of whatsoever rite with Eastern non-Catholic Christians, the Church has recently issued certain norms,[6] which we wish to remain in force.

Accordingly, in order that ecclesiastical discipline on mixed marriages be more perfectly formulated and that, without violating divine law, canonical law should have regard for the differing circumstances of married couples, in accordance with the mind of the Second Vatican Council expressed especially in the Decree *Unitatis Redintegratio*[7] and in the Declaration *Dignitatis Humanae*,[8] and also in careful consideration of the wishes expressed in the Synod of Bishops, we, by our own authority, and after mature deliberation, establish and decree the following norms:

1. A marriage between two baptized persons, of whom one is Catholic, while the other is a non-Catholic, may not licitly be contracted without the previous dispensation of the local Ordinary, since such a marriage is by its nature an obstacle to the full spiritual communion of the married parties.

2. A marriage between two persons, of whom one has been baptized in the Catholic Church or received into it, while the other is unbaptized, entered into without previous dispensation by the local Ordinary, is invalid.

3. The Church, taking into account the nature and circumstances of times, places and persons, is prepared to dispense from both impediments provided there is a just cause.

4. To obtain from the local Ordinary dispensation from an impediment, the Catholic party shall declare that he is ready to remove dangers of falling away from the faith. He is also gravely bound to make a sincere promise to do all in his power to have all the children baptized and brought up in the Catholic Church.

5. At an opportune time the non-Catholic party must be informed of these promises which the Catholic party has to make, so that it is clear that he is cognizant of the promise and obligation on the part of the Catholic.

6. Both parties are to be clearly instructed on the ends and essential properties of marriage, not to be excluded by either party.

7. Within its own territorial competence, it is for the Bishops' Conference to determine the way in which these declarations and promises, which are always required, shall be made; whether by word of mouth alone, in writing, or before witnesses; and also to determine what proof of them there should be in the external forum and how they are to be brought to the knowledge of the non-Catholic party, as well as to lay down whatever other requirements may be opportune.

8. The canonical form is to be used for contracting mixed marriages, and is required for validity, without prejudice, however, to the provisions of the

Decree *Crescens Matrimoniorum* published by the Sacred Congregation for the Eastern Churches on 22nd February, 1967.[9]

9. If serious difficulties stand in the way of observing the canonical form, local Ordinaries have the right to dispense from the canonical form in any mixed marriage; but the Bishops' Conference is to determine norms according to which the said dispensation may be granted licitly and uniformly within the region or territory of the Conference, with the provision that there should always be some public form of ceremony.

10. Arrangements must be made that all validly contracted marriages be diligently entered in the books prescribed by canon law. Priests responsible should make sure that non-Catholic ministers also assist in recording in their own books the fact of a marriage with a Catholic.

    Episcopal Conferences are to issue regulations determining, for their region or territory, a uniform method by which a marriage that has been publicly contracted after a dispensation from the canonical form was obtained, is registered in the book prescribed by canon law.

11. With regard to the liturgical form of the celebration of a mixed marriage, if it is to be taken from the Roman Ritual, use must be made of the ceremonies in the *Rite of Celebration of Marriage* promulgated by our authority, whether it is a question of marriage between a Catholic and a baptized non-Catholic (39-54) or of a marriage between a Catholic and an unbaptized person (55-66). If, however, the circumstances justify it, a marriage between a Catholic and a baptized non-Catholic can be celebrated, subject to the local Ordinary's consent, according to the rites for the celebration of marriage within the Mass (19-38), while respecting the prescription of general law with regard to Eucharistic Communion.

12. The Episcopal Conferences shall inform the Apostolic See of all decisions which, within their competence, they make concerning mixed marriages.

13. The celebration of marriage before a Catholic priest or deacon and a non-Catholic minister, performing their respective rites together, is forbidden; nor is it permitted to have another religious marriage ceremony before or after the Catholic ceremony, for the purpose of giving or renewing matrimonial consent.

14. Local Ordinaries and parish priests shall see to it that the Catholic husband or wife and the children born of a mixed marriage do not lack spiritual assistance in fulfilling their duties of conscience. They shall encourage the Catholic husband or wife to keep ever in mind the divine gift of the Catholic faith and to bear witness to it with gentleness and reverence, and with a clear conscience.[10] They are to aid the married couple to foster the unity of their conjugal and family life, a unity which, in the case of Christians, is based on their baptism

too. To these ends it is to be desired that those pastors should establish relationships of sincere openness and enlightened confidence with ministers of other religious communities.

15. The penalties decreed by Canon 2319 of the Code of Canon Law are all abrogated. For those who have incurred them the effects of those penalties cease, without prejudice to the obligations mentioned in number 4 of these norms.

16. The local Ordinary is able to give a *sanatio in radice* of a mixed marriage when the conditions spoken of in numbers 4 and 5 of these norms have been fulfilled, and provided that the conditions of law are observed.

17. In the case of a particular difficulty or doubt with regard to the application of these norms, recourse is to be made to the Holy See.

We order that what we have decreed in this Letter, given in the form of "Motu Proprio," be regarded as established and ratified, notwithstanding any measure to the contrary, and is to take effect from the first day of October of this year.

Given at Rome, at St. Peter's, March 31, 1970.

PAULUS PP. VI

1. Decree on Ecumenism, *Unitatis Redintegratio*, 3, AAS 57, 1965, p. 93; Cf. Dogmatic Constitution on the Church, *Lumen Gentium*, AAS 57, 1965, pp. 19-20.
2. Cf. *Decree on Ecumenism*, pp. 13-18, pp. 100-104.
3. Cf. AAS 58, 1966, pp. 235-239.
4. Cf. *ibid.*, p. 237.
5. Cf. *Argumenta de quibus disceptabitur in primo generali coetu Synodi Episcoporum, pars altera. Typis Polyglottis Vaticanis*, 1967, pp. 27-37.
6. Cf. Decree on Eastern Catholic Churches *Orientalium Ecclesiarum*, 18, AAS 57, 1965, p. 82; Sacred Congregation for the Eastern Churches: Decree *Crescens Matrimoniorum*, AAS 59, 1967, pp. 165-166.
7. AAS 57, 1965, pp. 90-112.
8. AAS 58, 1966, pp. 929-946.
9. AAS 59, 1967, p. 166.
10. 1 P 3:16.

Document III
Norms for Mixed Marriages in USA (Private)

The following "statement of the National Conference of Catholic Bishops on the implementation of the apostolic letter on mixed marriages" in the United States of America was issued on 16 November, 1970 and given the effective date of 1 January 1971.

Introductory Principles

The Fathers of the Second Vatican Council requested the Holy See to provide for the application of conciliar teaching to marriages which unite Catholics and those of differing religious convictions. Following discussions of this matter by the Synod of Bishops in 1967, the Holy See, after collegial consultation with the episcopal conferences, prepared a response to that request. And on March 31, 1970 Pope Paul VI issued *motu proprio* the Apostolic Letter Determining Norms for Mixed Marriages. The provisions of this apostolic letter, effective October 1, 1970, open the way to an improved pastoral approach in support of couples united or to be united in such marriages.

The National Conference of Catholic Bishops welcomes the apostolic letter and encourages its ready application within our country. We call to mind the principles upon which it is based and the values it seeks to uphold. Our statement is to be understood only with a view to the complete text of the *motu proprio*.

First of all, the apostolic letter recognizes the natural right of man to marry and beget children, and to exercise this right, free from undue pressure (cf. *Pacem in Terris*, no. 15).

Within marriage the Church seeks always to uphold the strength and stability of marital union and the family which flows from it. For "the well-being of the individual person and of human and Christian society is intimately linked with the healthy condition of that community produced by marriage and family. Hence Christians and all men who hold this community in high esteem sincerely rejoice in the various ways by which men today find help in fostering this community of life and perfecting its life, and by which spouses and parents are assisted in their lofty calling." (*The Church in the Modern World*, no. 47).

As the apostolic letter observes, the "perfect union of mind and full communion of life" to which married couples aspire can be more readily achieved when both partners share the same Catholic belief and life. For this reason, the Church greatly desires that Catholics marry Catholics and generally discourages mixed marriages.

Yet, recognizing that mixed marriages do occur, the Church, upholding the principles of Divine Law, makes special arrangements for them. And recognizing that these marriages do at times encounter special difficulties, the Church wishes to see that special help and support are extended to the couples concerned. This is the abiding responsibility of all. For "Christians should actively promote the values of marriage and family, both by example of their own lives and by cooperation with other men of good will. Thus when difficulties arise, Christians will provide, on behalf of family life, those necessities and helps which are suitably modern" (*Ibid.*, no. 52).

In a particular way, priests with a pastoral ministry to families and all persons engaged in the family life apostolate are to be commended for their attention to the specific needs of individual couples. Since these will vary, the apostolic letter stresses the importance of individualized support for diverse situations. It recognizes that ". . . the canonical discipline on mixed marriages cannot be uniform and must be adapted . . ." and "the pastoral care to be given to the married people and children of marriage" must also be adapted "according to the distinct circumstances of the married couple and the differing degrees of their ecclesiastical communion." Consequently, pastors, in exercising their ministry in behalf of marriages that unite Catholics and others will do so with zealous concern and respect for the couples involved. They should have an active and positive regard for the holy state in which the couples are united.

In such marriages, the conscientious devotion of the Catholic to the Catholic Church is to be safeguarded, and the conscience of the other partner is to be respected. This is in keeping with the principle of religious liberty (cf. *Declaration on Religious Freedom*, no. 3).

In all valid marriages the Church recognizes sacred and abiding values. For "the intimate partnership of married life and love has been established by the Creator and qualified by His laws. It is rooted in the conjugal covenant of irrevocable personal consent. Hence by that human act whereby spouses mutually bestow and accept each other, a relationship arises which by divine will and in the eyes of society too is a lasting one. For the good of the spouses and their offspring as well as of society, the existence of this sacred bond no longer depends on human decisions alone" (*The Church in the Modern World*, no. 48). So the sacred character of all valid marriages, including those which the Church does not consider as sacramental, is recognized. For those, too, manifest the hand of God, Who is the author of marriage, and should lead the couple to holiness of life. In preparing couples for mixed marriages, pastors should make clear to the partners the deep significance which the Church perceives in their intended union as "two in one flesh" (Mt 19:16).

In this regard, the broad areas of agreement which unite Christians and Jews in their appreciation of the religious character of marriage should be kept significantly in mind (cf. *Joint Statement on Marriage and Family Life in the United States*, issued by the United States Catholic Conference, the National Council of the Churches of

Christ, and the Synagogue Council of America, June 8, 1966).

In this context, it should be clearly noted that while Catholics are required to observe the Catholic form of marriage for validity, unless dispensed by their Bishop, the Catholic Church recognizes the reality of marriages contracted validly among those who are not Christians and among those Christians separated from us.

In addition to the sacred character of all valid marriages still more must be said of marriages between a Catholic and another baptized Christian. According to our Catholic tradition, we believe such marriages to be truly sacramental. The apostolic letter states that there exists between the persons united in them a special "communion of spiritual benefits." These spiritual bonds in which couples are united are grounded in the "true, though imperfect communion" which exists between the Catholic Church and all who believe in Christ and are properly baptized (*Decree on Ecumenism*, no. 3). Along with us, such persons are honored by the title of Christians and are rightly regarded as brothers in the Lord. In Marriages which unite Catholics and other baptized Christians, the couple should be encouraged to recognize in practical ways what they share together in the life of grace, in faith and charity along with other interior gifts of the Holy Spirit, and that in service to the same Lord they await the salvation which He promised to those who would be His followers.

A number of the particular difficulties faced by Catholics and other Christians in mixed marriages result from the division among Christians. However successful these marriages may be, they do not erase the pain of that wider division. Yet this division need not weaken these marriages, and given proper understanding they may lead to a deep spiritual unity between the spouses. Such couples should accept the painful aspects of Christian division insofar as these affect their lives together as a sharing in the suffering of the Church. Thus they should regard their personal efforts at understanding and patience as symbolic of and a participation in the broader efforts toward unity among the separated churches. Their own love as it reaches out to relatives and friends should have a healing effect in establishing closer relationships between groups of Christians who have been estranged due to divisions among them. In this way, such marriages, while encompassing within one home the divisions among Christians, nevertheless, like all sacramental marriages, should be seen as compelling signs of the mystery of Christ's abiding love for His Church, a love which continually seeks to reconcile. Finally, such couples, should they achieve such a perspective in regard to their marriage, can do much to intensify the longing among Christians for the day when all shall be one.

In order to aid these couples to come to this deep understanding of their married life together, when possible, their Catholic and other Christian pastors should jointly do all that they can to prepare them for marriage and to support them and their families with all the aids their ministry can provide. They can, for example, enliven the couple's appreciation of the virtue of fidelity, mutual trust, forgiveness, honesty, openness, love and responsibility for their children. In this way the past of the different Christian communities can best bring the couple to a keen awareness of all that they have in common as Christians as well as to a proper appreciation of the gravity of the differences that yet remain between their churches.

In their homes, these couples should be encouraged in practical ways to develop a common life of prayer calling upon the many elements of spirituality which they share with a common Christian heritage and expressing their own common faith in the Lord, together asking Him to help them grow in their love for each other, to bless their families with the graces they need, and to keep them always mindful of the needs of others. The example of parents united in prayer is especially important for the children whom God may give them. In regard to public worship together in each other's churches, pastors may explain to the couple the provisions made for this by the Holy See in the *Ecumenical Directory*.[1]

Beyond this, parents have the right and the responsibility to provide for the religious education of their children. This right is clearly taught by Vatican II: "Since the family is a society in its own original right, it has the right freely to live its own domestic religious life under the guidance of the parents. Parents, moreover, have the right to determine, in accordance with their own religious beliefs, the kind of religious education that their children are to receive" (*Declaration on Religious Freedom*, no. 5). It is evident that in preparing for a mixed marriage, the couple will have to reach decisions and make specific choices in order to fulfill successfully the responsibility that is theirs toward their children in this respect. It is to be hoped for their own sake that in this matter, the couple may reach a common mind. If this issue is not resolved before marriage, the couple, as sad experience has shown, find a severe strain in their marital life that can subject them to well-meaning but tension-building pressures from relatives on both sides. If this issue cannot be resolved, there is a serious question whether the couple should marry. In reaching a concrete decision concerning the baptism and religious education of children, both partners should remember that neither thereby abdicates the fundamental responsibility of parents to see that their children are instilled with deep and abiding religious values. In this the Catholic partner is seriously bound to act in accord with the faith which recognizes that, "This is the unique Church of Christ which in the Creed we avow as one, holy, catholic and apostolic. After His resurrection our Savior handed her over to Peter to be shepherded (Jn 21:17), commissioning him and the other apostles to propagate and govern her (cf. Mt 28:18f). Her He erected for all ages as 'the pillar and mainstay of the truth' (1 Tm 3:15). This Church, constituted and organized in the world as a society, subsists in the Catholic Church, which is governed by the successor of Peter and by the Bishops in union with that successor, although many elements of sanctification and of truth can be found outside her visible structure. These elements, however, as gifts properly belonging to the Church of Christ, possess an inner dynamism toward Catholic unity" (*Constitution of the Church*, no. 8). This faith is the source of a serious obligation in conscience on the part of the Catholic, whose conscience in this regard must be respected.

Specific Norms

This apostolic letter on mixed marriages leaves to episcopal conferences the further determination of specific questions. (The norms of *Matrimonia mixta* are not repeated here, nor are the special norms affecting the marriages of Eastern Catholics and marriages of Catholics with Eastern non-Catholic Christians. They are found elsewhere in these Appendices.)

Document IV
Implementation of Norms in the U.S.A.

In order to implement the mandate of Pope Paul's Motu Proprio, the NCCB sets forth the following for the dioceses of the United States.

I. Pastoral Responsibility

1. In every diocese, there shall be appropriate informational programs to explain both the reasons for restrictions upon mixed marriages and the positive spiritual values to be sought in such marriages when permitted. This is particularly important if the non-Catholic is a Christian believer and the unity of married and family life is ultimately based upon the baptism of both wife and husband. If possible, all such programs should be undertaken after consultation with and in conjunction with non-Catholic authorities.

2. In every diocese there shall be appropriate programs for the instruction and orientation of the clergy, as well as of candidates for the ministry, so that they may understand fully the reason for the successive changes in the discipline of mixed marriage and may willingly undertake their personal responsibilities to each individual couple and family in the exercise of their pastoral ministry.

3. In addition to the customary marriage preparation programs, it is the serious duty of each one in the pastoral ministry, according to his own responsibility, office or assignment, to undertake:

(a) the spiritual and catechetical preparation, especially in regard to the "ends and essential properties of marriage (which) are not to be excluded by either party" (cf. *Matrimonia mixta*, no. 6), on a direct and individual basis, of couples who seek to enter a mixed marriage, and

(b) continued concern and assistance to the wife and husband in mixed marriages and to their children, so that married and family life may be supported in unity, respect for conscience, and common spiritual benefit.

4. In the assistance which he gives in preparation for marriage between a Catholic and non-Catholic, and his continued efforts to help all married couples and families, the priest should endeavor to be in contact and to cooperate with the minister or religious counselor of the non-Catholic.

II. Declaration and Promise (M.P., no. 7)

5. The declaration and promise by the Catholic, necessary for dispensation from the impediment to a mixed marriage (either mixed religion or disparity of worship), shall be made, in the following words or their substantial equivalent:

"I reaffirm my faith in Jesus Christ and with God's help, intend to continue living that faith in the Catholic Church.

"I promise to do all in my power to share the faith I have received with our children by having them baptized and reared as Catholics."

6. The declaration and promise are made in the presence of a priest or deacon either orally or in writing as the Catholic prefers.

7. The form of the declaration and promise is not altered in the case of the marriage of a Catholic with another baptized Christian, but the priest should draw the attention of the Catholic to the communion of spiritual benefits in such a Christian marriage. The promise and declaration should be made in the light of the "indirect communion" of the non-Catholic with the Catholic Church because of his belief in Christ and baptism (cf. *Decree on Ecumenism*, no. 3).

8. At an opportune time before marriage, and preferably as part of usual premarital instructions, the non-Catholic must be informed of the promises and of the responsibility of the Catholic. No precise manner or occasion of informing the non-Catholic is prescribed. It may be done by the priest, deacon or the Catholic party. No formal statement of the non-Catholic is required. But the mutual understanding of this question beforehand should prevent possible disharmony that might otherwise arise during married life.

9. The priest who submits the request for dispensation from the impediment to a mixed marriage shall certify that the declaration and promise have been made by the Catholic and that the non-Catholic has been informed of this requirement. This is done in the following or similar words:

"The required promise and declaration have been made by the Catholic in my presence. The non-Catholic has been informed of this and obligation on the part of the Catholic."

The promise of the Catholic must be sincerely made, and is to be presumed to be sincerely made. If, however, the priest has reason to doubt the sincerity of the promise made by the Catholic, he may not recommend the request for the dispensation and should submit the matter to the local Ordinary.

III. Form of Marriage (M.P., no. 9)

10. Where there are serious difficulties in observing the Catholic canonical form in a mixed marriage, the local Ordinary of the Catholic party or of the place where the marriage is to occur may dispense the Catholic from the observance of the form for a just pastoral cause. An exhaustive list is impossible, but the following are the types of reasons: to achieve family harmony or to avoid family alienation, to obtain parental agreement to the marriage, to recognize the significant claims of relationship or special friendship with a non-Catholic minister, to permit the marriage in a church that has particular importance to the non-Catholic. If the Ordinary of the Catholic party grants a dispensation for a marriage which is to take place in another diocese, the Ordinary of that diocese should be informed beforehand.

11. Ordinarily this dispensation from the canonical form is granted in view of the proposed celebration of a religious marriage service. In some exceptional circumstances (e.g. Catholic-Jewish marriages) it may be necessary that the dispensation be granted so that a civil ceremony may be performed. In any case, a public form that is civilly recognized for the celebration of marriage is required.

IV. Recording Marriages (M.P. no. 10)

12. In a mixed marriage for which there has been granted a dispensation from the canonical form, an ecclesiastical record of the marriage shall be kept in the chancery of the diocese which granted the dispensation from the impediment, and in the marriage records of the parish from which application for the dispensation was made.

13. It is the responsibility of the priest who submits the request for the dispensation to see that, after the public form of marriage ceremony is performed, notices of the marriage are sent in the usual form to:
    (a) the parish and chancery noted above (12);
    (b) the place of baptism of the Catholic party.
The recording of other mixed marriages is not changed.

V. Celebration of Marriages Between Catholics and Non-Catholics

14. It is not permitted to have two religious marriage services or to have a single service in which both the Catholic marriage ritual and a non-Catholic marriage ritual are celebrated jointly or successively (cf. no. 13 of *Matrimonia mixta*).

15. With the permission of the local Ordinary and the consent of the appropriate authority of the other church or community, a non-Catholic minister may be invited to participate in the Catholic marriage service by giving additional prayers, blessings, or words of greeting or exhortation. If the marriage is not part of the Eucharistic celebration, the minister may also be invited to read a lesson and/or to preach (cf. the *Ecumenical Directory*, Part I, no. 56).

16. In the case where there has been a dispensation from the Catholic canonical form and the priest has been invited to participate in the non-Catholic marriage service, with the permission of the local Ordinary and the consent of the appropriate authority of the other church or communion, he may do so by giving additional prayers, blessings, or words of greeting and exhortation. If the marriage is not part of the Lord's Supper or the principal liturgical service of the Word, the priest, if invited, may also read a lesson and/or preach (cf. *Ibid.*).

17. To the extent that Eucharistic sharing is not permitted by the general discipline of the Church (cf. no. 11, *Matrimonia mixta*, and the exceptions in no. 39 of the *Ecumenical Directory*, Part I, May 14, 1967), this is to be considered when plans are being made to have the mixed marriage at Mass or not.

18. Since the revised Catholic rite of marriage includes a rich variety of scriptural readings and biblically orientated prayers and blessings from which to choose, its use may promote harmony and unity on the occasion of a mixed marriage (cf. *Introduction to the Rite of Marriage*, no. 9), provided the service is carefully planned and celebrated. The general directives that the selection of texts and other preparations should involve "all concerned including the faithful. . ." (*General Instruction on the Roman Missal*, no. 73; cf. 313) are especially applicable to the mixed marriage service, where the concerns of the couple, the non-Catholic minister and other participants should be considered.

VI. Place of Marriage

19. The ordinary place of marriage is in the parish church or other sacred place. For serious reasons, the local Ordinary may permit the celebration of a mixed marriage, when there has been no dispensation from the canonical form and the Catholic marriage service is to be celebrated, outside a Catholic church or chapel, providing there is no scandal involved and proper delegation is granted (for example, where there is no Catholic church in the area, etc.).

20. If there has been a dispensation from canonical form, ordinarily the marriage service is celebrated in the non-Catholic church.

Document V
Norms for Orientals with Orthodox in Orthodox Church

Decree: *Orientalium Ecclesiarum* Vat. II. Pope Paul VI, November 21, 1964. Effective: January 21, 1965 for Ruthenians, April 7, 1965 for Ukrainians.

This new marriage form is found in Article 18 of *Orientalium Ecclesiarum*, the Decree on the Eastern Catholic Churches of Vatican II. Article 18 states the following:

"To obviate invalid marriages when Eastern Catholics marry baptized Eastern non-Catholics, and in order to promote the stability and the sanctity of marriage, as well as domestic peace, the Sacred Council determines that the canonical form for the celebration of these marriages obliges only for liceity; for their validity the presence of a sacred minister is sufficient, provided the other prescriptions of law are observed."

The introduction of this new marriage form for Orientals affects the validity of a marriage, therefore it is very important that the date (January 21, 1965) be kept in mind when dealing with cases involving a *Byzantine Catholic and a baptized non-Catholic of an Eastern rite*. Chancery and tribunal officials must keep this new legislation in mind when dealing with cases involving individuals of this category.

Liceity: The liceity of such marriages remains in effect as found in the former law (*Crebrae Allatae* - May 2, 1949) whereby censures and other penalties are incurred if the regular prescriptions of the law are not observed. Neither can ordinaries dispense from this marriage form whereby they would grant permission for a Catholic to contract marriage *solely* or *first* before a non-Catholic minister (*communicatio in sacris*). It must be noted that Pospishil gives his opinion and makes a fine distinction when he states that although *communicatio in sacris* is forbidden, nevertheless, after such a couple has exchanged the marriage vows before a Catholic priest, thereby becoming recipients of the sacrament of matrimony, the rites performed in the Eastern dissident church cannot lead to a sacrament; therefore this is an extra-sacramental *communicatio in sacris*, which is permissible according to the above mentioned principle.

Document VI
Norms for Romans with Orthodox

The Sacred Congregation for the Oriental Church issued this decree on mixed marriages between Latin Rite Catholics and the Orthodox, February 22, 1967.

The increasing frequency of mixed marriages between Oriental Catholics and non-Catholic Oriental Christians in the eastern patriarchates and eparchies as well as in the Latin dioceses themselves and the necessity of coping with the inconveniences resulting from this, were the reasons why the Second Vatican Ecumenical Council decreed: "When Oriental Catholics enter into marriage with baptized non-Catholic Orientals the canonical form for the celebration of such marriages obliges only for lawfulness; for their validity, the presence of a sacred minister suffices, as long as the other requirements of the law are observed" (Decree on the Eastern Catholic Churches, n. 18).

In the exceptional circumstances of today, in which mixed marriages between the Catholic faithful and the non-Catholic Oriental faithful are taking place, the variety in canonical disciplines has brought about many grave difficulties both in the East and the West. For this reason petitions from various regions have been addressed to the Supreme Pontiff asking that he be pleased to unify canonical discipline in this matter by also permitting to Catholics of the Latin rite what has been decreed for Catholics of the Eastern rite.

His Holiness, our Lord Paul VI, by divine providence Pope, after mature reflection and diligent investigation, has resolved to agree to the petitions and desires addressed to him and, as a means of preventing invalid marriages between the faithful of the Latin rite and the non-Catholic Christian faithful of the Oriental rites, of showing proper regard for the permanence and sanctity of marriages, and of promoting charity between the Catholic faithful and the non-Catholic Oriental faithful, he has kindly granted that, when Catholics, whether they be Orientals or Latins, contract marriage with non-Catholic Oriental faithful, the canonical form for the celebration of these marriages obliges only for lawfulness; for validity the presence of a sacred minister suffices, as long as the other requirements of law are observed.

All care should be taken that under the guidance of the pastor such marriages be carefully entered into the prescribed registers as soon as possible; this prescription also holds when Catholic Orientals enter marriage with baptized non-Catholic Orientals according to the norm of the conciliar decree "On the Catholic Oriental Churches."

In conformity with the holiness of marriage itself, non-Catholic ministers are reverently and earnestly requested to cooperate in the task of registering marriages in the books of the Catholic party, whether of the Latin or Oriental rite.

Ordinaries of the place, who grant dispensation from the impediment of mixed religion, are likewise given the faculty of dispensing from the obligation of observing canonical form for lawfulness if there exist difficulties which, according to their prudent judgment, require this dispensation.

This same Supreme Pontiff has ordered the Sacred Congregation for the Oriental Church, of which he himself is the prefect, to make known to all this resolution and concession. Wherefore, the same sacred congregation, after also consulting the Sacred Doctrinal Congregation, at the order of His Holiness, has composed the present decree to be published in the *Acta Apostolicae Sedis*.

Meanwhile, in order that this new statute may be brought to the attention of those whom it concerns, whether they be Catholics of any rite whatever or Orthodox, the present decree will go into effect beginning from March 25, 1967, the feast of the Annunciation of the Blessed Virgin Mary.

Notwithstanding anything which in any way may be to the contrary.

Episcopal Faculties

The most important single faculty granted to bishops is that described in the motu proprio *De Episcoporum Muneribus* (June 15, 1966). The Latin text is found in the *Acta Apostolicae Sedis*, LVII (1966), 467-472. An English translation is in the *Canon Law Digest*, 1966 Supplement, under Canon 329. This faculty, based on the Decree *Christus Dominus* of the Second Vatican Council, gives to the diocesan bishops the faculty to dispense their faithful in particular cases from the general laws of the Church whenever they judge that it would be for their spiritual good, unless a special reservation has been made by the Supreme authority. For each new case that arises all that will be necessary is to consult this motu proprio to determine whether the particular faculty is there. A Handbook on all these faculties has been prepared by a special committee of the Canon Law Society of America. Copies can be obtained by writing to the headquarters of the CLS.

Document VII

Norms of Procedure on Nullity Cases
Motu Proprio, Causas Matrimonialis

Pope Paul VI, March 27, 1971, AAS 1971, Vol. 63, p. 441. Special Faculties were given, at different times, to England, Wales, Canada, USA, Australia, Belgium, Spain and other countries, so this special document was issued to standardize these laws, which was the purpose of this Motu Proprio-*Causas Matrimonialis*.

Marriage cases have always been given special care by Mother Church, and through them she endeavors to safeguard the holiness ,and true nature of the sacred bond of matrimony. The ministry of ecclesiastical judges shows forth clearly—though in its own special way—the pastoral charity of the Church, which is well aware how much the salvation of souls is sought in marriage cases.

Since the number of these cases is greatly increasing at the present time, the Church cannot but be very concerned about this matter. This increase of cases, as we said to the Prelates of the Sacred Roman Rota, "is a special sign of the decrease of the sense of the sacred nature of the law upon which the Christian family is based; it is a sign of the restlessness and disturbance of present-day life, and of the uncertain social and economic conditions in which it is lived. It is a sign therefore of the danger which may threaten the solidity, vigor and happiness of the institution of the family" (cf. *AAS*, LVIII, 1966, p. 154).

Mother Church trusts that the attention given by the recent Ecumenical Council to explaining and fostering the spiritual good and pastoral care of marriage may produce results with regard also to the firmness of the marriage bond; she moreover desires at the same time by the laying down of opportune norms that the spiritual well-being of many of her sons and daughters may not be damaged by the excessive lengthiness of matrimonial processes.

Therefore, while awaiting the fuller reform of the marriage process which our Commission for the Revision of the Code of Canon Law is preparing, we thought it well to issue certain norms on the constitution of ecclesiastical tribunals and on the judicial process, which will expedite the matrimonial process itself.

While other canonical norms concerning processes remain unchanged, we therefore on our own initiative and by our apostolic authority decree and lay down the following norms, which are to be faithfully observed from 1 October 1971 in all tribunals, including apostolic tribunals, until the new Code of Canon Law is promulgated.

Competent Forum

I.   The marriage cases of the baptized by proper right pertain to an ecclesiastical judge.

II.   Cases concerning the merely civil effects of marriage are the concern of the civil authorities, unless particular law lays down that such cases, if they are dealt with in an incidental and accessory manner, may be examined and decided by an ecclesiastical judge.

III.   All marriage cases concerning those persons mentioned in the *Code of Canon Law*, Canon 1557:1, no. 1, are judged by the Congregation, Tribunal, or special Commission to which the Supreme Pontiff entrusts them in each case.

IV.   1.   In other cases concerning the nullity of marriage the competent body is:

a) the tribunal of the place in which the marriage was celebrated; or

b) the tribunal of the place in which the respondent has an abode which is not transitory, which may be proved from some ecclesiastical document or in some other legitimate manner; or

c) the tribunal of the place in which *de facto* most of the depositions or proofs have to be collected, provided the consent is obtained both of the Ordinary of the place where the respondent habitually lives and of the Ordinary of the place in which the tribunal approached is situated, and of the president of the tribunal itself.

2. If the circumstances mentioned in 1.c) above occur, the tribunal, before admitting the case must inquire of the respondent whether he or she has any objection to the forum approached by the petitioner.

3. Should there occur a substantial change in the circumstances, places or persons mentioned in 1, the case, before its closure, may be transferred in particular cases from one tribunal to another equally competent one, provided both parties and both tribunals agree.

Constitution of Tribunals

V.   1. If it is impossible either in a diocesan tribunal or, where one is set up, in a regional tribunal, to form a college of three clerical judges, the episcopal conference is given the faculty of permitting in the first and second instance the appointment of a college composed of two clerics and one layman.

2. In the first instance, when a college as described in 1 cannot be set up even by adding a layman, in individual instances, cases concerning the nullity of marriage may be entrusted by the episcopal conference to one cleric as the sole judge. Such a judge where possible will choose an assessor and auditor for the case.

3. The episcopal conference can, in accordance with its statutes, grant the above mentioned faculties either through a group of members or at least one member of the conference, to be chosen for this purpose.

VI.   For the office of assessor and auditor in tribunals of any instance laymen may be used. The office of notary may be accepted by both men and women.

VII.   Lay people chosen for these offices should be outstanding in their Catholic faith and good character as well as their knowledge of canon law. When it is a question of conferring the office of judge upon a layman, as laid down in V,1, those who have legal experience are to be preferred.

Appeals

VIII.   1. The Defender of the Bond is obliged to appeal to the higher tribunal, within the time laid down by law, against a first sentence declaring the nullity of a marriage. If he fails to do this, he shall be compelled to do so by the authority of the president or the sole judge.

2. Before the tribunal of second instance, the 'defender of the bond' shall produce his observations stating whether or not he has any objection to make against the decision made in the first instance. The college shall, if it thinks it opportune, ask for the observations of the parties or of their advocates against those made by the 'defender of the bond.'

3. Having examined the sentence and having considered the observations of the Defender of the Bond and, if they were asked for and given, those of the parties

or of their advocates, the college by its decree shall either ratify the decision of the first instance, or admit the case to the ordinary examination of the second instance. In the first of the two cases, if no one makes recourse, the couple, provided there is no other impediment, have the right to contract a new marriage after ten days have elapsed from the publication of the decree.

IX.   1. If the decree of the college ratifies the first-instance sentence, the Defender of the Bond or a party who believes himself to be aggrieved has the right to make recourse to a higher tribunal within ten days from the date of publication of the decree, provided he presents new and serious arguments. These arguments must be placed before the third-instance tribunal within a month from making recourse.

2. The Defender of the Bond of the third instance, after hearing the president of the tribunal, can withdraw from the recourse, and in that case the tribunal shall declare the case terminated. If it is a party who makes recourse, the tribunal having considered the arguments adduced, within a month from the making of recourse shall either reject it by decree or admit the case to ordinary examination in the third instance.

Special Cases

X.   When there is proof from a certain and authentic document, not subject to any contradiction or exception, that a diriment impediment exists, and when it is also equally certain and clear that no dispensation from this impediment has been given, in these cases the formalities laid down in law can be omitted and the Ordinary, after the parties have been summoned and the 'defender of the bond' has intervened, can declare the marriage null.

XI.   With the same provisions and in the same manner as in X, the Ordinary can declare a marriage null also when the case was entered into on the grounds of lack of canonical form or lack of a valid mandate on the part of the proxy.

XII.   If the Defender of the Bond prudently considers that the impediments or defects mentioned in X and XI are not certain or that it is probable that there was a dispensation from them, he is bound to appeal against this declaration to the judge of second instance. The proceedings are to be transmitted to him and he is to be notified in writing that the case is a special one.

XIII.   The judge of second instance, with the sole intervention of the Defender of the Bond, shall decide in the same way as in X whether the sentence is to be confirmed or whether the case is to be proceeded with through the ordinary channels of law. In this latter case he shall send it back to the tribunal of first instance.

Transitional Norms

1. On the day on which the present apostolic letter comes into force, a marriage case which is proceeding before a higher tribunal by reason of lawful appeal after a

first sentence declaring the marriage null shall be temporarily suspended.

2. The Defender of the Bond of the tribunal of second instance shall make his observations on all that concerns either the decision given in the first instance or the proceedings completed in the second instance up to that date, and thereby state whether or not he has any objection to make against the decision made in the first instance. The college shall, if it thinks it opportune, ask for the observations of the parties or of their advocates against these observations.

3. Having considered the observations of the Defender of the Bond and, if they were asked for and given, those of the parties or of their advocates, and having examined the sentence of the first instance, the college by its decree shall either ratify the first instance decision or decide that the case must be proceeded with by examination in the second instance. In the former case, if no one makes recourse, the couple have the right, provided there is no other impediment, to contract a new marriage after ten days have elapsed from the publication of the decree. In the latter case the instance must be proceeded with until the definitive sentence is given.

We order that all that is decreed in this letter issued by us *motu proprio* be valid and firm, anything to the contrary notwithstanding, even if worthy of most special mention.

Given in Rome at St. Peter's, on March 28, 1971, Paulus P.P. VI.

Matrimonial Cases in the Eastern Churches

In an apostolic letter issued *motu proprio* by Pope Paul VI on September 8, 1973, norms are established for matrimonial procedure in the Eastern Churches. These norms were prompted by the same circumstances as those for the Latin Church (*Causas Matrimoniales*, March 28, 1971), namely, the pastoral need to simplify procedures for the more expeditious resolution of cases.

The prescriptions of the apostolic letter *Sollicitudinem Nostram* of Pius XII (January 6, 1950) remain in effect where they are not changed by the present document. The specific provisions follow those of *Causas Matrimoniales*.

(Excerpts from the commentary given by Reverend Raymond Bidagor, S.J., Secretary of the Commission for the Revision of the Code, on *Causas Matrimoniales*. This commentary was given during the publication ceremony of C.M. It is found in *Communicationes*, 1971, vol. III, no. 1, pp. 98-99. This is a translation from the original Italian.)

The most notable changes from the *Motu Proprio Causas Matrimoniales* can be found in the chapter dealing with Appeals. As is well known, Sentences of nullity of the marriage never become *res iudicata*. Since such cases deal with the state of the person they can always be re-examined for serious reasons, even after two Sentences have declared the nullity of the marriage. But the double conforming

Sentences produce the effect that the married couple who have obtained them have the right to contract a new marriage. In order for this right to become an actuality, the two steps of judgment must be pursued by the two distinct Tribunals, the ordinary Tribunal and the Tribunal of Appeal. Both these courts, in order to pronounce its own Sentence, are required to follow the same procedure—from the citation of the parties up to the publication of process and the actual discussion of the case. It is, therefore, a repetition of the judicial process before new judges.

After today's *Motu Proprio*, the Tribunal of Appeal which receives a Sentence from First Instance declaring the nullity of the marriage, has to proceed in a different manner. The Sentence of First Instance is immediately examined by the Defender of the Bond from the Tribunal of Second Instance; this Defender of the Bond must explain his observations before his Tribunal in order for him to declare if he has or has not anything against the decision pronounced in First Instance. The college, if it thinks it opportune, could request counter-observations from the parties or from their respective Advocates. After having examined the Sentences of First Instance, which must contain the motivations upon which it is based, and after having given thought to the observations of the Defender of the Bond and those of the parties and their Advocates—if asked—the college, by a decree, will either ratify the decision of First Instance or will submit the case to the ordinary examination of Second Instance. If the first course is pursued, says the Motu Proprio, and if no one makes an appeal, the spouses who are not prevented by any other reason, have the right to contract a new marriage after ten days from the application of the decree.

Let no one be ignorant of the importance of this new method. Matrimonial cases which are well founded when they are presented to ecclesiastical Tribunals can be concluded in a relatively brief time, and with every guarantee of full justice. Indeed this change, dictated by the personal interest of the Holy Father in order to supply a remedy for the actual difficulty which he has seen—as we said in the beginning—to exist in almost every diocese of the world, should move the members of the Tribunals to a greater solicitude towards expediting their proper duty and to an increased responsibility for the eternal salvation of souls which are depressed by problems so intimate and pressing, and which disturb the peace of family life and impede the spiritual peace to which they have a right.

Permit me to point out the great responsibility which, under this new procedure, is carried by the Defender of the Bond. Just as are the Judges, so the Defender of the Bond and in a way also the Advocates, are all bound to the unity of purpose of the Matrimonial process, that is, to ascertain with authority and to carry into practice truth and the right which corresponds to it as both relate to the existence or to the continuation of the marriage bond.

The Defender of the Bond, for his part, certainly must openly present all which in the process speaks in favor and not just that which speaks against the existence or the continuation of the marriage bond, but he, as anyone else who has any part in the process, must, without any exception as Pius XII said in one of his famous discourses to the Roman Rota, work to bring together all their actions to a single purpose: to establish truth.

The Motu Proprio has given to the Defender of the Bond or to the party who believes himself to be unjustly treated, the option to have recourse to a higher Tribunal against the decree of the college which ratifies the Sentence of First Instance. But this option must be pursued only within the limitations of existing law which limits have been fixed concerning a third appeal after two conforming sentences, that is, only by inducing new and grave arguments which must be quickly at hand. The right to have recourse must be exercised within ten days of the publication of the decree. Such a disposition was thought necessary by the legislator, and it emanates naturally from the very nature of cases which deal *de statu personarum*; since such is the case with matrimonial cases, as we have said before, that never pass *in rem iudicatam*.

Document VIII
NORMS FOR MIXED MARRIAGE IN CANADA
Formulated by Canadian Catholic Conference June 5-6, 1970. Effective August 1, 1970

I. The Canonical Form

General Principle: A Catholic should normally contract marriage in and before the Catholic Church (cf. note 1).

   A. The Ordinary of the Catholic party, or the Ordinary of the place where the marriage is to be celebrated, may dispense from the canonical form. In cases where the marriage is celebrated in a diocese other than that of the Catholic party, the "nihil obstat" of the Ordinary of the place where the marriage is to be celebrated, should be given.

   B. In order for the dispensations to be granted legitimately, the reasons for doing so should concern *in an important way* the good of the parties, especially their spiritual well being and the tranquility and peace of their personal and family relationships (cf. note 2).

II. Promises to be made by the Catholic Party

   A. The promises to be made by the Catholic party will be made orally (not in written form), and the presence of a witness is not necessary; the priest who prepared the couple for their marriage will certify to the Ordinary that these promises were sincerely made, and that he is morally certain that the Catholic party will be faithful to them (cf. Annex "B").

B. The celebration of a mixed marriage will not be authorized in those cases where:
   a. it is clearly evident that the Catholic party is not sincere in making the promises;
   b. the Catholic party refuses to promise to do his or her best to safeguard the Catholic faith and to see to the Catholic baptism and education of children to be born from the marriage.

III. *Preparation of the Non-Catholic Party*

The priest who prepares the couple for marriage will inform the non-Catholic party of the promises made by the Catholic party and will certify to the Ordinary that this has been done. He will see to it that the couple accept the ends and essential properties of Christian matrimony. He can make use of the formula given in Annex "B" for this purpose.

IV. *Annotation of the Marriage*

A marriage celebrated with dispensation from the canonical form will be recorded at the place where the marriage was celebrated (e.g. church, court house, etc.).

A marginal annotation will be made in the baptismal records of the place where the Catholic party was baptized (see Annex "A").

Record of the granting of the dispensation from the canonical form will be kept in the Chancery Office of the diocese granting the dispensation.

V. *Celebration of the Marriage*

A. The celebration of a mixed marriage in the Catholic Church should be presided by the Catholic priest. It is desirable that the non-Catholic minister be invited to take part in the ceremony in some way, according to norms to be drawn up in an Ecumenical Directory.
B. The celebration of a mixed marriage outside the Catholic Church—with dispensation from the canonical form—should be presided by the non-Catholic minister. It is desirable that the Catholic priest be invited to take part in the ceremony in some way.
C. Thus, the celebration of the marriage of a Catholic with a non-Catholic will be accompanied by various sacred rites; this will depend on whether the non-Catholic party belongs to a given Church, ecclesial community, or religion, and on the personal religious convictions of the parties.
D. In each case, it is the priest who will decide, after having consulted the couple, and in accordance with the directives given in Annex "C."

VI. Marriage Banns

In order to ensure greater cooperation between the ministers of both Churches, it is recommended that the practice be introduced of publishing the marriage banns in both Churches (Catholic and non-Catholic); this applies in places where it is customary to have such publications.

VII. Witnesses

Non-Catholics may be invited to act as witnesses to such a marriage or to assist the spouses in some other capacity.

Notes

1. Reasons in favor of maintaining or using the canonical form for mixed marriages:
    a) greater facility in ensuring that appropriate instructions have been given for the preparation of marriage;
    b) possibility of avoiding the celebration of premature and hasty marriages;
    c) greater order in parish records.

2. Among the many reasons for which the Holy See has granted dispensation from the canonical form since 1966, are the following:
    a) to keep the non-Catholic partner from breaking with his/her Church or religious body;
    b) to avoid the danger of having an invalid or illicit marriage celebrated outside the Church;
    c) promotion of better relations between the two families so that both may offer better support for the newly-married couple;
    d) *active* participation of the non-Catholic party in the life of his or her Church; for example, if the party were a Sunday School Teacher, Warden, Trustee, etc.
    e) local customs (e.g., in Canada the marriage is traditionally celebrated in the bride's church).

The other canonical reasons previously recognized in law for the dispensation from the impediments of mixed religion and disparity of worship (canon 1061) also apply in certain cases.

Concerning the procedure to be followed for the celebration of a marriage with dispensation from the canonical form, see Annex "A."

3. Notation in the Marriage Register

The following considerations seem to justify the proposed procedure:
    a) avoid unnecessary administrative work;

b) the Catholic priest cannot attend to a marriage which took place elsewhere;

c) the registration of all dispensations in the Chancery office which grants the dispensation and assigns a protocol number to it;

d) the plural used in the Latin text of the Motu Proprio is to be interpreted according to the general rules of Canon Law and, in certain cases, applies only to baptismal registers.

Annex "A"

Procedure for the Celebration of a Mixed Marriage with a Dispensation from the Canonical Form

1. The pastor (or the curate) of the Catholic party makes the prenuptial inquiry and completes the dossier which remains in the archives of the parish.
2. Using Form "V," the pastor or curate of the Catholic party requests from the Ordinary the dispensation required for a mixed marriage (mixed religion or disparity of worship, as the case may be), dispensation from the form, the nihil obstat, and, if necessary, the dispensation from other impediments. He indicates on the reverse side of Form "V" along with the reasons for requesting the other dispensations, the reasons for which he requests a dispensation from the canonical form, and mentions before what Church or civil institution the marriage is to be celebrated.
3. The pastor receives the regular rescript from the Chancery Office together with two copies of a document authorizing the celebration of the marriage outside the Catholic Church. The rescript is placed in the dossier, together with one copy of the authorization.
4. When advising the Catholic party that the dispensation has been granted, the pastor gives him or her one copy of the document authorizing the celebration of marriage before a minister other than a Catholic priest. The Catholic party is requested to forward a certificate of marriage as soon as possible after the ceremony.
5. When the marriage certificate is received, the pastor will advise the parish where the Catholic party was baptized. The following text may be used.

X _____, a Catholic baptized on
_____ in _____ Church,
_____ married Y _____
on _____ 19____ in _____
(Church, temple, Courthouse) after receiving a dispensation from the canonical form of marriage (Prot. No. _____).

Please make this annotation in your Baptismal Register and return this notice, certifying that the annotation has been made as requested.

Annex "B"

Declaration Concerning the Preparation of the Parties to a Mixed Marriage

(This form must be filled out by the priest who conducts the prenuptial inquiry. One copy is sufficient. It is to be sent to the Chancery Office with the petition for the nihil obstat, and will be returned to the parish to be included in the dossier.)

Names of the parties:

The Catholic party _____

The non-Catholic party _____

Member of _____

(Name of Church)

YES

    1. *Promise of the Catholic party*

The Catholic party has been carefully instructed concerning his responsibility to live according to his faith, to give witness to his faith, to avoid anything that could weaken his faith, and to do his best to have the children who will be born of the marriage baptized and educated in the Catholic faith. The Catholic party has explicitly promised to be faithful to these responsibilities.

YES

    2. *Preparation of the non-Catholic party*

The non-Catholic party has been instructed on the doctrine of the Catholic Church with regard to Christian marriage and recognizes that the marriage he wishes to contract is to be one and indissoluble. The non-Catholic party is aware of the responsibilities of the Catholic party with regard to religious practice and to the Catholic baptism and education of the children.

Describe briefly the non-Catholic party's attitude:

YES

    3. *Preparation for marriage*

Both parties have been adequately prepared for their forthcoming marriage.

YES

    4. *Opinion of the priest*

I am morally certain that the Catholic party will be faithful to these obligations.

Date   Signature of priest

Liturgical Celebration

General Principles

1. For all marriages celebrated in the Catholic Church, it is normal that the exchange of consent be accompanied by sacred rites which help the spouses to turn their minds and hearts to God, to discover God's love in their mutual love and to give thanks to Him.

2. However, no matter how keen our desire to share with non-Catholics the Church's means of grace, participation in the same sacred actions must always be respectful of truth. To avoid any ambiguity unworthy of an action which is directed to God and unbecoming of the persons who perform that action, the words, the acts, the chants and the responses of the ceremony must be in accord with the religious beliefs of both spouses. This respect for truth and for the convictions of the persons involved in *communicatio in sacris* is a primordial principle of ecumenism.

   Though it may be painful to the spouses that the divergence of their respective convictions appear at a time when they join together in marriage, they should be invited by the priest to acknowledge in humility this distressing reality and to accept the suffering that it brings instead of seeking to cover it up with false pretenses.

3. No one should be surprised that the Catholic Church should consider itself closer to one Church than to another and that, as a consequence, it should invite certain Christians to participate more fully in its worship. This difference of attitude does not stem from a judgment on persons but rather from the fact of a greater unity in faith and sacramental life.

   The marriage of a Catholic with a non-Catholic will therefore be differently accompanied by sacred rites depending on what Church, what community, what religion the non-Catholic partner belongs to, as well as upon the personal religious dispositions of those who are contracting marriage. This marriage could be celebrated within the Holy Sacrifice or even in the framework of the Celebration of the Word, or simply using the rites for marriage alone.

   This decision will be made for reasons in the religious or pastoral order and not for reasons foreign to faith, or to the spiritual good of the persons such as, for example, the desire of underlining the celebration of a marriage celebration or of following social conveniences.

   In some cases it will be necessary to recall that the sacred rites are not favors and consequently the decision to not accompany the marriage with a Mass is not because of an intention of penalizing those contracting a mixed marriage.

Catholic and Orthodox

A marriage of a Catholic to a Christian of an Oriental Church separated from the Roman Catholic Church may be celebrated within a Mass; in this particular circumstance, the Orthodox Christian may, if he has the required dispositions and *his own Church has no objections*, take part with the Catholic partner in the blessed Eucharist.

Catholic and Protestant

The differences in doctrine and the sacrament of life which exist between the Catholic Church and the churches and church communities in the West, generally lead one to celebrate the marriage of a Catholic with a Christian Protestant outside the ceremonies of Mass. Since Christian fiancees have nevertheless in common their faith in the Word of God, their marriage naturally fits into the framework of a Celebration of the Word.

Nevertheless, it may sometimes be desirable that the marriage of a Catholic with a Protestant Christian be celebrated within the Mass. This would particularly be the case when the spouses have requested it for motives which flow from a living and educated faith. The non-Catholic spouse nevertheless is not permitted to receive communion at this Mass and the priest will take care to inform the non-Catholic partner of this disposition and if necessary during the preparatory meetings for the marriage indicate the reasons for such a law.

Document IX
Norms For Processing Non-consummation Cases

Special Instructions of the Congregation of the Sacraments dealing with alterations in the procedure for Non-consummation cases, dated 7 March 1972. AAS Vol. 64, p. 244 ff.

I. General Faculty to Conduct the Process Super Rato et Non Consummato

It pertains exclusively to the Congregation of the Sacraments to examine the fact of non-consummation of marriage not only between Catholic parties, whether of the Latin or Eastern Churches, but also between a Catholic party and a non-Catholic party and between baptized non-Catholics, as well as to examine the existence of a just or proportionately serious cause for the granting of the pontifical favor of a dissolution.

By force of this instruction all diocesan bishops have the general faculty, for their own territory, to conduct the *super matrimonio rato et non consummato* process from the day when this instruction comes into effect until the promulgation of the revised *Code of Canon Law*, so that they no longer need to seek this faculty from the Apostolic See. In using this faculty the bishops should take into account articles 7 and 8 of the *Regulae Servandae* and carefully observe the following prescriptions:

a) The process is not judicial but administrative, and therefore it differs from the judicial process for cases of nullity. In the process a simple petition is made for a favor to be obtained from the concession of the Supreme Pontiff. Nevertheless, in view of the gravity of the matter, the truth of the fact of non-consummation is to be sought no less religiously and diligently than in strictly judicial matters, so that the Pope may use his supreme power with full knowledge of the case. It is for the properly deputed Instructing Judge, therefore, to gather proofs of non-consummation and of the existence of a just or proportionately serious cause for the concession of the favor. If from an examination of the acts of the process insufficient proofs are found, the Congregation may suggest to the bishop, according to circumstances, that the proofs be completed in accord with appropriate instructions.

b) Only the spouses may seek the dissolution; both may seek it or either one, even against the will of the other. Although it is the right of any member of the faithful to send the petition (which is always to be addressed to the Supreme Pontiff) directly to the Apostolic See it is expedient and always recommended that it be presented to the bishop. After considering the matter, he will see to the conduct of the process. Whenever it is a petition of one party alone, the other is to be heard extra-judicially before the process is begun, unless in particular cases another course seems opportune.

c) Before the process is conducted the bishop must be certain of the juridical basis of the petition and the opportuneness of undertaking the process. Likewise he should not fail to encourage the reconciliation of the parties, if this is possible, through the removal of the reasons for aversion and dissension, unless the facts and personal circumstances indicate that such an attempt would be useless.

d) The bishop should refer to the Congregation complicated cases or those with special difficulties of the juridical or moral order. The Congregation will weigh carefully all the circumstances and will communicate to the bishop the steps to be taken.

e) If it happens that a prudent doubt arises, from the examination of the petition, concerning the validity of the marriage, then it is for the bishop either to counsel the petitioner to follow the judicial order (or a declaration of nullity, in accord with the law) or—provided the petition is based on a solid and juridical foundation—to permit the *super rato et non consummato* process to be conducted. When, however, a case of nullity has been prosecuted on the grounds of impotence and, in the judgment of the tribunal, proof not of impotence but of non-consummation has emerged from the acts and evidence, then, upon the petition of one or both parties for an apostolic dissolution, all the acts should be sent to the Congregation together with the animadversions of the 'defender of the bond' and the *votum* of the tribunal and the bishop, based on legal and especially factual arguments. With regard to the *votum*, the bishop may follow that of the tribunal and add his signature to it, with the assurance of a just or proportionately serious cause for the dissolution, and the absence of scandal. If in the judgment of the tribunal, insufficient proofs of non-consummation have been obtained up to this point, in accord with the *Regulae Servandae* of May 7, 1923, the proofs should be completed by the instructing judge and the completed acts sent to the Congregation with the animadversions of the 'defender of the bond' and the *votum* of the tribunal and the bishop. If it is a question of another ground of nullity (e.g. defect of consent, force and fear, etc.) and in the judgment of the tribunal the nullity cannot be established but incidentally a very probable doubt emerges about non-consummation, it is the right of one or both parties to present a petition for the dissolution to the Supreme Pontiff and the instruction judge has the right to conduct the case in accord with the norms in the *Regulae Servandae*. Then all the facts, as above, should be sent to the Congregation together with the usual animadversions of the 'defender of the bond' and the *votum* of the tribunal and the bishop.

f) The bishop must be vigilant lest the parties, witnesses, or experts give false depositions or withhold the truth. He knows—and through him all interested persons should know—that the favor of dissolution cannot be granted unless two things are proved: that the marriage was actually not consummated and that a just or proportionately serious cause exists; in the absence of either or both the rescript is affected by *obreptio* and can in no way work to the advantage of the one who obtains it. It is clear that the pontifical dissolution never becomes definitive and a new marriage which may be entered after an invalid dissolution can always be declared null, if it later becomes known that the first marriage was actually *ratum et consummatum*.

II. Conduct of the Case and the Acts

With regard to the conduct of the case, the inquiry to establish accurately and expeditiously, whether it is true that the marriage was not consummated should foster the holiness and indissolubility of marriage. It therefore seems that the following emendations should be introduced in the norms for these processes in the *Code of Canon Law* and the *Regulae Servandae* of the Congregation for the Discipline of the Sacraments:

a) If, because of the size of the diocese or eparchy and especially because of the lack of priests who are experts in canon law, it is difficult to conduct the *super rato* process in the *curia* or tribunal, the bishop may, after prudent consideration and especially in more difficult cases, transfer his competence to conduct the process to the ministers of the regional, provincial, interdiocesan, or interritual tribunal (if any) or of the tribunal of a nearby diocese or eparchy which is capable of undertaking the process.

b) In cases of non-consummation both spouses must present witnesses who can testify to their probity and especially to their truthfulness with reference to the asserted non-consummation; the instructing judge may add other witnesses *ex officio*. A few witnesses may suffice, provided their concordant testimony can give valid proof and moral certitude. This is the case if they are persons above suspicion, agree among themselves, and testify under oath: indicating when, how and what they heard from the spouses or their close relatives about the non-consummation. It should not be forgotten that in these cases the moral argument is of great weight in attaining moral certitude concerning non-consummation.

c) The physical examination is to be employed if necessary for juridical proof of the fact of non-consummation. If, however, in accord with the decree of the Congregation of the Holy Office of June 12, 1942, the bishop judges there is full proof in view of the moral excellence of the parties and witnesses, after serious consideration of their spiritual disposition and other supporting arguments, the medical examination may be omitted; all these matters should be weighed before the examination is decreed to be useless. If the woman refuses, the physical examination should not be insisted upon. Finally, with regard to this examination, patriarchal synods and episcopal conferences have the faculty to establish additional norms according to local and other circumstances.

d) The procedural acts must be in writing and must be certified by notaries. With the bishop's consent the *curia* or tribunal may use tape recorders, in accord with current practice and technical progress, if their use seems to be useful and suitable for making a more accurate and certain record of the acts. The acts, however, may be given credence only if, although taken down by tape recorder, they satisfy the prescriptions expressly required by the law.

e) Differently from cases of nullity, because of the special nature of the *super rato* process, the assistance of advocates and procurators may not be sought. In response to the recommendations and the desires of some pastors, however, it is decreed that the parties—at their own request or by *ex officio* decree of the bishop—may use the services of counsellors or experts, especially ecclesiastics, in these cases. These may assist in drawing up petitions, in the conduct of the case, or in completing the acts of the process. Thus the good of souls may be assured more certainly, while the truth of non-consummation is protected. The designation of counsellors or experts, whether chosen *ex officio* or at the request of the parties, pertains to the bishop after he has heard the Defender of the Bond and informed the counsellors or experts beforehand. This is done by a special decree and with the requirement of secrecy lest the procedural acts become known to outsiders.

f) In writing the *votum pro rei veritate*, bishops should weigh the nature and qualities of the case in a concrete and practical manner, that is, by considering the special circumstances of the persons, the fact of non-consummation, and the opportuneness of the concession.

In cases of nullity, when the acts are sent to the Congregation for a dissolution (cf. no. I, e), or of non-consummation which are conducted with an extension of competence (cf. no. II, a), the archbishop or metropolitan of the regional, provincial, interdiocesan, interritual, tribunal or the bishop of the neighboring diocese or eparchy should before writing his *votum*, consult with the bishop of the petitioner who knows the conditions of his diocese or eparchy, at least with regard to the scandal which may arise from a pontifical dissolution. If the bishop judges that the scandal arises or has arisen without basis or reason, then he should try to prevent it or contain it with pastoral care and appropriate means.

g) All the procedural acts, both of the case and of the process, together with other documents which are not in Latin, may be drawn up in those vernacular languages that are widely used. Judicial acts and documents drawn up in a language that is not well known may be translated into one of the above languages.

The procedural acts and documents are to be sent to the Congregation in three copies, which may be photostatic copies, with certification of authenticity. The original manuscript shall be preserved in the archives of the *curia* or tribunal and is to be submitted, with appropriate precautions, only if this is expressly required by the Congregation.

Since it will contribute greatly to a more careful and expeditious solution of cases, it is hoped that copies of all judicial acts and documents will be typed and that the individual pages of the process, numbered and bound in a folder, will be guaranteed as to integrity and authenticity, with the certification of the actuary or notary of their faithful transcription.

III. Clauses Attached to Rescripts

After the pontifical dissolution of the bond of a non-consummated marriage has been granted, it is proper for the spouses to enter new marriages, provided this has not been prohibited. Such a prohibition may be expressed in two ways: an *ad mentem* clause (and in this case the *mens* can be of different kinds and is appropriately explained) or a *vetitum* clause.

a) The clause with the words *ad mentem*, which is prohibitory, is usually added when the fact of non-consummation depends on reasons of lesser significance, its removal is entrusted to the bishop, so that he may provide more suitably for pastoral needs. The bishop should not permit the remarriage of the party who asks for the removal of the clause unless after the prescribed regulations have been observed, the party is found to be truly ready to undertake the burdens of marriage and has promised that in the future he will fulfill his matrimonial duties in an honest and Christian manner.

b) In special cases, however, when the reason for non-consummation is a physical or psychic defect of major significance and seriousness, a *vetitum* for remarriage may be attached. Unless it so states in the rescript, this is not a diriment impediment but only a prohibiting impediment, the removal of which is reserved to the Apostolic See. Permission to remarry is granted if the petitioner, after making a petition to the Congregation and fulfilling the prescribed conditions, is shown to be capable of properly performing conjugal acts.

It is left to the bishop's judgment and pastoral consideration to inform the party with whom the second marriage is to be entered concerning either clause added to the rescript and later removed.

Document X
Procedure for Natural Bond Cases

Special Instruction of the Congregation for the Doctrine of the Faith concerning the procedure of natural bond cases, dated 6 December 1973.

(Sac. Cong. Doct. of Faith, Prot. no. 2717 68)

As is well known, this Congregation has subjected to lengthy investigation and study the question of the dissolution of marriage in favor of the faith. At length, after this careful investigation, His Holiness, Pope Paul VI, has approved new norms which express the conditions for the grant of the dissolution of marriage in favor of the faith whether the petitioner is baptized or converted or not.

I. The following three conditions *sine qua non* are required for the valid grant of the dissolution:

a) absence of baptism in one of the spouses throughout the entire period of conjugal life;

b) non-use of marriage after baptism, if the sacrament is received by the party who was previously non-baptized;

c) that the unbaptized person or the person baptized outside the Catholic Church leave to the Catholic party the freedom and opportunity to profess his or her own religion and to baptize and bring up the children as Catholics. This condition, in the form of a promise (*cautio*), is to be kept safely.

II. The following are required in addition:

1. That there be no possibility of restoring conjugal life, in view of the continuing radical and incurable separation.

2. That there be no danger of public scandal or serious wonderment from the grant of the favor.

3. That the petitioner be shown not to have been the culpable cause of the failure of a legitimate marriage and that the Catholic party, with whom the new marriage is to be contracted or validated, was not the guilty cause of the separation of the spouses.

4. That the second party in the prior marriage be questioned, if possible, and not be reasonably opposed to the granting of the dissolution.

5. That the party who seeks the dissolution sees to the religious formation of any children from the prior marriage.

6. That equitable provision be made, according to the norms of justice, for the previous spouse and any children.

7. That the Catholic party with whom the new marriage is to be entered lived in accord with his or her baptismal promises and is concerned for the welfare of the new family.

8. If it is a question of a catechumen with whom marriage is to be contracted, there should be moral certainty of the baptism which is to be received in the future, if the baptism itself has not taken place (which is preferable).

III. The dissolution is more easily granted where there is a serious doubt concerning the validity of the marriage, arising on other grounds.

IV. It is also possible to dissolve the marriage between a Catholic and an unbaptized person which was entered into with a dispensation from the impediment of disparity of cult, provided the conditions established in nos. II and III are verified and it is established that the Catholic, because of the particular circumstances of the region, especially the small number of Catholics, could not have avoided marriage and led a life proper to the Catholic religion in that marriage. It is necessary, in addition that this Congregation be informed concerning the public knowledge of the marriage celebrated.

V. The dissolution of a legitimate marriage entered into with a dispensation from the impediment of disparity of cult is not granted to a Catholic petitioner in order to enter a new marriage with an unbaptized person who is not converted.

VI. The dissolution of a legitimate marriage which was contracted or validated after a dissolution from a previous legitimate marriage is not granted.

In order that these conditions may be properly fulfilled, new procedural norms have been drawn up, and all future processes are to be carried out in accord with them. These norms are attached to the present Instruction.

With the establishment of the new norms, the earlier regulations for the conduct of these processes are entirely abrogated.

Dissolution of the Natural Bond of Marriage With No Conversion (S.C. Doct. Fid., 30 Aug., 1976) *Private*

(The reply is of interest because, after years of denying that the privilege of the faith could be applied to cases in which no conversion was had, the S.C. for the Doctrine of the Faith is back to the practice of earlier years.)

In your letter of August 10, of the current year, Your Excellency proposed the following question to this S. Congregation: whether a marriage which was entered into by a Catholic party and a non-baptized party after a prior dispensation from disparity of cult had been granted and the promises had been made, can be dissolved so that the Catholic party can contract a new marriage with a validly baptized non-Catholic party.

To the proposed question this S. Dicastery believes the response must be: *In the affirmative*. However, the Catholic party must do everything to bring about the conversion of the non-Catholic party by word and example.

Document XI

Norms for Processing Privilege of the Faith Cases

S.C. for the Doctrine of the Faith, Prot. N. 2717/68, 1973*

Procedural Norms for the Process of Dissolution of the Bond of Marriage in Favor of the Faith

Art. 1: The process which is to precede the granting of the favor of a dissolution of a legitimate marriage is conducted by the local Ordinary who is competent in accord with the prescription of the Apostolic Letter *Causas Matrimoniales*. IV, 1, either personally or through another ecclesiastic delegated by him. The Acts to be sent to the Holy See must contain proof of the fact of delegation or commission.

Art. 2: Allegations must not be simply asserted but proved in accord with the prescriptions of the canon law, either by documents or by trustworthy depositions of witnesses.

Art. 3: Both original documents and authentic copies must be certified by the Ordinary or by the delegated judge.

Art. 4: 1. In the preparation of questions to be asked of the parties and witnesses, the services of the defender of the bond or of some other person delegated for this function in individual cases must be employed. This delegation is to be mentioned in the Acts.

2. Before the witnesses are questioned they must take an oath to speak the truth.

3. The Ordinary or his delegate should ask the questions already prepared. He may add other questions which he judges appropriate for a better understanding of the matter or which are suggested by the responses already given.

When the parties or witnesses testify concerning facts not of their own knowledge, the judge should question them also concerning the reason for or the origin of their knowledge.

4. The judge must take great care that the question and the responses be accurately transcribed by the notary and signed by the witnesses.

Art. 5: 1. If a non-Catholic witness refuses to present himself or to testify before a Catholic priest, a document containing a deposition on the matter given by the witness before a notary public or other trustworthy person may be accepted. This is to be expressly noted in the Acts.

2. In order to decide whether this document is to be given credence, the Ordinary or the delegated judge should introduce sworn witnesses, especially Catholics, who know the non-Catholic witness well and are willing and able to testify to his truthfulness.

3. The judge himself should also express his opinion concerning the credence to be given to this document.

Art. 6: 1. The absence of baptism in one of the spouses is to be demonstrated in such a way that all prudent doubt is removed.

2. The party who says that he was baptized should be questioned under oath, if possible.

3. Moreover, witnesses and especially the parents and blood relatives of the party should be examined, as well as others, especially those who knew the party during infancy or throughout the course of his life.

4. Witnesses are to be questioned not only concerning the absence of baptism but also concerning the circumstances which make it believable or probable that baptism was not conferred.

5. Care should be taken to search the baptismal registers of places where the person who was said to be unbaptized lived during infancy, especially in churches which he frequented to acquire religious instruction or where the marriage was celebrated.

Art. 7: 1. If at the time the dissolution is sought the unbaptized person has already been admitted to baptism, at least a summary process must be conducted, with the intervention of the defender of the bond, concerning the non-use of marriage after reception of baptism.

2. The party should be questioned under oath concerning the kind of contract he or she may have had with the other party after the separation and especially asked

whether following baptism he or she had matrimonial relations with the other person.

3. The other party is also to be questioned, under oath if possible, concerning the non-consummation of the marriage.

4. In addition, witnesses, especially blood relatives and friends, are to be questioned, likewise under oath, not only concerning what has taken place after the separation of the parties and especially after the baptism, but also with regard to the probity and truthfulness of the parties, that is, concerning the credence which their testimony deserves.

Art. 8: The petitioner, if converted and baptized, should be questioned concerning the time and the intention which led him to receive baptism or to be converted.

Art. 9: 1. In the same case, the judge should question the parish priest and other priests who participated in the doctrinal instruction and in the preparation for conversion concerning the reason which led the petitioner to receive baptism.

2. The Ordinary should never direct any petition to the Congregation for the Doctrine of the Faith unless every reasonable suspicion concerning the sincerity of conversion has been removed.

Art. 10: 1. The Ordinary or judge should question the petitioner or the witness concerning the reason for the separation or divorce, namely, whether the petitioner was the cause or not.

2. The judge should include in the Acts an authentic copy of the divorce decree.

Art. 11: The judge or the Ordinary should report whether the petitioner has children from the marriage or other union and how he has provided or intends to provide for their religious upbringing.

Art. 12: The judge or the Ordinary should likewise report how the petitioner will make or intends to make equitable provision for the spouse and the children if any, in accord with the laws of justice.

Art. 13: The Ordinary or judge should gather information concerning the non-Catholic party from whom he may determine whether the restoration of conjugal life can be hoped for. He should not fail to report whether the non-Catholic party has attempted a new marriage after divorce.

Art. 14: The Ordinary should report expressly whether any danger is to be feared of scandal, *admiratio*, or calumnious interpretation if the dissolution were to be granted, either among Catholics or among non-Catholics, as if the Church in practice was favorable to divorce. He should explain the circumstances which make this danger probable in the case or exclude it.

Art. 15: The Ordinary should express the reasons which support the granting of the favor in the individual cases, at the same time always adding whether the petitioner has already attempted a new marriage in any form or is living in another union. The Ordinary should also report the fulfillment of the conditions for the grant of the favor and whether the promises mentioned in no I. c), were given. He should transmit an authentic document, with these promises.

Art. 16: The Ordinary should send to the Congregation for the Doctrine of the Faith three copies of the petition, all the Acts, and the information concerning which he is bound to report.

---

* A commentary on *Instructions and Norms for the Resolution of Marriages in Favor of the Faith* (A Practical Guide for Canonists) was published, February, 1979, by N.C.C.B. of Wash. D.C., and distributed to all bishops of the U.S.A. Since the commentary is not for publication, this information is available in your respective chancery.

Document XII
Jurisprudence

The jurisprudence of the Sacred Roman Rota provides the tribunals of the Church more than interpretative rules of law as decisional guidelines for particular cases. It serves also as a working exemplification of a methodology of canonical development through the rigorous discipline of the judicial process. This process is of inestimable value to the Church, particularly in these times when pastors and ecclesiastical judges are under such great pressure to apply the best of contemporary scholarship to meet the practical pastoral needs of the people. The logical analysis of law and facts, careful argumentation that thoroughly discusses the fruits of scientific investigation, the balancing of reasons for and against—these are the elements of a living and growing jurisprudence. More than merely in stated instances, such a process is assimilative, critical and in the precedents it often contributes greatly to confidence in the Church's judicial wisdom and stability in its law. In the words of Archbishop Aurelio Sabattani, formerly an Auditor of the Rota:

> Renewal is usually brought about by jurisprudence *sensim sine sensu*. Ordinarily, jurisprudence *"renovat iuventutem iuris"* not through noisy interventions or destructive propositions, not even by entirely new constructions, but slowly and surely, by humble labor, as that of the sea which imperceptibly sweeps away sand and pebbles from the beach so that the coastline is eventually modified. Thus jurisprudence imposes itself not *ratione imperii sed imperio rationis*. Jurisprudence covers cases not foreseen in the law, it perfects the rules of law by taking into account the progress of auxiliary sciences. . . . It can also correct previously accepted principles and maxims formulated at a time when a reality was insufficiently known and understood.

The Church needs its great tribunals where that law which must embody the Savior's sanctifying mission among men will not only be applied, but also interpreted, developed and grow. We need a living contemporary jurisprudence and the assurance born of a judicial methodology truly attuned to the needs of Christians in this age.

Notes on Canonical Jurisprudence

Definition: Canonical jurisprudence is the science and art of utilizing, interpreting, and supplying for the codified law by rescript and by judicial sentence.

> *Utilizing* means the fitting of a clear law to a corresponding situation. An example might be the fitting of C. 1081 (the canon which says that consent makes marriage) to the marriage of a severe schizophrenic, who, obviously, lacks the degree of discretion that would be necessary to give free consent to marriage.
>
> *Interpreting* means explaining the sense of a law that is obscure, at least as it applies to a particular situation. An example would be extending C. 1081 to the marriage of a sociopath, who probably, but not so obviously, lacks the due discretion for marriage.
>
> *Supplying* means creating a new norm where there is no express law. An example would be judging invalid the marriage of a sociopath or homosexual, not because he lacked due discretion (the consent required by C. 1081) but because he lacked due competence (the ability to function in marriage—not expressly required in the Code).

Significance of Definition: The general significance of defining jurisprudence as an art is that it gives to the local judge a degree of autonomy. One that must be used responsibly, of course, but still, it lifts the judge above the level of a mere enforcement officer. The local judge is not one who merely applies the judicial principles determined by higher courts. More specifically:

> *Utilization*—Occasionally a perfectly clear law goes unutilized. C. 1134, for example, says that, in a convalidation ceremony, the parties must personally recognize the former ceremony as invalid. It is only recently, however, that this law has been widely utilized in the United States to declare invalid ceremonies where a party viewed the convalidation as a mere blessing of an already valid marriage.
>
> *Interpretation*—C. 17 points out that there are two interpreters of law: the legislator and the judge. When the legislator officially interprets a law, the interpretation has the same force as the law itself but when a judge interprets

a law it does not have the force of law and affects only the parties involved in the case.

This is true per se. But per accidens, namely by the force of consuetudinary law, the interpretations of judges can become law. If in other words, all judges hand down like decisions over a period of forty years, the interpretation is then tantamount to law. Or, to put it another way, the original law, at that point, may no longer be regarded as obscure. Later judges should view it as a clear law to be utilized according to the generally accepted sense.

The Code (C. 18) recommends that, in interpreting a law, the judge should look to various sources: other similar laws, the purpose of the law, the circumstances and the mind of the legislator. Interestingly, it does not recommend that he look to the interpretations of other judges, even rotal judges.

Supplementation—When there is a lacuna or deficiency in the law, the Code views this situation as somewhat more urgent and delicate than it does an unclear law that needs interpreting. To fill the lacuna C. 20 suggests four sources, one of which is the practice of the Curia, which in our case means the jurisprudence of the Rota.

Rotal supplementation does not, of course, have legal force but only suppletive force. A Rotal supplementation, in other words, is a priori recommended as safe. It has something more than its own intrinsic wisdom (which is all a supplementation by any other court has) to recommend it. This "Goodchurchkeeping Seal of Approval" awards a certain dignity to the Rota. On the other hand, it should not rob the local court of its independence, or make it excessively reliant on the Rota, because ultimately the real value of jurisprudence is not extrinsic (based on authority) but intrinsic (based on the merits of the legal argument).

There would seem to be only one occasion where a Rotal supplementation would be binding on a lower court and that would be when the following three conditions are verified: 1) some suppletory norm is required. 2) the lower court, using the other sources mentioned in C. 20, cannot supply its own norm and 3) the lower court cannot disprove the legitimacy of the Rota's norm.

Development: Like any other science, jurisprudence is dynamic and always evolving. It does this in many ways: by newly utilizing forgotten laws, by finding new applications for old laws, by restoring laws or principles which were once in effect but were not included in the Code, by expanding the sense of a principle to include new situations, and occasionally by giving a more restrictive interpretation to a law. In recent years, the behavioral sciences, with their insights into psychic disorders and the effect of those disorders on the consensual and functional capabilities of people, have been widely utilized by jurists in the development of jurisprudence.

The Roman Rota: The Roman Wheel, as this great Tribunal is called, is most likely referred to as "The Wheel" either because the judges originally sat in a circle, or because there was a circle on the chamber floor at Avignon where the title is first known to have been used (circa A.D. 1350), or because the cases under consideration were moved from judge to judge on a bookstand which was on wheels. At any rate, the Rota has not only retained the name but still uses the wheel as its logo.

History: The Rota dates back at least to the twelfth century, though in those days the auditors, who were the Pope's chaplains, were only auditors and not judges as they are today. In the early days, in other words, the Pope's chaplains sat in an auditorium and took or audited the testimony, but only the Pope judged the cases. Today a judge on the Rota is still referred to as an auditor, but he has, of course, full judicial power.

There are twenty such auditors today. Eleven of them are Italian; and there is one from each of the following countries: Belgium, Canada, Colombia, France, Lebanon, Poland, Spain, Switzerland and the United States. They are listed in the *Annuario Pontificio* according to the date of their Rotal appointment and are assigned cases according to that listing in turns or boards of three in such a way that what might be called the first case would be heard by the three senior auditors, the next case by the second, third and fourth auditors and so on. The senior man on each turn is the Ponens or Commissioner and the sentence is frequently cited by referring to him: one might, for example, refer to a case "before Wynen" or "coram Wynen."

In 1870 when the Italian army invaded Rome the doors of the Rota were closed and they did not open again until 1908 when the Rota was revived by Pope Pius X. This marks, as it were, the beginning of the Rota's modern era.

Published Sentences: Volume I of the Rota's published sentences contains the decisions of 1909, the year following the Rota's revival. Each volume number, therefore, always lags eight numbers behind the year, so that Volume 50, for example, contains the decisions for the year 1958.

The Work Load: The Rota as might be expected, took on an increasing number of cases during the first several decades of its modern era. The 1923 volume contains 36 decisions, the 1933, 77 decisions, the 1943, 93 decisions and the 1953, 126 decisions (though 178 cases were actually sentenced that year).

Around this time there seems to have occurred a kind of marriage case explosion. In one year the Rota increased its decision load by better than 40%, and it published 251 decisions in 1954. This, in itself, was a dramatic jump, but was even more impressive because there was no proportionate increase in the number of auditors judging the cases. From the beginning of 1950 to the end of 1954 the number of auditors increased only from fourteen to seventeen. Bonet came to the Rota in May of 1950 and Pinna was appointed early in 1952. Lamas became an auditor early in 1954 but he was the only judge added to the Rotal staff during that expansive year of 1954.

On October 16 of that same year, the Holy Father issued a rescript (A.A.S. XXXXVI, 614) by which he derogated C. 1599 1,1° as it applied to Italy, thus disallowing the Italian Tribunals to appeal their cases to the Rota in second instance, as had been their right along with the other Tribunals of the world. In that same rescript Pope Pius XII suggested that Italy begin to make use of its regional Tribunals for second instance and he also ordered that a court of appeal be established in Rome to hear cases on appeal from the Vicariate and a couple of other dioceses.

This rescript apparently had the desired effect of lightening the Rota's work because the Rota issued only 236 sentences in 1957 and just 224 in 1968.

In the 1970's interest in bringing a case to the Rota diminished. Special procedural laws were granted to several countries facilitating a more local settlement of marriage cases. In some individual instances, where a third instance judgment, usually provided by the Rota, was needed, another court, closer to home, was appointed in the Rota's stead. The result of all this is that the work load of the Rota is now less than it was in 1953. In 1976 the Rota judged only 155 cases.

Citing a Rotal Decision: The year 1954 also introduced a new way of citing rotal decisions. Up to 1953 the decisions were numbered in Roman numerals both in the Table of Contents and in the text, and a citation would include the volume number, the decision number and the page number. In 1954, however, the decision number was dropped altogether from the text, and received an Arabic number in the Table of Contents. Since it was dropped from the text it has also commonly been dropped from the citation and a sentence formerly referred to as XX, XXXV, 323 is now generally cited simply as 20, 323. In formal citations, the numbers are preceded by S.R.R.D. (Sacrae Romanae Rotae Decisiones).

Indexing: The indexing of rotal decisions also saw a change in 1954. Up until 1953 each volume of decisions contained two indexes. One was a long summary (it comprised 32 pages in the 1953 Volume and 66 pages in the 1950 Volume) of all the jurisprudence contained in the volume. This was called the *Index Rerum Notabilium* and amounted to a cursillo in jurisprudence. The other index was called the *Tabula Rerum* and was a brief listing (a page and a half in 1953) of all the sentences under each principal ground for nullity. In 1954 and 1955 the Index was discontinued and only the Tabula retained.

In 1956 a new system was introduced, namely the *Index Rerum Analyticus* which was a kind of expanded tabula listing both the generic and specific grounds with references to the pertinent sentences. Under the heading of amentia, for example, the 1956 index (which was four pages long) listed the following subheadings: homosexuality, lucid interval, paralysis, phrenasthenia and moral imbecility, psychasthenia, manic-depressive psychosis and schizophrenia.

In 1957 the *Index Rerum Analyticus* was retained but was lengthened to twenty pages in order to include a precis of the specific point of law under each subheading.

This is by far the best indexing system to date. Under the old system neither the index nor the tabula was of much use, the first being too long and the second too short. The analytical index of 1956 was a definite improvement and the 1957 edition offers us finally a highly functional system of indexing. In 1962 the word "Analyticus" was dropped, but otherwise the Index remained unchanged. The *Index Rerum* of 1967 still contained about 20 pages, and followed the format of the 1957 volume.

Value: The Rota is certainly the chief source of canonical jurisprudence for all other courts. It has set the tone and established virtually singlehandedly the traditional jurisprudence to which all other Tribunals turn. And it has done so with masterly finesse and thoroughness, especially in the area of utilizing the law.

In the areas of interpreting and supplying, rotal auditors, as might be expected, often take divergent positions on a given question. Generally, however, they are thorough, excellent theoreticians, and especially considering their distance from the people involved, remarkably empathetic. Local judges, on the other hand, though sometimes inferior as theoreticians, nevertheless have their own pragmatic strengths. Their understanding of the capacities of people, an understanding gained from broad, clinical experience, seems especially acute and real; and they have a high awareness and sensitivity to local conditions and their importance.

The challenge, at any rate, is the same for every judge, both rotal and local. He must know his own culture and his own times. He must be able to perceive, and to weigh, and to create suitable, enlightened norms by which justice can be rendered. He must avoid the extremes of being insensitive on the one hand, and pandering on the other; of being too theoretical on the one hand, and too intuitive on the other. He must be neither too legalistic nor too romantic, neither too demanding nor too excusing. He must, above all, show forth the ability of the Church to treat people as individual persons of the community and not just as cases or stereotypes. Only in this way can jurisprudence continue to be the "ars boni et aequi" for each succeeding generation.

Also cf. "Jurisprudence in Canon Law" by Arthur Caron, *The Jurist*, Vol. XVIII. I. Jan. 1958, pp. 88-97; and *A Survey of Recent Rotal Jurisprudence on Psychological Cases*, James A. McEnerney, S.J., 1973.

Document XIII
The Diocesan Tribunal

The common complaint among laymen who have a marriage case is that the pastor or assistant does not understand them or their case. They fail to realize that the life of a pastor is one of manifold dimensions: instructing, administering the sacraments, building, financial worries, etc., so much so that it is impossible for him to be an expert in the matrimonial field. The pastor of souls is not expected to understand all the details of matrimonial procedure; nevertheless, there are certain fundamental principles that every priest should know and understand in matrimonial procedure. The following is a brief resume of some of these fundamentals:

Personnel

The personnel of the diocesan tribunal are the following: Officialis, Judges, Promoter of Justice, Defender of the Bond, Notary, Procurator and Advocate.

The Officialis

The bishop or archbishop is the Presiding Judge of the tribunal; however, according to the Canon Law prescription the bishop appoints one to take his place. This person is called the Officialis who shares with the bishop all the powers on judicial matters. Therefore, the Officialis is also the Presiding Judge of the Tribunal and in this capacity he functions as one person with the bishop. He may also exercise the delegated powers which the bishop grants to him upon his appointment.

The Judges

Besides the Presiding Judge, Canon Law requires that the Ordinary appoint other Judges to the Tribunal who help to decide the cases that come to their attention. Three Judges are required for deciding formal cases. Some cases of a criminal nature require five Judges. (If judges are selected in a Synod, they are called Synodal Judges; if chosen outside the Synod they are called Pro-Synodal Judges. They should not number more than twelve in a diocese.)

The Promoter of Justice

The Promoter of Justice may be considered the diocesan attorney. He has the responsibility to uphold the common good. Thus, if it is known publicly that a certain marriage is invalid, and that scandal has resulted from the parties cohabiting, it is the duty of the Promoter of Justice to petition the nullity by bringing forth witnesses and other proofs to substantiate his claim; or, he can enter a cause for nullity to a Tribunal when the parties involved are prohibited by law from acting as Plaintiffs (e.g., non-Catholics) and the Promoter of Justice is convinced that the public good requires the intervention of the Tribunal. Moreover, among his other duties, he must follow the progress of a case during a trial and see to it that the proper procedure is followed in the case. Usually this office is filled by the Defender of the Bond.

The Defender of the Bond

The Defender of the Bond is the attorney for the Church; his office is similar to that of the State's Attorney or Prosecuting Attorney in a criminal case. He is a very important member of the Tribunal. He is the defender of the law, insofar as he sees to it that the law is always upheld. For example, when a certain marriage is attacked to be invalid, he defends the marriage bond by the application of the proper canons. He also prepares the questionnaires for the examination of the witnesses. These questions, in turn, are proposed to the witnesses by one of the judges (or by the Auditor appointed by the Officialis) in the judicial examination. He also points out the flaws in the evidence offered by the plaintiff, by calling witnesses of his own, etc.

The Notary

The Notary is an official who, in a formal trial, puts into writing the replies of the witnesses. He must put to writing either the exact words of the witnesses or the substance of them as dictated by the judge or auditor. The Notary keeps a record of the entire trial. His name and seal attest to the authenticity of every judicial act or deposition. If his signature is not on the judicial act, this act is considered null. It is also advantageous for the Notary to take shorthand.

Procurator-Auditor

The Procurators or Auditors are appointed by the Ordinary, to serve as lawyers for the parties in the case. One is appointed for each of the parties—namely, the Plaintiff and Defendant. If the Defendant does not select one, the Presiding Judge will appoint one or leave the defense to the Defender of the Bond.

The Procurator-Auditor assists in contacting witnesses; he takes the necessary steps during the trial to promote the cause of the client, without however, jeopardizing the truth in any way; when the case is closed he will, by a written brief, seek to advance the case of his client. This brief will be answered in writing by the

Defender of the Bond. If necessary he may write a second brief which is handled in the same manner. The Procurator-Auditor may leave the defense of the marriage to the Defender of the Bond.

Document XIV

Marriage Procedure

The fourth Book of the Code of Canon Law gives the procedure on handling marriage cases. Some are simple, others are complicated and require more study. In summary, we have the following types of procedure:

I. Simple Administrative Procedure

This procedure is called simple because there is *no court procedure* of any kind here. It consists merely in a judgment made by the Ordinary or his delegate based upon the documents or affidavits presented. For example, in deciding questions of nullity based on the *lack of canonical form* (Defect of Form). Pauline privilege cases are decided in the same way. Here again the Ordinary or his delegate makes a judgment on the proof of both parties in the marriage in question based on the evidence presented to them.

II. The Formal Procedure

The formal process is more complicated than the others. The case is usually admitted for trial by three judges. In all such cases, (1) careful investigation must be made to determine whether a particular court is competent[1] to handle it; (2) the judges must determine whether there is a case according to the law (an impediment) as a basis of nullity in this particular case; (3) that there is a possibility of proving the case by competent witnesses, documents, testimony, etc. Following the acceptance of the case and after the Procurators are appointed, the session is held for "joining the issues" (*litis contestatio*). At this meeting the Presiding Judge (Officialis) together with the Defender of the Bond and the Procurator of the parties, determine the exact point in question to be solved in the case.

The testimony of the parties and the witnesses are then taken. All the witnesses are heard in the presence of the three judges of the court (or auditor), the Defender of the Bond and Notary. When all the testimony has been taken and all the proof submitted, the case is declared closed. Afterward, the Procurator and the Defender of the Bond must submit their written briefs. These together with all the testimony gathered, are submitted to the three judges. (Copies are made for each.)

The decision of the Judges is based entirely upon the facts contained in the case.

Judges are reminded here to remember the well-known axiom *"Quod non est in actis, non est in mundo."* If the Judges uphold the validity of the marriage, their decision will be considered: "Negative." If the Judges declare the marriage null, the decision of the Judges will be considered: "Affirmative."

In either the affirmative or negative decision, the case is not considered settled as yet, because the law requires two concordant decisions.

For example, if (1) the decision of the Judges is "Affirmative" the law requires the Defender of the Bond to appeal the case to the higher court (Court of Appeal or Court of Second Instance). If this Appellate Court likewise gives an "Affirmative" decision, the marriage case in question is considered null and the case is considered settled. If (2) the decision of the Judges of the First Court is "Negative," the Plaintiff has the right to appeal the case to the Court of Appeals, but is not obliged to do so. He may abide by the decision. If the Plaintiff does appeal his case to the Appellate Court and this Court would reverse the decision (i.e. First Court: "Negative"—the Second Court: "Affirmative"), the case has to be appealed further (for two concordant decisions) to the Court of Third Instance, namely to the highest court, the Roman Rota.

III. Summary Procedure

The Summary Process, in brief, means that the testimony is heard by the Ordinary or his delegate after the Defender of the Bond has reviewed the case and the parties to the marriage in question have been notified or cited. This procedure is used in all cases that come under Canon 1990, namely, disparity of cult, Order, solemn vows, ligamen, consanguinity, affinity and spiritual relationship. If any of these cases become too complicated then it is processed according to the Formal Procedure mentioned above. The Defender of the Bond has the right to appeal the decision of the Judge to the court of appeal. Courts of appeal are selected by the Holy See for each diocese. The court is also called the Appellate Court.

IV. Special Procedure

The Special Procedure pertains to cases which are sent to Rome for a decision:

I. Non-Consummation Cases

1. The Ordinary no longer needs permission from the Holy See to begin such a case. Cf. Document IX, Appendix.

2. The decision is not made by the local ordinary or Tribunal, but the case is sent directly to Rome and the decision is made by the Sacred Congregation.

II. Privilege of the Faith

These cases also follow this formal procedure, except that (1) the Defender of the Bond need not be present at the hearings of the witnesses; however, he prepares the necessary questionnaire in the case, (2) neither Judges nor Pro-curators are appointed, and (3) the decision is not given by the Ordinary or the Tribunal but by the Sacred Congregation.

1. A tribunal is competent if it (1) is the diocese in which the marriage in question took place or (2) is in the diocese of the defendant, or (3) in the case of a mixed marriage, is in the diocese of the Catholic party; and (4) a woman who has separated with ecclesiastical approval may choose the diocese in which she is, otherwise, she must follow the domicile of her husband. There are some other exceptions.

Document XV
How To Begin a Formal Case

Between 1940-1950 Canon Law was at its peak. Every seminary had a com-prehensive course in this field. Scripture was in the background. Since then Scripture assumed the place of priority in seminaries. Canon Law has not only a second place in the curriculum today but it seems to occupy the lowest place on the rostrums.

Scripture rightfully belongs where it is. Unfortunately, Canon Law has been put in the background, as if it had no importance in the seminary curriculum. Fortunately, despite this indifference the Canon Law Society of America and some Societies of other countries are holding the lifeline to this all important subject. I regret to express this comment, but the many inquiries I have received from priests and chanceries since the end of Vatican Council II, indicates a lack of knowledge among many ecclesiastics of the basic elements of Canon Law on marriage.

Pope Paul VI was also alarmed about this situation of apathy and ignorance of the law when he issued several instructions on this subject. He said in the Motu Proprio, *Causas Matrimoniales*, "Marriage cases have always been given special care by Mother Church . . . The Ministry of the ecclesiastical judges shows forth clearly . . . the pastoral charity of the Church. Since the number of these cases is greatly increasing at the present time, the Church cannot but be very concerned about this matter."

Due to the lack of proper pastoral instructions on marriage in the seminaries, it seems that many newly ordained priests do not know how to go about introducing a marriage case to their tribunal. Therefore, for justice, charity, and the salvation of souls, which is our concern, I wish to propose the following to those who need such guidance. It is very simple and is not time consuming.

Every person has a right to be heard by the Church in matrimonial problems. Especially so when he or she seeks an annulment. After a brief interview, all one must do is to give the person the following guidelines, putting the burden on him or her, and have them submit this in writing to some responsible person in the tribunal for evaluation.

The priest should also give some information on what an annulment really is, and the procedure involved. The following is the guideline and annulment information which is used by our Metropolitan Archdiocese of Pittsburgh (Byzantine Rite).

Preparing A Marital Case History
Matrimonial Tribunal
Metropolitan Archdiocese of Pittsburgh

This is not a questionnaire. It is an arrangement of topics which are of concern in a Tribunal process. Please give specific information on the points which follow. Omit any item which does not pertain to your case. Number your responses according to the number given each item. It is suggested that you prepare a preliminary draft and then revise it for clarity. A typed resume would be appreciated if at all possible. Please try to contain your statement to six pages. You should keep a copy for yourself. When returning the resume by mail, use the address given above.

A. Identification and Background:

For the writer:

1. Present legal name, (maiden name), complete address, phone, birthday, religion of baptism, religion presently practiced, present marital status.
2. Education, religious education, professional training, present employment.
3. Name of parents, essential facts about parents, description of home life.
4. Description of personality, medical history which has a bearing on the marriage.

For the other party to the marriage:

5. Present legal name, (maiden name), complete address, phone, birthday, religion of baptism, religion presently practiced, present marital status.
6. Education, religious education, professional training, present employment.
7. Name of parents, essential facts about parents, description of home life.
8. Description of personality, medical history which has a bearing on the marriage.

B. Courtship:

1. Meeting, length of acquaintanceship before marriage, basis of interest, development of serious relationship, degree of intimacy.
2. Intention to marry: who proposed, willing acceptance by the other party, length of engagement period, objections to the engagement from other parties, preparations for marriage.
3. Discussion between parties about: the nature of marriage, obligations of marriage, of lifelong, faithful marriage.
4. Discussion between parties about children: how many, when, agreement to delay children.
5. Problems in courtship: disagreements, personality clashes, involvement with other parties; family interference, any breaking of the engagement.
6. Presence of pregnancy before marriage.
7. Any pressures impelling either party to enter marriage.

C. Wedding:

1. *For a Catholic party who attempted marriage before a civil official or minister of another religion*: date, reasons, circumstances of this attempted marriage.
   For validation of this type of marriage: reasons which brought the couple to have the marriage rectified in the Church, any pressure to do so, attitude of the priest toward the validation, attitude of the couple to each other at time of this validation, their attitudes toward marriage at the time of validation.
2. *For marriage of two non-Catholic parties*: date, place of celebration, type of official who witnessed the marriage.
3. *For a marriage celebrated in the Catholic Church*: details on arrangements, instructions for marriage, consent of the parents, priest's attitude toward the marriage, date and place of marriage.
4. Anything unusual in connection with wedding rehearsal, ceremony, reception.
5. Honeymoon: where, how long, consummation by physical union, reactions of both parties.

D. Married Life:

1. Life style: residence, with whom, first adjustments to married life, financial situation.
2. List the problems which arose in the marriage: nature, cause, efforts to overcome the problems.
3. Situations of personality change, drinking, associations with others, attitudes toward each party's family.

4. Children born to the marriage: number, when, attitude toward children, treatment of them.
5. Sickness caused by problems in the marriage, medical consultations, psychiatric treatments, marriage counseling.

E. Separation and Divorce:

1. Length of time lived together, number of separations, length of separations, what brought about any reconciliations.
2. Cause of final separation: date, who initiated the separation.
3. Divorce: who filed, grounds, contested, date divorce was granted, where.
4. Remarriage: *For the writer*—have you married again, when, to whom, where, children born of this marriage.
   Remarriage: *For the other party*—has the other party married again, when, to whom, where, children born of this marriage.
5. Witnesses who can support allegations: complete names, addresses, relationship to parties in the case.

(Please sign and date your statement.)

Document XVI
The Annulment Procedure

Canon No. 1 (Crae. All.) 1012 (CIC) of the Code of Canon Law

Christ the Lord has raised to the dignity of a sacrament the matrimonial bond contracted between baptized persons.

For this reason then there can be no valid marriage contract between baptized persons unless the same is also a Sacrament.

Paragraph 48 of the Church in the Modern World:

The intimate partnership of married life and love has been established by the Creator and qualified by His laws. It is rooted in the conjugal covenant of irrevocable personal consent. Hence, by that human act whereby spouses mutually bestow and accept each other, a relationship arises which by divine will and in the eyes of society too is a lasting one. For the good of the spouses and their offspring as well as of society, the existence of this sacred bond no longer depends on human decisions alone.

For God Himself is the author of Matrimony, endowed as it is with various benefits and purposes. All of these have a very decisive bearing on the continuation of the human race, on the personal development and eternal destiny of the individual members of the family, and on the dignity, stability, peace, and prosperity of the family itself and of human society as a whole. By their very nature, the institution of Matrimony itself and conjugal love are ordained for the procreation and education of children, and find in them their ultimate crown.

Thus a man and a woman, who by the marriage covenant of conjugal love "are no longer two, but one flesh," render mutual help and service to each other through an intimate union of their persons and of their actions. Through this union they experience the meaning of their oneness and attain to it with growing perfection day by day. As a mutual gift of two persons, this intimate union, as well as the good of the children, imposes total fidelity on the spouses and argues for an unbreakable oneness between them.

What is an annulment?

In the *Catholic Church* (Byzantine and Roman) a marriage is considered valid when:

1. It is celebrated in a Marriage Ceremony which is legally accepted in the eyes of the Church;

2. Both partners in the marriage were free to marry each other;

3. Each partner intended from the beginning of the marriage to accept God's plan for married life as that plan is taught by the Church;

4. Each partner had the physical and/or psychological ability to live up to the consent initially given to the marriage;

If any one of the requirements is lacking from the beginning of the marriage, then the Church Tribunal, acting as the Bishop's representative, can declare that marriage to have been invalid from its very beginning.

It must always be kept in mind, however, that merely because a marriage case is accepted for consideration by the Tribunal that fact *does not mean that a Church Annulment will always be granted.*

What is the Archdiocesan Tribunal?

Somewhat like civil governments, the Church has a system of Courts. These Church Courts are called Tribunals.

In each diocese the Bishop is the chief Teacher and chief Priest for that portion of God's People over whom he has been placed as Shepherd. At times in his role as Teacher and Priest it becomes necessary for the Bishop to give judgment whether the teaching and sanctifying mission of the Church is correctly being carried out in practice. This necessity then gives the Bishop the role of being the Chief Judge concerning the practice of the Christian Gospel as the Church intends it to be practiced.

Since the Bishop of a diocese, however, cannot personally act as Judge in all these matters, he delegates certain priests to set up a Tribunal to handle this aspect of the Bishop's work.

Most of the problems presented to the Tribunal for judgments are those which deal with the validity of the Sacrament of Marriage. Persons will contend that their marriages were not really sacramental Christian marriages in the eyes of the Church. Their contention is that these marriages never really existed, that they are null and void. The work of the Tribunal, therefore, for the most part exists in an attempt to arrive at the truth of such contentions. To do so requires that such marriages be proved *null and void* before the Judges of the Tribunal.

To help the person present such proof, a priest or priests is assigned to each case as an Advocate to build up evidence for the case. Because of the long-standing teaching of the Church concerning the holiness of married life, however, another priest called the Defender of the Bond of Matrimony is also assigned to each case. His function is to see to it that the teaching of the Church is preserved in practice.

During the annulment process, then, several priests will be involved in each marriage case. The final decision—whether or not this particular marriage is to be considered valid in the eyes of the Church—is made by the priest or priests delegated as Judge by the Bishop. Before any case comes to this final judgment stage the following usually happens in each case:

1. The person petitioning for the annulment is interviewed by one of the priests on the Tribunal staff, or the Pastor.

2. The other partner of the marriage in question likewise is interviewed if this is at all possible;

(These two steps are taken for the Tribunal to determine the "grounds" on which the validity of the marriage is to be "attacked.")

3. When sufficient evidence is gathered, the case is then presented to one or more Judges who decide whether or not to accept the case;

If the case is accepted, the priest who acts as Advocate then formally petitions the Tribunal to accept this case for consideration based on the evidence contained in the acts of the case;

If the case is not accepted at this stage, then more evidence must be gathered, if this is at all possible;

4. When so accepted and after both the Advocate and the Defender of the Bond of Matrimony have asked for the Tribunal's judgment, the case then goes to the Judge or Judges who give the final decision;

The evidence spoken of above is gathered by the Tribunal from witnesses who have been supplied by the person asking for the annulment. These witnesses must be able to give their testimony concerning the alleged grounds for the invalidity of the marriage.

The above description of the Tribunal gives a mere outline of what the Tribunal is and how it operates. The time involved in this process may be long due to several reasons—e.g. the difficulty met in contacting witnesses, the difficulty met in obtaining certain Church, civil or medical records which may be needed, or the large number of similar cases gathered before the Tribunal. Whatever can be done to arrive at the truth in such matters will be done.

How much money is involved?

It is often said by persons who know little or nothing of Church Tribunals that someone has to have a lot of money in order for their marriage case to be considered by the Church. What is even sadder is that more people believe such rumors. The fact, however, is that such is not true.

But as would be expected, expenses are incurred in the running of the Tribunal. There are salaries to be paid to the Tribunal staff. There are costs incurred by the Tribunal office for mailing letters and other material, stationery, stamps and telephone bills. Heating and electricity, etc. are also costly to run such an office operated for annulment procedures. This is all done for people whose marriage has been a failure. Therefore, the person asking for the annulment is expected to bear some of this burden.

The total average expenses incurred by the Tribunal in each trial case are approximately $1,000.00. The tribunal would expect an offering, not of $1,000 but $300.00 for the ordinary case. Of this amount $300 covers only the minimal expenses. If medical experts, such as psychiatrists, psychologists, etc. are employed by the Tribunal court, this must be borne by the Petitioner. If the Petitioner is financially unable to assume these minimal expenses, arrangements can be made through the pastor of the Petitioner. Installments are also possible. When the case is introduced into the Tribunal by the Pastor, the Petitioner is asked to make a deposit of $35.00 toward Court costs.

Certain cases cannot be judged by the Archdiocesan Tribunal, but must be referred to Rome. This does not happen frequently, but when it does, the person is asked to pay the amount of tax which is asked by Rome. This amount is somewhat greater than that asked by our Tribunal.

What Documents or Records are Needed?

For each marriage case under consideration the Tribunal needs the following documents:

1. *Recent copies* of the Baptismal Certificate of each partner in the marriage, if each partner was baptized in the Catholic Church;
2. A copy of the marriage license;
3. A copy of the civil divorce decree.

These documents should be sent in to the Tribunal by the person as soon as possible after the initial interview. This will help save time in the processing of the case since no final decision will be given unless these documents have been presented to the Tribunal. The only exception to this is the case in which no Civil Divorce has been obtained.

At times it may be necessary for the Tribunal to have certain medical records concerning treatment given previously to one or both of the marriage partners. In order for the Tribunal to obtain such records it will be necessary for the party concerned to sign a release from professional secrecy.

What is expected in the Testimony?

After the initial interview the party interviewed will be asked to send to the Tribunal a short report on why he or she thinks the marriage should be declared invalid. This report should be no more than three pages in length. In this report should be given only those facts of the marriage which would have a bearing on the alleged invalidity of the marriage. (Such facts would be details concerning the courtship and the preparations made for the marriage, the details of the marriage itself, details concerning separations which may have occurred in the marriage, and the reasons for the final break-up of the marriage.)

Witnesses to these facts must be supplied by the person asking for the annulment. These witnesses should be persons who have firsthand knowledge of these facts. These witnesses should also be contacted beforehand by the person asking for the annulment and informed that they may be contacted for their testimony by the Tribunal. Unless such witnesses are supplied the Tribunal, there is very little that can be done in the annulment process.

INDEX